DEMOCRACY REINVENTED

INNOVATIVE GOVERNANCE IN THE 21ST CENTURY

ANTHONY SAICH
Series editor

This is the ninth volume in a series that examines important issues of governance, public policy, and administration, highlighting innovative practices and original research worldwide. All titles in the series will be copublished by the Brookings Institution Press and the Ash Center for Democratic Governance and Innovation, housed at Harvard University's John F. Kennedy School of Government.

Decentralizing Governance: Emerging Concepts and Practices
G. Shabbir Cheema and Dennis A. Rondinelli, eds. (2007)

Innovations in Government: Research, Recognition, and Replication
Sandford Borins, ed. (2008)

The State of Access: Success and Failure
of Democracies to Create Equal Opportunities
Jorrit de Jong and Gowher Rizvi, eds. (2008)

Unlocking the Power of Networks: Keys to High-Performance Government
Stephen Goldsmith and Donald F. Kettl, eds. (2009)

Ports in a Storm: Public Management in a Turbulent World
John D. Donahue and Mark H. Moore, eds. (2012)

Agents of Change: Strategy and Tactics for Social Innovation
Sandeijn Cels, Jorrit de Jong, and Frans Nauta (2012)

The Persistence of Innovation in Government
Sanford Borins (2014)

The PerformanceStat Potential: A Leadership Strategy for Producing Results
Robert D. Behn (2014)

Democracy Reinvented: Participatory Budgeting and Civic Innovation in America
Hollie Russon Gilman (2016)

Democracy Reinvented

Participatory Budgeting and Civic Innovation in America

Hollie Russon Gilman

Ash Center for Democratic Governance
and Innovation
John F. Kennedy School of Government
Harvard University

BROOKINGS INSTITUTION PRESS
Washington, D.C.

The Brookings Institution is a private nonprofit organization devoted to research, education, and publication on important issues of domestic and foreign policy. Its principal purpose is to bring the highest quality independent research and analysis to bear on current and emerging policy problems. Interpretations or conclusions in Brookings publications should be understood to be solely those of the authors.

Library of Congress Cataloging-in-Publication data

Names: Gilman, Hollie Russon.
Title: Democracy reinvented : participatory budgeting and civic innovation in America / Hollie Russon Gilman.
Description: Washington, D.C. : Brookings Institution Press, 2016.
Identifiers: LCCN 2015029122| ISBN 9780815726821 (paperback) | ISBN 9780815726838 (epub) | ISBN 9780815726845 (pdf)
Subjects: LCSH: Budget—United States—Citizen participation. | Democracy—United States. | BISAC: POLITICAL SCIENCE / Civics & Citizenship. | POLITICAL SCIENCE / Public Policy / Economic Policy. | BUSINESS & ECONOMICS / Economics / General. | POLITICAL SCIENCE / Public Policy / General.
Classification: LCC HJ2051 .G49 2016 | DDC 352.4/80973—dc23 LC record available at http://lccn.loc.gov/2015029122

9 8 7 6 5 4 3 2 1

Typeset in Adobe Garamond

Composition by Westchester Publishing Services

For my parents, Gail M. Russon and Stephen Gilman

Contents

Acknowledgments

This work is a result of a collective effort spanning several cities, institutions, and mentors. Throughout, I have felt enormously lucky to have a network of support, expertise, and guidance.

This book took a tremendous amount of nurturing (from the academy to the field to policy and back to thinking and experimentation). It originated at the John F. Kennedy School of Government's Ash Center for Democratic Governance and Innovation at Harvard University. The ideas presented in this book originated there, and my growth as a person and as a thinker was nurtured and supported.

I am indebted to my dissertation committee members Archon Fung, Claudine Gay, and Dennis Thompson. Claudine Gay inspired me to believe my doctoral program was a place I could pursue my passions. Dennis Thompson's commitment to the values of deliberative democracy formed and fueled those passions. Archon Fung's advice and example taught me a great deal about how to approach the world: with critical analytic insight, a spirit of collaboration, and kindness to all.

I benefited from several courses at Harvard that provided fertile learning ground and influenced my worldview as well as from conversations with individuals who included Eric Beerbohm, Yochai Benkler, Nolan Bowie, Susan Crawford, Ryan Enos, Peter Hall, Jennifer Hochschild, Marshall Ganz, Larry Lessig, Jane Mansbridge, Nancy Rosenblum, Michael Sandel, Roberto Unger, Tom Wall, to name but a few.

The inspiration, incubation, and sustained support for this research comes from Harvard's Ash Center. Special thanks to Tim Burke, Elena Fagotto, Gigi Georges, Daniel Harsha, Bruce Jackan, Christina Marchand, Marty Mauzy, Kara O'Sullivan, Francisca Rojas, Jennifer Shkabatur, and Juanne Zhao.

New York University's Governance Lab (GovLab) inspired me to believe that this book was a worthy endeavor, one that could serve as part of a larger conversation about open governance and civic innovation. Special thanks to Beth Noveck, Shankar Prasad, and Stefaan Verhulst for their kindness, support, talent, and sense of fun. This book would not exist without their visionary thinking in the emerging field of open government. I thank them for their personal encouragement.

I am indebted to New America and the Open Technology Institute, where I learned about the nuances of the digital era, especially the necessary challenge involved in bridging the realms of technology and public policy. Particular thanks to Anne-Marie Slaughter, Alan Davidson, Reid Cramer, Mark Schmitt, Alissa Black, Georgia Bullen, and Laurenellen McCann.

I was lucky to receive detailed feedback, edits, and comments on this manuscript from Michael Freedman-Schnapp, Adam Lebowitz, Matt Leighninger, Josh Lerner, Carolyn Lukensmeyer, Quinton Mayne, Tiago Peixoto, K. Sabeel Rahman, Donata Secondo, Carmen Sirianni, Paolo Spada, Jannon Stein, Brian Wampler, and Sondra Youdelman. I am grateful for their editing inputs.

Without the early inspiration of faculty at the University of Chicago, including Charles Lipson, John Mearsheimer, Herman Sinaiko, and many others, I may have failed to acquire a belief in the power of ideas and the value of political science and theory to improve society. Michael Dawson opened my eyes to the world of graduate school and to an awareness of the intersection of technology and democracy. I remain grateful for their support.

I am fortunate to have the wisdom offered by, and the faith and support of, a variety of advisers, thought leaders, and collaborators. These include my passionate colleagues at the Office of Science and Technology Policy: Todd Park, Tom Kalil, Nick Sinai, Katie Dowd, John Farmer, Brian Forde, Vivian Graubard, Raph Majma, Marina Martin, Jen Pahlka, Ryan Panchadsaram, Doug Rand, Aden Van Noppen, and Nicole Wong. My thanks to the entire Open Government team, including Lisa Ellman and Remington Gregg, as well as to those in the broader community, including Anna Burger, Tom Glaisyer, Hahrie Han, Ginny Hunt, Dave Karpf, Kate Krontiris, Jed Miller, Tina Nabatchi, Andrew Rasiej, Alec Ross, Andrea Batista Schlesinger, Pat Scully, Micah Sifry, Matt Stempeck, Nicole Summers, Martin Tisne, Ari Wallach, and Darrell West. I remain grateful for several edits to earlier versions, including from Lindsay Brine, Phil Caruso, Jennifer Glickel, Samantha Gordon, and Erin Nitti. I am also appreciative for the support I received from William Finan, Janet Walker, and C. Elliott Beard at Brookings Press, and Melody Negron at Westchester Publishing Services.

I also want to thank Merit Janow, Daniel McIntyre, and Anya Schiffrin at Columbia University for their support. Sonal Shah has been a friend, mentor, and collaborator. The Beeck Center, which she leads, has been a source of creative inspiration and encouragement.

I remain in awe of those working to advance these causes around the country, including Shari Davis, Michael Freedman-Schnapp, Maria Hadden, Alexa Kasdan, Josh Lerner, Chris Osgood, Abi Vladeck, Sondra Youdelman, in addition to the countless volunteers, civic leaders, foundations, and public servants.

The people who volunteer their time, each and every day, to come together to try to address seemingly intractable public problems served to inspire me in pushing this work forward. Their joy, patience, and exuberance remind me of the power of human ingenuity and that grassroots democracy is very much alive in the United States and beyond.

Finally, to my stoic, talented, and good-natured partner, Daniel Benaim. His insight, whether from 30,000 feet in the air or in our living room, has fueled this, and so many other, endeavors. His kindness, unwavering support, and eloquence never cease to amaze me. And, especially, to my first teachers, Gail M. Russon and Stephen Gilman, who enabled me to explore the world backed by their unrelenting support and love.

DEMOCRACY REINVENTED

1

Civic Innovation and Democratic Discontent

I was forced to go.[1]

That was how one teenager in Boston grimly described his reason for attending an experimental pilot program in youth participatory budgeting. On an unseasonably warm spring day, after a seemingly endless winter, it was easy to see why he might want to be anywhere other than a community center in East Boston's inner city. A staffer from the mayor's office—who looked only a few years older—valiantly tried to convince this reluctant participant that the meeting mattered for his community.

The young man stayed. He stayed for the whole meeting, then for a slice of pizza afterward, then for several months as a volunteer. He worked with city officials to turn ideas submitted by Boston residents into viable projects for municipal capital infrastructure—everything from park benches to school computers. Later, young Bostonians, aged twelve to twenty-five years old, voted on these projects. A total of $1 million was allocated for these projects.

Programs like this one do not represent a sudden or wholesale transformation in the nature or structure of self-government. Across the country, people have always worked to strengthen their communities and volunteered their time for civic ends. Yet in some of America's largest municipalities, policymakers, citizens, and administrators are working toward a reinvigorated and even reinvented model

---

1. All quotes were directly transcribed by the author from firsthand encounters and conversations with relevant participants. Some are consolidated. All names have been changed to provide anonymity. For more detail regarding research methodology, please see appendix.

of democracy exemplified by the experience of the young man in Boston.[2] This book explores efforts to reconceive the institutional space between citizens and government through innovative mechanisms for empowered civic engagement. It seeks to offer an extended scholarly reflection on one of these experiments, participatory budgeting, as a democratic innovation in the United States.

Participatory budgeting (abbreviated hereafter as PB) stands on the cusp of becoming a major national trend with the potential to shape how public budgets are decided in the United States. It empowers citizens to identify community needs, to work with elected officials to craft budgeted proposals to address these needs, and to vote on where and how to allocate public funds. A news story in the *New York Times* described it as "revolutionary civics in action."[3]

PB leads directly to the spending of public money. Citizens work directly with government officials, who translate the input that these citizens provide into concrete policy outcomes. This stands in contrast to other models of civic engagement that put citizens in an advisory or consultative role. The power of PB derives, in part, from its ability to create a space for civic engagement that is directly tied to government decisionmaking. Importantly, PB programs in the United States are also extending a vote to those who are typically disenfranchised, including the undocumented and those under the age of eighteen.

In interviews conducted by the author, many community activists who sit on community boards (CB), block associations, and parent teacher associations (PTAs), repeatedly noted that they found PB to be the most meaningful civic engagement they had ever experienced. One woman in New York City's Harlem neighborhood praised the process, saying: "I finally got to see how the sausage is made."

This book studies participatory budgeting as part of a larger set of civic experiments and innovations. Across localities, in the United States and beyond, civic experiments are reengaging citizens to develop public goods, co-create, and share resources. These endeavors are known by a variety of names, including "civic tech," "open government," and "community renewal." What many of these processes have in common is that they open up a new channel of communication between citizens and elected officials and among citizens themselves. Taken together, these developments present an opportunity for democratic deepening that

2. Throughout this book, the term "citizen" denotes someone with the political standing to exercise voice or give consent over public decisions, not legal citizenship.

3. Soni Sangha, "Putting in Their 2 Cents," *New York Times,* March 30, 2012 (www.nytimes.com /2012/04/01/nyregion/for-some-new-yorkers-a-grand-experiment-in-participatory-budgeting.html); Soni Sangha, "The Voters Speak: Yes to Bathrooms," *New York Times,* April 6, 2012 (www.nytimes .com/2012/04/08/nyregion/voters-speak-in-budget-experiment-saying-yes-to-bathrooms.html).

strengthens communities and rebuilds "civic muscles"—the insight and inspiration that can arise from robust civic engagement.

Among these varied civic innovations, PB is a noteworthy and prominent example. It gives citizens a more direct voice in spending, gives elected officials more accurate information about voter preferences, and gives government technocrats more complete information about public wants and needs. Participatory budgeting is not, however, a time-saving innovation. It is resource intensive. Its civic appeal lies precisely in the deliberative process and the surrounding information ecosystem it creates. The outputs of PB—specific, executed projects—are less illustrative of that value than its broader outcomes, which include enhanced "civic rewards" such as greater civic knowledge and transformed relationships.[4] As this book discusses, PB is effective at engaging citizens to form new civic relationships and become meaningful participants in democracy. This includes people who have never before engaged in the civic realm—I call these "new citizens" and detail their participation in chapter 4. Perhaps PB's greatest democratic contribution comes in creating a new process for how citizens and institutions share information, interact, and make public decisions. If it can be institutionalized, PB has the opportunity to create a sustainable structure for robust, transparent citizen engagement between elections.

The rise of participatory budgeting also reflects an increasing public interest in collaborative governance, wherein citizens—often with the aid of new technologies—are empowered as co-producers of public policy and agents who inform decisionmaking. "In collaborative governance, policy design aims to 'empower, enlighten, and engage citizens in the process of self-government,'"[5] says Carmen Sirianni. Lessons from PB provide a framework that can be applied to other innovations in governance and public policy, as explored in chapter 8.

Addressing the Democratic Trust Deficit

> The downgrade reflects our view that the effectiveness, stability, and predictability of American policymaking and political institutions have weakened.[6]

With these words, Standard & Poor's Financial Services downgraded the creditworthiness of the United States from a rating of "AAA" to "AA+" for the first

---

4. See Bach and Matt (2005) on the "theory of additionality," where they distinguish between single outputs and aggregate outcomes.

5. Sirianni (2009, p. 39).

6. Nikola G. Swann, John Chambers, and David T. Beers, "United States of America Long-Term Rating Lowered to 'AA+' Due to Political Risks, Rising Debt Burden; Outlook Negative," Standard & Poor's, August 5, 2011 (www.standardandpoors.com/ratings/articles/en/us/?assetID=1245316529563).

time. Although ordinary citizens do not issue a collective rating of their confidence in the U.S. government, available evidence suggests that they too are los-
ing faith in government.[7] In a 2013 survey, government dysfunction surpassed
the economy as the single problem Americans were most likely to list as the country's most serious. Similarly, Harvard's Institute of Politics found that Americans between the ages of eighteen and twenty-nine possess a record-low level of
trust in government institutions.[8] In a 2014 Gallup survey, only 17 percent of
adults expressed a great deal of confidence in the president. Only 10 percent expressed a great deal of confidence in Congress.[9]

Conventional wisdom suggests that most citizens do not want to be politically engaged. Many political scientists agree. These experts argue that not only
do citizens not want to engage in politics, but also they are ill equipped to make
rational policy decisions.[10] Kenneth Arrow's famous "impossibility theorem"—
positing that there is no rationally acceptable way to construct social preferences
from individual preferences—has been especially influential.[11] Similarly, Philip
Pettit's "discursive dilemma" states that individuals in deliberative settings are
so alienated from policy concerns that they can potentially support policies that
are inconsistent with their own beliefs.[12]

Citizens' declining faith in political participation comes at a moment when
remarkable advances in communications technologies offer increased agency
in social and commercial spheres.[13] In the United States, there are 103.1 mobile
phones for every 100 people.[14] Sixty-four percent of Americans have smart phones,
and penetration rates are rising.[15] In 1969 all of NASA had access to less com-
puting power than a single smart phone does today.[16] Digital technologies have
accelerated the flow of communication and reduced barriers to entry for collective action, introducing new possibilities for organization and activism in a
networked world. Large-scale aggregation of goods, as exemplified by Amazon
.com, has changed shopping habits. More goods are available on demand in real

7. See Shrupti Shannon, "The GovLab Index: Trust in Institutions," Governance Lab, November 6,
2013 (http://thegovlab.org/govlab-index-trust-in-institutions-updated/); Gallup (2014).

8. Harvard Institute of Politics, "Low Midterm Turnout Likely, Conservatives More Enthusiastic,
Harvard Youth Poll Finds," April 29, 2014 (www.iop.harvard.edu/Spring-2014-HarvardIOP-Survey).

9. See Gallup (2014).

10. Hibbing and Theiss-Morse (2002); Waltzer (1999).

11. See Arrow (1988).

12. See Pettit (2001).

13. See Fung, Gilman, and Shkabatur (2013).

14. CTIA—The Wireless Association, "U.S. Wireless Quick Facts" 2015 (www.ctia.org/your
-wireless-life/how-wireless-works/wireless-quick-facts).

15. Aaron Smith, "U.S. Smartphone Use in 2015," Pew Research Center, report, April 1, 2015
(www.pewinternet.org/2015/04/01/us-smartphone-use-in-2015/).

16. Kaku (2011, p. 21).

time, creating an expectation among consumers of hyper-convenience and instant gratification. Parallel, collaborative production, as exemplified by Wikipedia, is transforming knowledge creation and learning.[17]

But these remarkable social innovations have yet to penetrate the sphere of politics. The ways in which citizens engage with government institutions remain largely unchanged.[18] Some critics of democracy warn that voting every two years seems to continue to be the alpha and omega of civic participation. In this model of minimal engagement, they suggest, citizens are purposefully alienated from the decisionmaking that most affects their lives.[19] Given these critiques, it can be argued that the predominant model of contemporary representative democracy—with its overwhelming focus on elections—does not sufficiently empower people to express their preferences between trips to the polls, provide the most effective flow of governance information to citizens, or keep decisionmakers informed of public preferences, beyond limited poll sampling. Citizens increasingly expect instant feedback, but government institutions little changed from models developed in the eighteenth and nineteenth centuries are unprepared to provide it.[20]

Some argue that such Weberian hierarchical-bureaucratic models have been unable to foster inclusive and robust relationships between citizens and their elected officials.[21] At a minimum, these models seem poorly suited for the fast pace of organization in the age of social networks.[22] They are struggling to fulfill basic democratic imperatives that the will of the people is effectively expressed and that citizens have transparent and accurate information about governance.[23]

Engaging citizens in governance is difficult. In Max Weber's famous phrase, "politics is the strong and slow boring of hard boards."[24] To effectively engage citizens in politics and capitalize on the dispersed wisdom of the multitude, innovation will have to extend beyond devices and gadgets to encompass democratic processes.[25]

---

17. See Fung, Gilman, and Shkabatur (2013); Noveck (2009).

18. See discussion on collaborative governance in Sirianni (2009, pp. 39–65).

19. See Thomas Meaney and Yascha Mounk, "What Was Democracy," *The Nation*, June 2, 2014 (www.thenation.com/article/179851/what-was-democracy?page=0,3).

20. See Noveck (2009).

21. Zajac and Bruhn (1999); See Peters (1996) on more participatory, alternative models of governance.

22. See Noveck (2009).

23. Moynihan (2007). It is for this very reason that some scholars posit that participation can undermine representative government; see Lynn (2002).

24. In "Politics as Vocation" (2004).

25. See Noveck (2009).

While civic life has not experienced the same technologically driven seismic shifts as other sectors, both in the United States and around the globe, citizens are working together to leverage new approaches and digital tools—from crowd-funding civic projects to creating the civic equivalent of the "sharing economy"—to strengthen their communal life.[26] Chapter 8 of this book offers a rubric laying out these diverse initiatives and their implications.

National governments are seeking to build on these developments. In 2011 President Obama launched the Open Government Partnership with seven other nations. To date a total of sixty-six nations have signed on to the endeavor. Countries in this multilateral partnership commit to greater citizen participation, collaboration, and transparency in governance. Each member country is required to submit a national action plan outlining its domestic open government commitments. According to President Obama, "empowering citizens with new ways to participate in their democracy" is critical to the effort.[27] My research suggests that participatory budgeting can be an important tool in efforts at open and inclusive governance, in the United States and globally. To that end, as a policy advisor on open government and innovation in the White House Office of Science and Technology Policy (OSTP), I worked to incorporate participatory budgeting into the second National Action Plan, which the United States submitted as part of the Open Government Partnership.[28] The National Action Plan, released in December 2013, features a commitment to promote community-led PB, as explored further in chapter 7.[29] The post-2015 Development Agenda of the United Nations Development Program (UNDP) has led to an ongoing international effort to formulate sustainable development goals (SDGs).[30] SDG 16.7 calls on signatories to "ensure responsive, inclusive, participatory and representative decision-making at all levels."[31] Chapter 8 extends the analysis in placing PB within an emerging set of civic tech experiments aimed to deepen civic engagement in governance.

---

26. See Davies (2014) for the definition of civic crowdfunding.

27. President Obama's speech to the United Nations in September 2011; quoted in Nikki Sutton, "President Obama on Open Government: 'The Essence of Democracy,'" *Open Government Initiative* (blog), September 20, 2011 (www.whitehouse.gov/blog/2011/09/20/president-obama-open-government -essence-democracy).

28. Obama White House (2013).

29. Obama White House (2013, p. 10).

30. United Nations Economic and Social Council, "Millennium Development Goals and Post-2015 Development Agenda" (http://www.un.org/en/ecosoc/about/mdg.shtml).

31. See United Nations, Sustainable Development Knowledge Platform, "Open Working Group Proposal for Sustainable Development Goals" (https://sustainabledevelopment.un.org/sdgsproposal).

Participatory Budgeting

While participatory budgeting (PB) is just now taking root in the United States, it traces its origins to a unique initiative started in 1989 in Porto Alegre, Brazil, by the leftist Partido dos Trabalhadores (Workers' Party, henceforth PT).

After twenty-one years during which Brazil was governed by a military dictatorship, participatory budgeting offered the country a means by which to reimagine the state: it "would help relegitimate the state by showing that it could be effective, redistributive, and transparent."[32] Since 1989 PB has spread to over 1,500 sites worldwide—and the World Bank and United Nations have supported it as a "best practice" in democratic innovation.[33]

In its original campaign for participatory budgeting, the PT outlined four basic principles guiding PB: (1) direct citizen participation in government decisionmaking processes and oversight; (2) administrative and fiscal transparency as a deterrent for corruption; (3) improvements in urban infrastructure and services, especially aiding the indigent; and (4) a renewed political culture in which citizens would serve as democratic agents.[34] Recent research convincingly demonstrates that in the last twenty years PB has enhanced the quality of democracy in Brazil, improving governance and empowering citizens.[35] Other positive outcomes linked to specific uses of PB in Brazil include increased municipal spending on sanitation and health, increased numbers of CSOs, and decreased rates of infant mortality.[36]

Participatory budgeting gives citizens the opportunity to learn about government practices and to come together to deliberate, discuss, and substantively affect budget allocations.[37] PB programs are implemented at the behest of citizens, governments, nongovernmental organizations (NGOs), and civil society organizations (CSOs) to give citizens a direct voice in budget allocations.[38] Scholars have suggested that when people take part in participatory deliberative engagements, they are better equipped to assess the performance of elected officials on both the local and the national levels.[39]

Participatory budgeting can take on different forms, depending on where and how it is implemented. But PB programs share certain basic traits:

32. Goldfrank (2007a, p. 95).
33. Porto Alegre's PB was named one of the "best practices" in urban planning in 1996 at the UN Habitat II conference (Goldfrank 2006).
34. Goldfrank (2002).
35. Touchton and Wampler (2014).
36. Touchton and Wampler (2014, p. 1444); Gonçalves (2014).
37. Shah (2007).
38. Wampler (2007b).
39. Pateman (1976); Santos (2005).

1. *Information sessions*: Citizens are given access to information about the cost and effect of different government programs.

2. *Neighborhood assemblies*: Citizens articulate local budgetary needs.

3. *Budget delegates*: Some sign up to directly interact with government officials and draft viable budget proposals.

4. *The Vote*: A larger group of residents vote on which projects to fund.

Throughout the PB process citizens have unfiltered access to government information and elected officials. Where such programs work, citizens leave with new relationships with their neighbors, a new understanding of their elected officials, and a deepened sense of solidarity and community. In the United States, taking part in PB is a matter of citizen self-selection rather than elected representation.

Some forms of participatory democracy already exist in the United States, including nonbinding consultative mechanisms for citizen feedback within school boards, neighborhood policing, and urban planning, to name but a few.[40] To clarify what is unique about participatory budgeting, however, I offer a bounded definition that focuses on three aspects in particular: participatory budgeting is (1) a replicable decisionmaking process whereby citizens, (2) deliberate publicly over the distribution of, (3) limited public resources, arriving at decisions which are then implemented.[41]

Under this definition, the PB process is more than one single ad hoc event, such as a citizen jury or a deliberation day.[42] Importantly, deliberation and decisionmaking is done in public, in contrast to closed processes such as jury duty. Finally, monies are clearly delineated so that a set amount of funds will be allocated. This stands in contrast to citizen feedback with respect to vague or undisclosed funds that lack direct mechanisms for transparency and accountability.

Participatory Budgeting in America

It took two decades for the practice of participatory budgeting to migrate from Brazil to the United States. Its official arrival can be traced to a single ward in Chicago, where an alderman used $1.3 million of his discretionary funds to make American civic history.[43] Within five years what began in one Chicago ward is

40. Fung (2004); Berry and others (2006); Sirianni (2009).
41. Adding bounded resources to the definition differentiates PB in the United States from PB in Brazil, where it often does not control a clear amount of set aside resources.
42. Crosby, Kelly, and Schaefer (1986); Fishkin (1993); Ackerman and Fishkin (2005).
43. See Weeks (2000) for large-scale deliberative processes in the early 1990s that engage citizens to address municipal budget concerns in Eugene, OR, and Sacramento, CA. For other examples of U.S.-based citizen engagement on budgeting, see Center for Priority Based Budgeting 2015 (www.pbbcenter .org/).

rapidly growing.[44] In 2015 Boston, Chicago, and New York City allocated $40 million dollars through PB. For 2015–16 the process is expected to grow, including with five new wards in Chicago alone.[45] As Josh Lerner, co-founder and executive director of the nonprofit Participatory Budgeting Project (PBP), which seeks to support the implementation of PB in the United States and Canada, noted in 2014, "in the United States, the number of PB participants and dollars allocated has roughly doubled each year since 2011."[46] PBP, working with community partners, has helped introduce, advance, and sustain PB's growth from Brazil to the United States.[47]

Much of this book's research focuses on the pilot year program on participatory budgeting in New York City (hereafter PBNYC) that ran during 2011 and 2012. As outlined in chapter 3, the New York City Council had a long history of nontransparent use of discretionary funds—closely determined by the Speaker of the City Council. Breaking with tradition, in 2011 four council members came together, across party lines, to implement a PB process that now serves as an instructive model for participatory budgeting efforts throughout the country. Just as Porto Alegre's 1989 experiment sparked international interest, New York's 2011 pilot project elevated the stature of PB in America.

Participatory budgeting appears to be a rising force in municipal democracy in the United States. The mayors of Chicago and New York have pledged to greatly expand it. Cities from Boston and Cambridge, in Massachusetts, to Long Beach, San Francisco, and Vallejo, in California, are adopting PB.[48] Cities across the country, including Detroit, continue to explore adoption.[49] Greensboro, North Carolina, is launching a process.[50] St. Louis ran its first pilot in 2013.[51]

44. Scruggs (2014). See the Participatory Budget Project, "Examples of PB" 2015 (www.participatory budgeting.org/about-participatory-budgeting/examples-of-participatory-budgeting/). During 2014–15, estimates of PB in North America included $45 million.

45. See www.pbchicago.org for more information on the Chicago expansion.

46. Lerner (2014, Kindle edition, 468–69).

47. For more information see Lerner (2014) and PBP's mission statement; "Our mission is to empower people to decide together how to spend public money. We create and support participatory budgeting processes that deepen democracy, build stronger communities, and make public budgets more equitable and effective"; Participatory Budget Project, "Mission & Approach" September 2015 (www.participatorybudgeting.org/who-we-are/mission-approach/).

48. See PB experiments in a Phoenix high school, Zocalo Public Square, "How Would Students Spend the Principal's Money," *Time*, March 11, 2015 (http://time.com/3740510/phoenix-budgeting-experiment/).

49. See Detroit People's Platform: Participatory Budgeting 2015 (www.detroitpeoplesplatform.org/resources/participatory-budgeting/).

50. See Greensboro Participatory Budgeting (greensboropb.org/).

51. Participatory Budgeting St. Louis, "Your Money, Your Voice!!!" 2015 (http://pbstl.com/), and Jessica Lussenhop, "Participatory Budgeting—St. Louis Launches Pilot Project in 6th Ward," *River*

Boston is pairing PB with programs in "Internet Democracy," including civic crowdfunding and the first youth-driven process, as reviewed in chapter 6.[52]

In the fall of 2014, nearly half of the members of the New York City Council, representing nearly four-and-a-half million residents, launched PB efforts.[53] In 2015 New York residents allocated roughly $32 million to be spent through PB.[54] The White House issued a pledge to support the growth of PB, using existing federal community funds at the end of 2013 as part of its international effort to support open government initiatives.[55] Cities, such as Buffalo, New York, are already exploring how to use Community Development Block Grants (CDBG) from the U.S. Department of Housing and Urban Development (HUD) to fund PB programs.[56]

PB has proved popular, in part because of the political benefits it offers politicians who embrace it.[57] I argue that PB offers communities a new space for information flow and civic engagement, connecting community-level action to larger questions of governance and decisionmaking. This space holds appeal not only for citizens, but also for their elected political representatives. In fact, as discussed in chapter 3, some of the citizens who participated in the first year of PB in Chicago felt that the process was focused more on creating networks of support for their alderman than promoting genuine engagement in decisionmaking.

PB also gives elected officials crucial crowd-sourced information that would otherwise be prohibitively difficult to obtain, while citizens, in turn, get to learn about their neighborhoods, see how governance works, and actively participate in the formation of public policy. When assessing projects vying for funding in PB assemblies, citizens often canvas entire neighborhoods, closely examining conditions at every park and school in the district. Participatory budgeting encourages civic creativity as the participatory process has the potential to be more inventive than the existing urban bureaucratic process.

Front Times, April 3, 2013 (http://blogs.riverfronttimes.com/dailyrft/2013/04/participatory_budgeting _can_th.php).

52. Boston Department of Youth Engagement and Employment, "Youth Lead the Change," 2015 (http://youth.boston.gov/youth-lead-the-change/).

53. Ginia Bellafante, "Participatory Budgeting Opens Up Voting to the Disenfranchised and Denied," *New York Times,* April 17, 2005 (www.nytimes.com/2015/04/19/nyregion/participatory-budgeting-opens -up-voting-to-the-disenfranchised-and-denied.html).

54. New York City Council, "Participatory Budgeting," 2015 (http://council.nyc.gov/html/pb/home .shtml).

55. Obama White House (2013).

56. See Change.org, "Implement Participatory Budgeting in Buffalo," 2015 (www.change.org /p/mayor-byron-brown-implement-participatory-budgeting-in-buffalo?source_location=update_footer &algorithm=promoted).

57. See Lerner (2014).

Information and communications technologies (ICTs) have the potential to streamline the process. Yet the use of ICTs should not prevent people from experiencing the painstaking rewards and gaining the kinds of knowledge that come from in-person participation in civic dialogue. One current challenge is the limited suite of tools available for effective online deliberation. Ideally, PB will help catalyze support for nonprofit tools that better provide these opportunities and reduce barriers to entry for participants.

An Unlikely Innovation

Given the resources and effort it requires, PB can be said to represent an unlikely exemplar of twenty-first-century innovation. Many technological innovations are designed to streamline processes, removing the human touch. In our increasingly automated society, participatory budgeting provides an alternative approach. By design, the process is "high touch," requiring elected officials to devote resources and time and encourage face-to-face engagement. Its innovation is bringing people back in—not through a groundbreaking technology or tools but through a deliberative mechanism that seeks to marshal civic and political will to reinvent the current budgeting process and reengage citizens in democracy. This book aims to explain the paradox presented by an innovation that actually both creates and depends on what some might consider inefficiency.

Participatory budgeting requires significant resources from elected officials, community-based organizations, and citizens. These include the commitment of time from citizens who choose to serve as budget delegates in the effort to craft viable budget proposals for their neighbors. Delegates choose not only to devote their time, which is a scarce resource, but also sometimes even provide in-kind donations such as food.

In some respects, conventional budgeting is more streamlined than PB. However, the conventional approach has its own significant shortfalls, some of which PB addresses. In the normal course of governance, little time and few resources are devoted to providing transparent information to citizens. Citizens are not empowered participants or contributors of local knowledge. Funding for projects is often delayed until needs have become so serious that they can no longer be ignored. Organizations with preexisting relationships with elected officials—and well-connected lobbyists—are sometimes first in line to receive funds. This is due, in part, to the limited capacity of staff in the offices of council members to engage with larger swaths of their districts. The current model remains resilient. Participatory democratic experiments must contend with institutional inertia, with limited resources for public engagement, and with the influence of entrenched interests, including officials' reluctance to forgo control over the allocation of resources.

In the United States, many local officials receive discretionary funds through highly opaque processes. As is discussed in chapter 3, prior to major transparency reforms in 2014,[58] New York City Council members received from $3 million to $12 million per annum in discretionary funds. These monies were not tied to district need but rather often reflected the whims of the speaker and the city council. Council members then have discretionary authority regarding how this money is spent. A report by Citizens Union on the New York City Council in 2012 contended: "The current discretionary funding process, while improved from a decade ago, remains flawed and needs additional reform."[59]

New York City was not alone in these practices. Local officials throughout the United States receive sizable amounts of discretionary funds subject to little or no oversight. The same holds, mutatis mutandis, for Chicago. Sometimes oversight comes only in the form of prosecution: between 1972 and 2009 thirty Chicago aldermen were indicted and convicted of federal crimes ranging from income tax evasion to extortion, embezzlement, and conspiracy.[60]

The participatory budgeting process is effective partly because it is not as "efficient" as these less transparent approaches. PB is both labor intensive and time intensive because it involves the hard work of coalition building and direct dialogue. I dub these latter "civic rewards." Among the most valuable of these rewards is learning how expensive and inefficient government projects can be. Government, by its mandate to be just and equitable, cannot necessarily function like other sectors. This can prove to be beneficial for the public. Ultimately it is the process itself, and the experience of participation, that makes PB such an important phenomenon. PB provides opportunities for civic knowledge, strengthened relationships with elected officials, greater community inclusion, and leadership combined with skill development. Studying the above-mentioned "civic rewards" and other factors in participatory budgeting can, in turn, inform other civic and social innovations.

By their very nature, innovations tend to adapt and evolve. Political ecosystems change. Methods and means are constantly adjusted. New actors emerge. This study of a relatively recent innovation in U.S. political practice provides, by necessity, a snapshot of how things were done in particular times and places. The latest versions of participatory budgeting will already differ from those detailed here. Nonetheless, this book seeks to draw lessons from these shifting, incipient attempts.

58. Council of the City of New York, "Council to Vote on Landmark Rules Reform Package," press release, May 14, 2014 (http://council.nyc.gov/html/pr/051414stated.shtml).

59. Fauss (2012, p. 4).

60. Gradel and others (2009, p. 1).

Overview

This book studies participatory budgeting and its implications for democracy and public policy, situating PB within a broader framework for understanding civic and democratic innovation—a set of principles which can then be applied, as appropriate, to other innovations in governance, information, and public policy. I have put forward three core ingredients that I view as essential for understanding PB: (1) substantive participation, (2) deliberation, and (3) opportunities for institutionalization. These criteria can be incorporated into holistic strategies for assessing the effectiveness and legitimacy of various other innovations in civic process. The nature and objectives of programs will vary,[61] as will the political context, but many other civic innovations rest on one or more of these same criteria.

This introductory chapter frames the challenge of declining trust in government and argues that PB and other civic innovations can help reinvigorate and strengthen democracy. Chapter 2 discusses the international origins of participatory budgeting and presents a normative argument for the value of citizen engagement. Chapter 3 discusses the rise of participatory budgeting in the United States, with an emphasis on its founding in Chicago and New York.

The chapters that follow consider in depth the three criteria I have articulated for assessing participatory budgeting: participation, deliberation, and institutionalization. Chapter 4 discusses in depth PB's pilot year in New York City and offers a typology of its participants. Specifically, I argue that PB plays a crucial role in generating "new citizens" who have not previously participated in elections or engaged in public political discourse. Chapter 5 explores the role of deliberation and dialogue in PB, as illustrated in New York's pilot year. Chapter 6 considers innovations to the practice of PB through findings from Boston's youth-driven process, highlighting that innovation can take the form of mechanisms—innovation or civic tech is not only driven by digital tools.

The concluding chapters place the findings within a broader theoretical context of civic innovation and civic technology, including policy recommendations for PB and a rubric for assessing civic and social innovations, presenting PB as one technique within a broader toolkit. Chapter 7 offers policy recommendations for institutionalizing civic innovation.

How much can PB achieve? If it is restricted to funding parks and school construction, it will not reach its potential. To reinvigorate local democracy, PB must encompass major budgetary questions, up to and including urban redevelopment,

---

61. For example, not all civic innovations require deliberation; some might even lose community buy-in if overly institutionalized.

zoning, and social welfare spending. At the same time, if PB is to be more than a passing trend, it will need to be made part of a permanent routine practice. Building on discussion throughout the book, chapter 7 considers the use of information communication technologies (ICTs) in PB and civic innovation for greater institutionalization and scale in the United States and internationally. This includes a suggestion that as PB expands, it will need to become less resource-intensive while still creating robust opportunities for substantive civic participation. Chapter 8 puts forward a broader framework to understand civic tech and innovation beyond PB. The conclusion offers questions for further research and argues for more vigorous effort and experimentation to reengage citizens in governance to improve the long-term health of democracy.

If properly understood and supported, participatory budgeting has the potential to strengthen local democratic practice and to alter the current relationship between citizens and local government. Yet this will only be possible if we ask and answer the right empirical questions and if we approach the inquiry with the right normative framework. I hope this book will be a contribution to this vital ongoing discussion.

As one civil society leader noted on completion of the pilot PBNYC process:

> I've been working on the budget for fifteen years in New York City, where the budget dance is so entrenched. I've seen a radical change in the last few months. People are talking about this and imagining a budget process that is modified and doesn't involve the highest paid lobbyists. Opening up the imagination of what is possible is the biggest achievement of participatory budgeting and shame on me for not thinking it was possible.

2

Origins: A More Participatory Budget Approach

In the realm of political imagination, participatory democracy has plenty of romance. Perhaps for that reason alone, we wizened North Americans seldom discuss it. But perhaps we should. As we consider the polarization, deadlock, cynicism, and outright corruption that infects the eighteenth-century machinery through which we try feebly to govern ourselves in the twenty-first, we would all do well to look beyond Alexandria.[1]

In attempting to address what ails U.S. democracy, lessons can be learned from the Global South. For example, even many of our most advanced theories of participatory democracy typically overlook the seemingly mundane world of budgets and fiscal policy as arenas for citizen engagement. These issue areas may be seen as too complex and unwieldy for ordinary citizens. Participatory budgeting's success stems from its ability both to translate complex issues into more easily digestible policy questions and to draw on citizens' expertise regarding their immediate surroundings, thus bringing the scale of politics back to the local level. Importantly, budgets embody policy intentions.

This chapter issues a normative appeal for participatory budgeting (PB) as a democratic innovation that enables political participation and deliberative expression. Through deeper engagement at the local level, contemporary citizens can realize some of the virtues of the polis as outlined by Aristotle and Arendt.[2] The current political science literature stages a debate between a populist wing,

---

1. Fung (2011, p. 867). Alexandria here refers to the epicenter of culture and politics in Greek antiquity, founded by Alexander the Great in 332 BC. Fung, quoting Richard Rorty, uses it figuratively to make an analogy to the most prominent contemporary example of democracy.

2. Dahl (1967); Arendt (1998).

which urges greater participation by citizens in the processes of government, and an elite-oriented side, which is skeptical about the public's capacity for and commitment to direct democracy. My sympathies are with those arguing for an expanded role for ordinary citizens in the everyday practice of self-government. But with its emphasis on budgeting and fiscal policy, my project departs from some literature to explore an arena that at times has been neglected by theorists like John Stuart Mill, Benjamin Barber, and Carole Pateman.

In this chapter I place PB within a context of a broader civic innovation ecosystem. This chapter outlines a definition of PB and sketches its trajectory from its origins in Brazil to more recent experiments in the United States. I present participatory budgeting as decisionmaking that occurs at a distinctively local level, where citizens can study a focused set of problems while drawing on their expertise as inhabitants of the local community.

Participatory budgeting began in Brazil as a project of a new, left-leaning government headed by the Partido dos Trabalhadores (Workers' Party, henceforth PT).[3] One aim of PB in Brazil was to help reimagine the relationship between citizens and the state. The dynamics that gave rise to Brazilian PB differ from the roots of similar efforts in the United States in three critical respects: (1) Brazilian PB was instituted in the aftermath of a military dictatorship; (2) it was influenced by Marxist and liberation theology and initiated by a specific political party;[4] and (3) it pertained to a larger share of the budget. The "genetics" of Brazilian PB do not succinctly conform to a deliberative ideal.[5] As PB has continued to evolve in Brazil, it has developed multiple local variations highly dependent on the local context.

This genesis contrasts with that of participatory budgeting in the United States, which began as part of a broader good governance agenda,[6] was not tied to a specific political party or ideology, and was intended to disperse a limited set of municipal discretionary funds. In the United States, PB leverages the North American tradition of participatory planning, community engagement, and small grants. These processes are, by design, focused on educating citizens, providing learning opportunities, and facilitating small-group discussions. Informed by these practices, speech and deliberation have been a vital component of PB's starting formula in the United States.

---

3. Participatory Budgeting Project, "Participatory Budgeting: Where Has It Worked?" (www .participatorybudgeting.org/about-participatory-budgeting/where-has-it-worked/).

4. Santos (1998); Abers (2000); Avritzer (2002, 2009); Baiocchi (2001, 2002); Goldfrank (2011, 2007a); and Wampler (2007c) provide more detailed discussions of the origin of PB.

5. Many thanks to Paolo Spada for collaborative work on this schema.

6. An agenda that features a vision of greater political inclusion, including for previously marginalized citizens.

Status Quo Citizen Engagement

Popular rhetoric about U.S. politics describes a body populace that is disengaged and disillusioned. This is not new. Indeed, for quite some time mainstream political science has contended that such disillusionment actually constitutes coherent and reasonable behavior, since rational citizens perceive the opportunity costs and seek to minimize the time and effort they expend on democratic participation and deliberation.

Joseph A. Schumpeter initiated much of this line of thought when he challenged what he called the "classical doctrine," arguing instead that citizens in democracies are largely ignorant of politics and easily manipulated by political elites.[7] Therefore, average citizens ought not to be involved in policy decisions. Following the tradition of Max Weber, Schumpeter presents democracy as an affair for elites, with channels for popular participation properly kept to a minimum. Anthony Downs expounded what he called "the rationality of electoral ignorance," arguing the costs of citizens' educating themselves about politics outweigh the potential benefits.[8] In these views, citizens rationally rely on heuristics and party cues to determine their preferences.[9] Any participation above the minimum threshold of voting is viewed as inefficient.

This argument has been updated for the twenty-first century. Now it is argued not so much that people are uninterested in politics, but rather that they are content to elect governments they see as offering competent, technocratic management.[10] Politics is the realm of efficient service delivery—not a place for civic engagement. When citizens do engage in politics it is almost always through elections, yet even acquiring information for such elections is rendered irrational in many political science literatures.

Party identification is the primary heuristic that citizens use for making political decisions.[11] Often partisan allegiance precedes views on policy, with party cues determining preferences.[12] Citizens are influenced by the party preferences of their families, friends, and neighborhoods. Research argues that elites target those voters who are most likely to be influential, such as those with higher levels of income or education.[13]

---

7. See Schumpeter (1942).
8. See Downs (1965).
9. Fiorina (1975).
10. Hibbing and Theiss-Morse (2002).
11. Green, Palmquist, and Schickler (2002).
12. Goren, Federico, and Kittilson (2009); Fiorina (1975).
13. Rosenstone and Hansen (1993).

Partly in reaction to the cynicism of modern political science, an alternative perspective in political theory advocating strong participation emerged. Carole Pateman's work offers a stark contrast with Schumpeter's elite-centered conception of democracy, countering it with a more participatory alternative.[14] She buttresses her claims for a multidimensional participatory democracy with citations from Mill and Jean-Jacques Rousseau, theorists who appreciated what Schumpeter misses.[15]

Similarly, Benjamin Barber calls for a "strong democracy" that can enable individuals to achieve an existential "human freedom" found only in the political sphere.[16] In this conception, democracy offers more than simply the smooth delivery of services. This "strong democracy" articulated by Barber and others who share this vision for a more politically engaged public have proposed a host of creative institutions such as deliberative opinion polls or more substantive citizen juries.[17] Some advocates of these options argue they should be coupled with nonpartisan and expert information to foster more informed decisionmaking. Bruce Ackerman and James S. Fishkin have proposed an annual "Deliberation Day," in which citizens would be encouraged to participate in small, diverse group discussions about the nation's political future.[18] Deliberation Day is inspired by a series of social science experiments, titled "Deliberative Polls," that were aimed at more robustly engaging citizens to participate in electoral decisions.[19]

Although theorists have put forth norms for increased participation in a broad variety of political interactions, budgets are sometimes missed as opportunities for meaningful civic engagement. Archon Fung and Erik Olin Wright articulated a concept of empowered deliberative democracy in which Brazilian PB is given as one compelling example among others that included: neighborhood governance in Chicago to check urban bureaucratic power over public schools and policing; Wisconsin Regional Training Partnership (WRTP/BIG STEP), which enables organized labor, firms, and government to assist workers in employment transitions; and Panchayat reforms in West Bengal and Kerala in India that have created both representative and direct channels to empower local villages.[20] Fung and Wright's concept of "empowered deliberative democracy" places PB in dialogue with diverse initiatives meant to give citizens an additional voice in decisionmaking.[21]

14. Pateman (1976).
15. Pateman (1976).
16. Barber (1984, p. 311).
17. Fishkin (1993); Fishkin and Farrar (2005).
18. Ackerman and Fishkin (2005).
19. Ackerman and Fishkin (2005).
20. Fung and Wright (2001).
21. Fung and Wright (2001, p. 7).

Civic Innovation beyond Participatory Budgeting

Innovations to re-engage citizens are occurring in practice as well as in theory. PB represents one example within a thriving civic ecosystem aimed at more inclusive and participatory governance. Communities have undertaken numerous experiments in strengthening governance, comprising civic, social, and democratic innovations. As discussed further in chapter 8, PB represents one manifestation of a broader emerging civic infrastructure for experimentation and reform.[22] Box 2-1 gives examples of various types of civic innovations in order to place PB within a broader context. The consistent theme across these examples is openness toward experimentation and a desire to augment the status quo. Importantly, people are redefining what a community is—place-based and networked. A community can collectively share goods, build a park, or envision policy for a new government. The innovation is often in an improvement in process, knowledge sharing, or resource allocation. It is not simply confined to generating a new app or deploying the Internet. Examples are diverse by design. For example, City Hall to Go in Boston is a refurbished truck that delivers city services directly to people. This includes everything from voter registration to birth certificates. The program helps build trust—showing that government can work for the people.

A More Participatory Approach

Participatory budgeting (PB) is a compelling example to understand civic innovation more broadly in large part because it directly ties citizens to public decisionmaking. It has also spread and grown across the globe. PB gives citizens opportunities to learn about government practices and to come together to deliberate, discuss, and ultimately decide on budget allocations.[23] Through participation in PB, citizens become educated about budget processes and engaged in politics. Ideally, PB can lead to greater accountability and transparency as citizens leave the process with more knowledge and experience in governing and holding officials accountable. The World Bank has conjectured that PB, especially in developing democracies, has the potential to limit government inefficiency and curb clientelism, patronage, and corruption.[24] Recent research convincingly

---

22. For an expanded take on this subject, see my work with New America, in particular with their Open Technology Institute, focusing on civic innovation.

23. Shah (2007).

24. Shah (2007); see also Goldfrank (2012).

BOX 2-1
Various Civic Innovations

Economy—Resources, Goods, Services
Innovations are changing the way people share, acquire, and effectively produce resources and goods.

Collaborative Funding For example, Citizinvestor: An online platform that crowdfunds public sector projects.[a]

Sharing Economy For example, Time-banked currency: Alternative currency where the unit of exchange is person hours.[b]

Government—Institutions and Process
Government institutions are exploring ways to increase participation, transparency, and collaboration internally and externally.

Collaborative Decisionmaking For example, Participatory budgeting: Empowers citizens to make binding recommendations on spending public money.

Process Improvement For example, City Hall to Go: A refurbished truck in Boston that delivers city services directly to people.[c]

Communities—Local, Online and Off, and Context Specific
As locality reemerges as a sphere for civic life, community-based innovations increasingly tie place-based interventions—whether digital or physical—to the needs of individuals and collectives.

Knowledge Transfer For example, Makerspaces: Workshops that provide space with industrial equipment for communal use.[d]

Co-creating For example, OldWeather.org: A crowdsourcing project that began by enrolling citizens to collectively transcribe old British ship logs to determine climate patterns.[e]

---

[a] See Citizinvestor.com for more details.
[b] TimeBanks.org offers a central knowledge bank on such projects around the world.
[c] City of Boston, "City Hall to Go" (www.cityofboston.gov/cityhalltogo/).
[d] MakerSpace.com sponsors public events promoting do-it-yourself technology tinkering called Maker Faires and maintains a directory of shared workshops (http://spaces.makerspace.com/).
[e] It has since expanded, involving collaboration between several national-level agencies in the United States and the United Kingdom to make historical weather data available for research, while continuing to enlist citizen participation in processing archival material.

demonstrates that in the last twenty years PB has enhanced governance, citizens' empowerment, and the quality of democracy in Brazil.[25]

While countless participatory and deliberative engagements can be cited, even several involving budgeting, the form of "participatory budgeting" discussed and found in its current manifestations harken back to a specific process that first originated in Brazil. Thirteen Brazilian cities introduced PB programs in 1989. By 2013 this kind of PB could be found in more than 1,500 municipalities worldwide.[26]

Participatory budgeting is highly adaptable. It has many different manifestations suited to the specific geopolitical contexts in which it is implemented. PB programs are implemented at the behest of citizens, governments, nongovernmental organizations (NGOs), and civil society organizations (CSOs) to give citizens a direct voice in budget allocations.[27] The scale at which PB is implemented can differ from national to local to municipal levels. The enabling organization that shepherds PB can vary as well, ranging from such actors as a political party like the PT, which brought PB to Brazil, to international NGOs such as the World Bank Institute.[28] Local, social, political, and economic environments condition the effects of PB on empowerment, decentralization of decisionmaking authority, and accountability.[29]

As mentioned in chapter 1, I have adopted the following definition of PB:

Participatory Budgeting is a (1) replicable decisionmaking process whereby citizens, (2) deliberate publicly over the distribution of, (3) limited public resources, arriving at decisions which are then implemented.[30]

PB thus contrasts with standard public budget making, in which bureaucrats or elected politicians decide the allocation of public resources. There is also a more nuanced contrast with less empowered forms of deliberation that are not binding. These include deliberative polls, structured town halls, or large-scale participatory events, such as those that AmericaSpeaks used to convene and conduct.[31]

---

25. Touchton and Wampler (2014).
26. Sintomer and others (2010); Goldfrank (2012); Spada (2013).
27. Wampler (2007a).
28. See Goldfrank (2012).
29. Wampler (2007b).
30. This definition is my own. The addition of bounded resources to the definition differentiates PB in the United States from PB in Brazil, where it often does not have a clear amount of resources. As Sintomer, Herzberg, and Röcke (2014, pp. 29) note, "there is no recognized definition of participatory budgeting, either political or scientific, explaining the minimum criteria they must satisfy." See Wampler (2012a) on PB as a set of priciples that can generate social change.
31. See Fishkin (1993); AmericaSpeaks was a nonprofit organization (1995–2014) that organized large-scale deliberative dialogues to engage citizens on key policy issues. See AmericaSpeaks, "AmericaSpeaks:

The positive impacts of participatory budgeting in local government are due, in part, to its ability to empower typically marginalized members of society, offering them an avenue to take part in politics. PB often provides poor and historically excluded citizens with a critical venue for decisionmaking and involvement. At its best, PB makes government more responsive to the needs of these typically excluded groups and more accountable to them in terms of resource allocation and delivery.

For those who take part in PB, its participatory and deliberative aspects can serve as citizenship training, providing a kind of learning whereby citizens leave with more knowledge, increased self-efficacy, and fewer antidemocratic attitudes.[32] Scholars have suggested that when people engage in participatory deliberation they are better able to assess the performance of elected officials on both local and national levels.[33]

The Local Level

Participatory budgeting is especially powerful because it engages citizens with complex political issues on the local level. In contrast, some democratic innovations aiming at broader participation face the challenge of integrating individual-level participation into the scale of contemporary politics in the United States.[34] Contemporary democracies face challenges of building inclusive governance given bureaucratized governments tasked to make policy for large populations.[35] Governance is viewed as a matter of technocratic elites grappling with interdependent, highly challenging problems. PB's strength as a democratic innovation lies in its focus on municipal budgets, which constitute the scale at which citizens can be experts.

PB positions citizens as empowered experts in their local settings, where they do not necessarily need to bring in outside expertise or experience to be able to accurately assess community needs. The local level can become the focal point for integrating participatory mechanisms back into politics.[36] It may offer the

A Legacy of Critical Innovations in Deliberative Democracy and Citizen Engagement," online pamphlet, 2014 (https://dl.dropboxusercontent.com/u/6405436/AmericaSpeaks_Legacy.pdf).

32. See Almond and Verba (1965).

33. Santos (2005); Abers (2000).

34. Athens, the largest city-state in ancient Greece, had its quorum for its assembly fixed for some purposes at 6,000. (There were around 6,000 total seats in the Pnyx, where the Ecclesia, or assembly, met.) The city had an estimated 40,000 adult male citizens. For Plato, 5,040 was the maximum number of people for a unit of government. The polis, with its strengths and weaknesses, was inescapably local. See Dahl (1967), cited in Fung (2011); Hansen (1983, p. 25); Plato, *Laws* 5.738a.

35. See Zajac and Bruhn (1999).

36. Peters (1996).

best hope in the United States for the reinvention of a polis for modern citizens.[37] As Robert Dahl noted in his presidential address to the American Political Science Association in 1967:

> In this vision, the city-state must be small in area and in population. Its dimensions are to be human, not colossal, the dimensions not of an empire but of a town, so that when the youth becomes the man he knows his town, its inhabitants, its countryside as well as he knows his own college or university.[38]

Participatory budgeting is conceptually powerful because it suggests that better institutional design and structure can more effectively engage citizens in politics. Unlike the vision of New England democracy that arose from villages, PB is an urban governance innovation. The PB process groups residents into units small enough so that individuals can be local area experts on issues in their own neighborhoods. By breaking up questions of complex budgetary needs into neighborhood-level needs assessments, PB recasts politics on a more human scale. Through PB, citizens are able to know their neighborhoods, their neighbors, and their elected representatives. PB may not solve the problem of citizen engagement in a highly bureaucratic world, but it may nonetheless foster better democratic conditions.

These better democratic conditions include material outputs—the built projects that emerge from the PB process and better address community needs than the status quo budget process. Other better democratic conditions may include renewed civic spirit in a particular community or renewed faith in elected officials. Participatory budgeting is an attempt to rescue politics from elitism. I argue that PB enables new channels for deepening democracy and for empowering citizens to take on new social roles.

While the material outputs of participatory budgeting are modest thus far in the United States, I argue that its immaterial "civic rewards" are substantial. Some of these include the ability to transcend ordinary social roles and thus think more creatively and collaboratively. PB fosters opportunities for citizens— as architects of their collective life—to use speech and reason to combat traditional power dynamics. On the local level, PB creates micro-spaces in which citizens can use speech and reason to create new forms of engagement and participation.

---

37. A Greek city-state and now considered by some as the Platonic ideal for political life.

38. Dahl (1967, p. 954). This article is his presidential address to the American Political Science Association, delivered on September 7, 1967, in Chicago. Cited in Fung (2011, p. 858).

Why are speech and reason so important? Speech is an expression of human freedom.[39] Drawing on Aristotle's discussions of Athenian democracy, the twentieth-century political philosopher Hannah Arendt focused on speech as a uniquely human capacity that enables politics. She articulated how this worked in the early city-state, the polis: "To be political, to live in a polis, meant that everything was decided through words and persuasion and not through force and violence."[40]

Speech and reason free humanity from the need to determine decisions through sheer force. In a modern democracy, force is not necessarily simply physical; it can also include monetary and political influence.[41] Contemporary theorist Roberto Unger also draws on the Aristotelian vision of the engaged polis, expanding it in terms more appropriate for the twenty-first century: "In a deepened democracy people must be able to see themselves and one another as individuals capable of escaping their confined roles."[42]

Such an escape from our "confined roles" is another means of expressing freedom. Unlike Arendt, Unger does not primarily focus on small, personal polities; rather, he outlines the "bigness" of the political sphere as the place where humans can be free. The political is deeply personal: for Unger, bigness is important because it enables an otherwise unrealized expression of our humanity. Speech also enables people to think more creatively—to think on a bigger scale than that of day-to-day tasks.

When they engage in participatory budgeting, citizens find themselves suddenly interacting with their elected officials in nontraditional roles. PB asks for civic creativity and opens up spaces for it. People from widely diverse backgrounds are given the well-worn Silicon Valley exhortation to "think outside the box." One contemporary obstacle to establishing the more "authentic" political communities favored by Arendt and Unger is the lack of space for face-to-face political discourse and for concrete experience in self-government. Indeed, creating such spaces is perhaps even more challenging in the digital age. Yet there is hope that innovations like PB can level the playing field and enable more people to experience self-government.

Participatory budgeting creates several opportunities for building important relationships. It can improve democratic conditions by renewing the civic spirit in a community, strengthening ties between neighbors, renewing faith in elected officials, and transforming the relationships between citizens and their elected officials. These civic rewards can be intangible and difficult to quantify. Will

39. Arendt (1998, p. 27).
40. Arendt (1998, p. 27).
41. Such as the role of lobbying outlined in Lessig (2011).
42. Unger (1998, p. 256).

these new relationships build new and deeper sustained forms of political engagement? Can pilot programs become sustained beyond one-of-a-kind or ad hoc experiments? Institutionalizing PB on a long-term basis can translate these civic rewards into lasting political reform.

Why Participatory Budgeting?

Understanding participatory budgeting requires identifying the potential interests of various stakeholders in the process. Local government officials may want to implement PB, for example, in order to (1) promote government transparency, (2) encourage civic education, (3) create new channels for feedback with a potential for greater equity in resource distribution, or (4) achieve electoral success. Citizens may want to participate in PB in order to (1) gain information, (2) gain access to political leaders and policy, (3) gain control over service delivery, (4) form new social capital and networks in their neighborhoods, or (5) exert civic leadership or fulfill a perceived civic obligation. Civil society organizations may want to engage in PB in order to (1) strengthen the impact of their own programs, (2) expand their networks, (3) influence political leadership and policies, or (4) expand their programmatic agendas and priorities.

In some manifestations of PB, such as those found in Brazil and developing democracies, international NGOs can have incentives to help support the process. This help ranges from a consulting role to directly embedding themselves in the process. Many of these NGOs discuss PB as part of a larger programmatic strategy to reduce corruption and clientelism, promoting better service delivery within a larger framework of reform of government transparency and accountability. Yet NGOs implementing PB run the risk of imposing a top-down structure on what has typically been a bottom-up process.[43] In some municipalities that have adopted PB the business community becomes involved in order to support more open government. Sometimes local commerce associations come together to have members work on a specific topic in the PB process.

Any discussion of participatory budgeting should acknowledge the ideological components of PB's origins. Its roots lie in the post-authoritarian left in Brazil, in a political situation that grew out of twenty-one years of rule by a military dictatorship. New thinking revolved around the concept of "radical democracy," also known as "direct democracy," "deepening democracy," and "democratizing democracy."[44] In the original campaign for participatory budgeting the PT party in Brazil outlined four basic principles for PB. It had to involve (1) direct

---

43. See Goldfrank (2012).
44. Goldfrank (2007a).

citizen participation in government decisionmaking processes and oversight; (2) administrative and fiscal transparency as a deterrent for corruption; (3) improvements in urban infrastructure and services, especially in aiding the indigent; and (4) change in political culture so that citizens could be democratic agents.[45]

Participatory budgeting was conceived in an ideological tradition stuck between two models—a Soviet-style centralized powerful state, on the one hand, and a minimal state, on the other.[46] Emerging out of these extremes, PB offered a way to reimagine the state: "Participatory budgeting would help re-legitimate the state by showing that it could be effective, redistributive, and transparent."[47] Since then the process has expanded and grown into a variety of forms.[48]

Participatory Budgeting in Brazil

While most of the literature credits the rise of "Brazilian style participatory budgeting" to the efforts of the PT in Porto Alegre in 1989, some scholars offer a different view.[49] According to these accounts, Brazilian municipal governments in Lages,[50] Boa Esperança,[51] and Pelotas[52] started experiments to submit their budgets for public discussion in the late 1970s.[53] Recife started experimentation in the early to mid-1980s.[54]After winning control of thirty-six municipalities in the 1988 election, the PT experimented with citizen budget councils in thirteen cities total, including in areas beyond Porto Alegre such as Ipatinga and Santos.[55] Four of these municipal processes (Teresina, Ipatinga, Vitória, and Porto Alegre) are still active after twenty-six years. Earlier efforts by another party, the Movimento Democrático Brasileiro (MDB), to engage citizens in budgeting also contributed to shaping PB.[56]

Nonetheless, the actual design of PB was forged by civil society and the PT's municipal administration in Porto Alegre.[57] Using the formal nomenclature of "participatory budgeting" for this specific process became fashionable in the

---

45. Goldfrank (2002).
46. Dutra (2002).
47. Goldfrank (2007a).
48. See Goldfrank (2012); Ganuza and Baiocchi (2012); Peck and Theodore (2015).
49. Goldfrank and Schneider (2006); Goldfrank (2007a).
50. Lesbaupin (2000).
51. Baiocchi (2001).
52. Goldfrank and Schneider (2006).
53. Goldfrank (2007a).
54. See Souza (2001).
55. Abers (1998); Goldfrank (2007a, p. 92).
56. Goldfrank (2007a).
57. Baierle (1998); Baiocchi (2001).

1990s.[58] PB gained international fame after Habitat II: the Second United Nations Conference on Human Settlements in Istanbul in 1996 cited Porto Alegre's participatory budgeting as one of forty-two best practices in urban governance throughout the world.[59]

The leftist PT took advantage of the confluence of three factors that made Brazil ripe for PB at this moment in time: (1) a history of participation in civil society, (2) decentralization, and (3) democratization. Brazil constituted a unique country in that, although it was governed by an authoritarian regime, it not only allowed opposition parties to exist, but also—in contrast with neighboring authoritarian regimes—devolved power to the municipal level via relatively transparent mayoral elections. Brazil had maintained a civic infrastructure that provided opportunities for citizens to participate in governance, including local health councils and federal policy conferences.[60]

The end of authoritarian rule spurred further desire for citizen-focused governance. The new Brazilian Constitution of 1988 mandated many forms of participatory engagement and strongly supported citizen participation, even though it did not include a specific provision for participatory budgeting. Devolution of power and de facto fiscal autonomy to the local level is a paramount structural condition for implementing PB. Arguably, the emergence of PB can be attributed to the combination of lack of public trust in a defunded national government and devolution of power to the local level. In the first years that PB was implemented in Porto Alegre—in 1989 and 1990—fewer than one thousand citizens participated in it. In 1992 participation began to increase sharply, from eight thousand participants at the beginning of the year to more than twenty thousand citizens participating in PB by the time of the PT's reelection that same year. PB can grow quickly as it gains momentum and legitimacy in the eyes of citizens.

The original structure of PB in Porto Alegre serves as an instructive PB paradigm. Figure 2-1 shows the basic structure and design of PB in Brazil. The PB structure evolved after 2002 to include only one round of regional plenary assemblies.

In Porto Alegre, the first portion of the process involved a series of neighborhood assemblies in sixteen regions of the city.[61] There were two assemblies: a public works assembly and a thematically organized one.

In the public works assembly, citizens discussed, debated, deliberated, and voted on budget priorities and to elect representatives who would move on to

58. Goldfrank (2007a, p. 93).
59. Goldfrank (2007a).
60. See Avritzer (2009).
61. After 2002, this number was altered.

Figure 2-1. *The Structure of PB in Brazil*

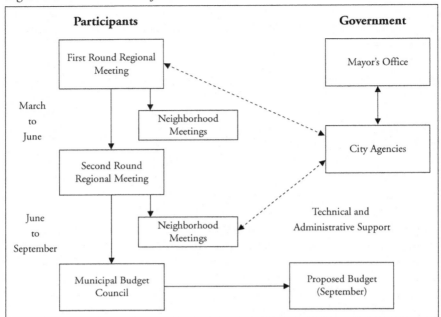

Source: Wampler (2007c), p. 53.

the next levels of the process. In the thematic assembly, citizens discussed policies grouped together under large themes with a broader impact on politics beyond the municipality. Examples of themes included transportation, health, and education, to name but a few.

A second layer, known as the regional budget forum, followed this initial level of engagement. Elected representatives participated in these forums by consolidating the list of priorities from the neighborhood assemblies and mapping out priorities for their regions. Elected representatives in thematic budget forums had similar responsibilities. Citizens were invited to attend as observers.

The third level of engagement was that of the Conselho do Orçamento Participativo or municipal budget council (henceforth COP), to which each regional forum elected two councilors. The COP is where decisions about the distributions of funds were made. It was also open to citizen observers. Within the COP, a process of deliberation and debate determined distributive rules to govern the PB for the following year. In addition to deciding on the distribution of funds, the COP was tasked with monitoring implementation of projects. The COP served the function of both transparency and accountability under the control of the citizens. The next steps after the COP involved voting on public works projects and submitting the final budget proposal to the mayor's office and the city legislature.

An examination of the two forums confirms PB's dual goals of (1) high-quality service delivery of goods to citizens, and (2) deepened democratic engagement. The public works forum enables citizens to see a direct link between their involvement and concrete improvements in their areas. Citizens can observe their impact on city policy and feel that their efforts are efficacious. After its initial adoption of PB, Porto Alegre established a successful track record of implementing projects within two to three years. The quick turnaround of projects in these early years of PB demonstrated that the process could support increased accountability.

In the public works forums, citizens craft the agenda and determine the priorities for their region. Because the process is broken down into localities, citizens are able to use specific knowledge of their own local areas. Through their participation, citizens learn governance. The idea of democracy as self-government can become a reality within the scope of this process.

In Porto Alegre's implementation of PB, the public works forum allows citizens to see the tangible results of their efforts in projects achieved throughout the city, while the broader thematic councils provide opportunities for deeper democratic engagement. First, the government provides citizens with detailed information about current spending priorities and policies. Second, participants debate the current set of government policies. Citizens do not present new proposals; rather, they deliberate on the merits of current policies. They discuss spending priorities without independently proposing new policies. Civic education for participants is a component of the thematic councils.

Scholars who have studied the inner workings of the PT to uncover the origins of PB discuss various reasons for its implementation, including the confluence of "ingenuity and self-interest of leftist political entrepreneurs."[62] Some analyze relationships between extant civil society and elected officials.[63] One common thread throughout the scholarly literature is the contention that, over the course of the 1980s, Brazilian civil society became more robust, taking on new forms and deploying more diffuse yet strategic tactics for citizen engagement.[64] Civil society pushed for participatory engagement and hoped to foster citizen deliberation—leading to the inclusion of CSOs with elected officials.[65]

62. Fung (2011, p. 859).
63. Abers (1998, 2000).
64. Wampler and Avritzer (2004).
65. Baierle (1998); Wampler and Avritzer (2004).

While scholars disagree on the causal mechanisms and conditions that led to PB in Brazil, a consensus has emerged that PB in Porto Alegre was the starting point of the specific form of PB we know today. PB's origins in Porto Alegre has served as a model for structuring PB elsewhere, including in the United States. Throughout this book, I examine the initial pilot projects of PB in the United States as marking another turning point in PB's history.

Defining Success

Acknowledgment that Porto Alegre constitutes the birthplace of PB compels an assessment of its impact there. Some potential indicators of success include: (1) greater citizen education, (2) greater investment in meeting the needs of lower-income citizens, (3) greater transparency and accountability in the budget process, and (4) a deepening of citizen engagement and furthering of democratic opportunities for citizens.

Adalmir Marquetti notes that PB has a redistributive effect with respect to lower-income neighborhoods.[66] In the 1970s and 1980s, the majority of Porto Alegre's investment of resources was directed to middle-class neighborhoods. By contrast, spending in Porto Alegre under PB has concentrated in poorer pockets within the municipality. Poorer locales now receive more spending per capita than wealthier areas. Yet Marquetti's analysis, looking at census data over ten years of PB, shows that redistribution becomes visible only several years after the implementation of PB.[67]

Several scholars have identified a range of successful outcomes associated with PB. Gianpaolo Baiocchi, Patrick Heller, and Marcelo K. Silva use a matched-pair analysis to compare successes in cities that adopt PB with others that do not.[68] The results show that in all but one pair, civil society outcomes related to PB were superior to those in cities without PB.

In Brazil, PB has been shown to improve governance, reinforce democracy, and contribute significantly to the well-being of the poorest citizens.[69] Touchton and Wampler connect the presence of PB in a given locality with increased municipal spending on sanitation and health, increased numbers of CSOs, and decreased rates of infant mortality.[70] Similarly, Sonia Goncalves found that Brazilian municipalities that implemented PB channeled a larger fraction of their

---

66. Marquetti (2002).
67. See also Wampler (2007b, p. 36).
68. Baiocchi, Heller, and Silva (2011).
69. Touchton and Wampler (2014).
70. Touchton and Wampler (2014, p. 1444).

total budget to investments in sanitation and health services, with a pronounced reduction in infant mortality.[71]

Gauging the success of participatory budgeting is intricately related to the criteria used for evaluation. For example, Brian Wampler's set of criteria involves "engaged deliberation, social justice, and active citizens."[72] He understands PB's success through this lens, looking at various indicators, including citizen efficacy and mobilization of low-income residents.[73] Wampler's surveys assess the degree to which the involvement of citizens in PB proves efficacious, including in influencing and improving service delivery.[74] His depiction of successful PB requires strong networks of CSOs that exert political pressure to implement the process and move it forward. He suggests that social movements in Brazil have viewed participatory mechanisms as useful tools for organization.

Other scholars buttress this conclusion by highlighting the role of Brazil's twenty-one years under military dictatorship in producing the conditions for civil society to work cooperatively together through participatory mechanisms.[75] Leonardo Avritzer notes not only that the presence of a robust civil society is critical for PB, but also that these CSOs and their members should infuse the PB process with practical skills embedded in their preexisting organizational structures for its success.[76] Rather than looking for a one-size-fits-all approach to PB, Avritzer suggests certain social and political constraints influence success.[77]

While Avritzer contends that civil society must provide the primary impetus for PB, Rebecca Abers argues that the state must induce civil society organizations to be active participants in PB.[78] Moreover, the state is a critical actor in encouraging participation by typically marginalized citizens who had not engaged previously in politics.

Some scholars take a less sanguine view of PB. Benjamin Goldfrank notes that "participatory budgeting does not always strengthen the state with respect to the market."[79] In Brazil, the PT was able to use PB as a way to both legitimate its party and expand its support within Brazil's poorest demographic communities. Yet this strategy proved to be unsustainable in the face of the economic crisis of the late 1990s. The result was that the PT was constricted in its ability to redistribute funds downward. In a paper written with Aaron Schneider, Goldfrank

71. Gonçalves (2014).
72. Wampler (2007b, p. 26).
73. Wampler (2007a).
74. Wampler (2007c).
75. Moynihan (2007).
76. Avritzer (2002).
77. Avritzer (2006, 2009).
78. Abers (2000).
79. Goldfrank (2007a, p. 117).

analyzes PB as a politically driven process, subject to its own forms of partisanship with an eye toward competitive institution building.[80]

It can sometimes be difficult to understand the precise causal mechanisms that drive these results. One challenge to isolating causal effects is variance in local city conditions. Paolo Spada argues that a clear impact of PB on public spending cannot be currently identified.[81] The initial introduction of PB has a demonstrable effect only on the probability of reelection for the party of the mayor implementing PB.[82]

Luciano Joel Fedozzi and Kátia Cacilda Pereira Lima note in their examination of PB in Brazil:

> The data reinforces the possibilities and the importance of participatory democracy in the Brazilian development model which is historically exclusionary and authoritarian. On the other hand, the results indicate serious limitations to the possibilities of participation—as a means to democratise the application of public resources—in local contexts and underprivileged regions of the country.[83]

The above quote confirms what some have argued: there are significant possibilities for change, but the changes will be slow.

Participation beyond Latin America

Participatory budgeting has the ability to serve as an important model for citizen engagement throughout the developing world. Successful versions have been implemented globally within political structures as diverse as those found in Bangladesh and South Africa to take just two examples.[84] One lens to understand these PB variants includes: those in which the state is legally mandated to implement a direct form of citizen engagement through a constitutional arrangement and those in which citizens achieve an implementation of participatory mechanisms via external pressure in the form of domestic or international organizations.[85] In the post–Cold War era, some newly formed democracies added participatory mechanisms directly into their constitutional structures. For example, Bulgaria created robust mechanisms for direct citizen engagement in

---

80. Goldfrank and Schneider (2006, p. 8).
81. Spada (2010).
82. Spada (2010).
83. Fedozzi and Pereira Lima (2014, p. 162).
84. See Dias (2014); Shah (2007).
85. Fölscher (2007c); McNulty (2012).

decisionmaking, including at community meetings, through regulated contact with mayors, and via referendums.[86]

Three broad imperatives in some newly formed democracies encourage the adoption of PB: (1) an increase in the forms of legitimate participation,[87] (2) a trend toward transparency,[88] and (3) a trend toward fiscal decentralization.[89] PB can help strengthen or legitimate these goals. International organizations often partner with local NGOs to implement a variety of PB processes. The precise form, how it is mobilized, and the degree to which the process is binding—either legally or politically—differ across geopolitical contexts.

Bangladesh offers an interesting example. A democracy since 1971, its constitution includes both fundamental rights and "pledges ownership of the republic to the people," yet it offers few constitutional mechanisms for citizen engagement.[90] In 2000 in Sirajganj, Bangladesh, a form of PB was implemented by the United Nations Development Program (UNDP) and the United Nations Capital Development Fund (UNCDF) in conjunction with the local government.[91] The budgeting project revolved around *parishads,* or unions, the smallest units of local government. The project began with block grants of $6,000 for each union to allocate for ward-level projects.

South Africa provides another illustrative example. Mechanisms for citizen engagement were constitutionally mandated in the wake of the end of apartheid. While it does not fit my definition of PB, it reflects the broader movement toward participatory policy in budget making. The Municipal Systems Act of 2000 requires municipalities to interact with communities regarding service delivery, performance management, integrated development planning, and the budget process.[92] At least ten months before the start of the financial year, mayors must put out public timetables for budget deadlines and enter all deadlines for consultative and participatory mechanisms into the public record. Municipalities are legally bound to make annual budgets public, including any supporting documents, and to invite public submissions on the budget from community stakeholders.[93] However, a formalized, legalistic, or top-down mandate within itself is not enough to guarantee robust civic engagement in budgetary decisionmaking.

86. Fölscher (2007c); Novkirishka-Stoyanova (2001). Bulgaria is also a signatory to the European Charter of Local Self-Government.
87. Moynihan (2003); Olivo (1998).
88. Moynihan (2007).
89. Robinson (2004).
90. Fölscher (2007a, p. 160).
91. Rahman, Kabir, and Razzaque (2004).
92. Shall (2007).
93. Shall (2007).

In newly formed democracies PB helps institute mechanisms for transparency and bottom-up democracy, which is particularly valuable in countries with a history of corruption.[94] The goal is often more effective service delivery and greater responsiveness to the needs of the local citizen.[95] Citizen participation improves social accountability by altering the incentive structure for officeholders. Because it deepens citizen engagement, PB gives public officials a sense of accountability to new eyes watching them. Development organizations seeking to implement PB in political systems with a limited history of civic accountability in institutional decisionmaking highlight the potential for PB to lead to greater government transparency and accountability.[96]

In addition to addressing concerns for greater accountability and transparency as well as improved service delivery and reduced corruption, PB also answers a normative argument for a higher quality of democracy. In contrast to other innovations aimed solely at ameliorating corruption, PB also deepens democracy. Participants in PB ideally leave equipped with the tools, or "civic rewards" as I argue, to be more engaged citizens in the future.[97] This is especially critical in developing democracies that lack a strong foundation for relationships between citizens and the state.[98]

Within developing democracies, PB offers opportunities and challenges. In many of the implementing countries, new constitutional orders call for an increase in participatory political structures. The World Bank has called for beneficiary feedback from all their programs by 2018.[99] While they promise more participatory mechanisms, many of these countries are united by a shared history of centrally controlled bureaucracies. Therefore, ensuring that officials at the local level have access to the money and power necessary to implement PB mechanisms may be difficult. Case studies looking at PB in developing democracies consistently cite the lack of capacity or fiscal autonomy of officials on the local level as an impediment to PB.[100]

When foreign NGOs and governmental organizations do the primary work to implement PB, the risk arises that domestic civil society will be unable to successfully monitor the process when these external bodies leave. Under these circumstances, the process may face additional questions about its legitimacy as a

94. Edstrom (2002).

95. McGee and others (2003).

96. Fölscher (2007c).

97. See also Julien Talpin. 2011. *Schools of Democracy: How Ordinary Citizens (Sometimes) Become Competent in Participatory Budgeting Institutions* (United Kingdom: ECPR Press).

98. McGee and others (2003).

99. World Bank, "Citizen Engagement," brief (www.worldbank.org/en/about/what-we-do/brief/citizen-engagement).

100. Shall (2007).

bottom-up grassroots endeavor and whether PB is being implemented in response to the needs of the citizens.

Conclusion

The traditional elites know perfectly well that this practice gives real content to democracy, ending privileges, clientelism, and ultimately the power of capital over society. . . . Besides deepening and radicalizing democracy, participatory budgeting also is constituted by a vigorous socialist impulse, if we conceive socialism as a process in which direct, participatory democracy is an essential element, because it facilitates critical consciousness and ties of solidarity among the exploited and oppressed, opening the way for the public appropriation of the State and the construction of a new society.[101]

This statement by Olívio Dutra, the mayor who first implemented PB in Porto Alegre and was then elected governor of the state of Rio Grande de Sul, illustrates the role of ideology in the first wave of PB. An understanding of the particular Marxist ideology that shaped the PT and that party's decision to first institute PB enriches the study of early "Brazilian style PB."

Participatory budgeting takes on a different flavor in each place where it is implemented. Structural factors shape the process. Is an NGO or a political party instituting it? What is the nature and format of funding? To date, several design differences between the most common structure of PB in Brazil and forms of PB found in the United States can be identified: (1) the nature of the relationship with a city council and a nonpartisan framework, (2) deliberative versus representative structures, and (3) resource-bounded efforts.[102] Unlike in Latin America, in the United States PB is too nascent for longitudinal impact to be seen yet.

In Brazil, PB structures can sometimes exist in friction with the citizen's council. In Chicago and New York City, it has been the councilors or aldermen themselves who have instituted PB. Its first implementation in the United States, at the behest of one Chicago alderman, was instituted with neither a strong partisan nor ideological framework. The New York City process is bipartisan, in distinct contrast with the partisan framing of PB in Brazil. Citywide processes are emerging—as seen in Boston, Massachusetts, or Vallejo, California—but to date these have been limited to endeavors that involve small amounts of public monies.

101. Quoted in Goldfrank (2007a, p. 95).
102. For more information on these design differences see Paolo Spada and Hollie Russon Gilman, "PBNYC Design in Comparative Perspective," *International Conference on PB*, March 2012, New York City.

In its current versions in the United States, deliberation is front-loaded, with more of an emphasis placed on moderated dialogue and small group deliberation than representation. For early PB projects in the United States, deliberation is integrated throughout project formation, whereas in early Brazilian processes, deliberation was sometimes contained until immediately before the vote. In Brazil, PB often has a structured representative system—as seen in the Conselho do Orçamento Participativo (COP)—and employs large group assemblies. PB pilots in the United States have not elected community representatives in PB, whereas there is an elected assembly in Brazil.[103] Thus far, PB in the United States has dealt only with small discretionary budget portions of municipal districts, whereas Brazilian PB usually involves a larger portion of an entire city budget. The structure and overall organization of PB in the United States, which is consistently evolving, is explored in depth in chapter 3. Distinct political and institutional factors, such as funding structures and amounts, will shape where and how PB is executed in the United States.

Despite differences between U.S. PB and Brazilian PB, several similar issues arise regarding participation, deliberation, and institutionalization as explored in the next chapters. These institutional factors are salient as PB continues to spread across the globe. In 2014, Paris implemented the largest version of PB in Europe. The municipal government has set aside €426 million to be spent between 2014 and 2020 based on the decisions of residents; the allocation in 2014–15 was roughly €20 million.[104] As PB continues to spread across the globe, lessons from the United States will be added to those learned in Brazil and elsewhere.

This book argues that PB in the United States should be considered not merely as a successor to Brazilian PB, but also as part of a larger framework of contemporary civic innovation taking shape inside the United States today. Chapter 8 further explores the implications of this trend. PB may find additional support and resonance as part of a broader ecosystem—and, in turn, contribute to the overall push for democratic renewal. The following chapters provide an in-depth study of PB pilots in the United States, and New York City in particular, in order to identify potential broader lessons for civic innovation and civic engagement.

---

103. When Chicago began its pilot year, the initial plan included elected representatives, but this was quickly abandoned as the realities of the process unfolded, as discussed in chapter 3.

104. Richelle Harrison Plesse, "Parisians Have Their Say on City's First €20m 'Participatory Budget,'" Cities, *The Guardian*, October 8, 2014 (www.theguardian.com/cities/2014/oct/08/parisians-have -say-city-first-20m-participatory-budget).

3

Participatory Budgeting Comes to America

Participatory Budgeting (PB) in the United States began in a single Chicago ward, when Alderman Joe Moore instituted it as a pilot project in 2009–10.[1] As the alderman tells it, he discovered this process at the meeting of the U.S. Social Forum in Atlanta in 2007 at workshops organized by members of the Participatory Budgeting Project (PBP), became enamored of its value for democracy and civic engagement, and realized that the modest discretionary funds he received as a council member could provide the funding.[2] Within Chicago, it took another few years before other aldermen began to sign on to the process in 2012.[3] A more detailed description of how Alderman Moore and other U.S. municipal officials came to adopt PB in the first place is offered by Josh Lerner, a key actor in PB's arrival in America and co-founder of the PBP.

The first year of any democratic experiment is critical for informing future implementations and guiding the overall trajectory of an innovation. The first year is when public interest is the highest, everything is new, and anything seems possible. As with all disruptive innovations, the first year of the process in Chicago

---

1. As discussed in chapter 1, across America other large-scale, deliberative experiments engaging citizens in public budget decisions have already taken place. See Weeks (2000) for discussions in Eugene, Oregon, and Sacramento, California. For other opportunities and resources to engage citizens in budget decisions, see Peak Democracy, "About Us: Our Mission" (www.peakdemocracy.com/about_us). Additionally Kahn (1997) offers a glimpse of a very different type of participation in budgeting during New York City's Progressive Era. In distinction from these other efforts, the form of PB I describe self-identifies as a variant of a form of PB imported from Brazil.

2. Summers (2011); Secondo and Jennings (2014); See also Lerner (2014) for discussions of PBP's advocacy to bring PB to the United States.

3. PB Chicago, "Voting Results for 2012–2013" (www.pbchicago.org/2012-2013-cycle.html).

was imperfect. Yet it set an important precedent for the further diffusion of PB in the United States. PB in Chicago set the stage for PB in New York City and beyond. In this chapter, some of the variables that influenced participatory budgeting in Chicago are sketched out.

Elected officials exist within political economies that shape any politically innovative process. These political ecosystems are critical engines of change, even as they themselves are systems continually in flux. The goal is not to understand all political dynamics and idiosyncratic politics at the district level but rather the basic process structure—in order to extract and refine it for potential replication, adaptation, and scale. To isolate the effects of PB on discretionary spending, I compare this spending in the initial Chicago ward that piloted PB before and after its introduction. I also use a second lens for understanding PB projects, examining the *nature* of the projects themselves. This more textured approach includes a typology of "innovative" and "conventional" PB projects, as discussed throughout the chapter.

The projects split evenly, with half of the projects classifiable as innovative and half as conventional. Many of the conventional projects closely tracked those from previous years, while many innovative projects address tangible needs. This suggests that citizens themselves can effectively determine how to spend capital funds and that fears of genuine citizen engagement in decisionmaking appear to be unwarranted. The chosen projects pursued in Chicago's pilot year reflect the will of ward residents more directly than similar ones implemented in years without PB. Further, the participatory process has the potential to be more creative than the normal urban bureaucratic process. At its best, PB is self-legitimating: through PB, citizens confer legitimacy on a governance structure that genuinely engages people. The very act of implementing PB can send a signal of greater government transparency and citizen accountability as elected officials, public servants, civil society, and other constituents take notice.

In this chapter I outline how participatory budgeting came to Chicago, its structure there, and the basic properties of Chicago's process, with results and lessons learned. This chapter lays out a foundation for understanding institutional factors critical for implementing PB across the United States.

Background

Chicago aldermen often have personal relationships with their constituents and serve effectively as "mayors" of their wards, with significant decisionmaking power. Since 1994, aldermen in Chicago have been receiving "menu money" in the amount of roughly $1.3 million per ward per annum for infrastructure projects.[4] This "menu money" is disbursed equally to all fifty wards in Chicago in a need-blind allocation. After learning about the power of PB in Brazil, in part thanks to outreach from PBP and other CSOs such as Cities for Progress, Alderman Moore decided in 2009 to cede a portion of his discretionary funds for infrastructure to the PB process.[5] The alderman was intrigued by the opportunity to try this experiment in the United States.

Corruption has been a recurring problem in Chicago. Its Democratic Party machine has a history of wielding power; Richard J. Daley served as mayor from 1955 to 1976, and his son Richard M. Daley served from 1989 to 2011.[6] Not only mayoral politics but also ward-level politics have been rife with political scandals. From 1972 to 2009 thirty Chicago aldermen were indicted and convicted of federal crimes ranging from income tax evasion to extortion, embezzlement, and conspiracy.[7] At first glance, this might not seem like the most fertile ground for a democratic innovation focused on transparency and accountability. Yet the publicity attached to being the first person to implement PB in the United States—in Chicago of all places—created a powerful incentive that helped convince the alderman to adopt the practice.[8]

The alderman had been serving the ward since 1991. He took a calculated risk that PB would be favorably received.[9]

From Theory to Implementation

In spring 2009 about forty leaders of diverse local service organizations, schools, religious institutions, block clubs, and other civic groups were invited to form a steering committee for the ward's PB pilot.[10] The nonprofit organization, Participatory Budgeting Project (PBP), which champions PB in the United States and Canada, worked to adapt the process imported from Brazil to the municipal ward level in the United States by providing education, technical assistance, and research and evaluation.[11] PBP worked to provide the support and expertise to enable PB to grow and flourish in the United States, which included giving

4. Summers (2011); City of Chicago, "Capital Improvement Program" (www.cityofchicago.org /city/en/depts/obm/provdrs/cap_improve.html).

5. See Lerner (2014); Baez and Hernandez (2012, p. 320).

6. Roger Biles, "Machine Politics," *Encyclopedia of Chicago* (website), 2004 (www.encyclopedia .chicagohistory.org/pages/774.html).

7. Gradel and others (2009).

8. Summers (2011).

9. Thank you to demographer Rob Paral, principal of Rob Paral and Associates in Chicago.

10. See Summers (2011).

11. Lerner and Secondo (2012); Lerner (2014).

presentations about previous implementations of PB throughout the world, helping to draft guidelines for Chicago, and leading workshops for the steering committee.

The steering committee had responsibilities for each phase of the process, including planning meetings, facilitating small group discussions, and structuring the vote. The steering committee met in the evenings for meetings that usually lasted between one and two hours; over time, the numbers in attendance dropped from the initial group of roughly forty. The original rulebook was crafted by PBP, the steering committee, and the alderman's office. It outlined four stages of the process: (1) neighborhood assemblies (October–November), (2) community representative meetings (November–March), (3) voting assembly (March), and (4) implementation and monitoring (April–December).

The original rulebook stated that community representatives would be elected at the neighborhood assemblies. It called for a "bus tour," led by the alderman's office, to assess needs within the ward, similar to the caravans in Brazil, whereby citizens would go into the field to observe what the greatest needs might be for specific projects.

As the process progressed, the steering committee, in conjunction with the alderman's office and PBP, amended some of the rules. The biggest changes involved abandoning the election of community representatives. Instead, participants were able to self-select to serve as community representatives, without a specific maximum number of representatives. Another amendment added a second round of neighborhood assemblies in March, pushing the voting back from March to April. The bus tour was eliminated as part of the process as was the limit of fifteen project proposals per committee. The original six themes of the committees were changed to more aptly reflect projects put forth at the neighborhood assemblies. The themes that emerged were: (1) streets, (2) transportation, (3) public safety, (4) traffic safety, (5) parks and environment, and (6) art and other projects. These changes to the rulebook made the process more responsive to on-the-ground realities and needs.[12]

The members of the steering committee played an integral role in every phase of the PB process. They facilitated the neighborhood assemblies and the budget committees. This included publicizing and chairing neighborhood assemblies—even doing the setup and cleanup for them. For the vote, they worked at voting stations doing setup, cleanup, and voter registration; welcoming attendees; and leading the oral project presentations.

12. See PB Chicago, "Participatory Budgeting in Chicago Rulebook, 2012–2013" (www.pbchicago .org/uploads/1/3/5/3/13535542/pbchi_rulebook_screen_oct_3_2012.pdf).

The Process

Understanding the mechanics of PB in Chicago is critical to assessing PB's adoption and spread throughout the United States. PB in Brazil often included mayoral involvement, two thematic committees, and elected representatives. The theoretical design of the Chicago process was altered throughout its initial implementation in order to reflect community realities. For example, the original plan called for a set number of elected community representatives. In reality, community representatives were not voted upon, and there was no set number. Similarly, a second round of neighborhood assemblies that was not in the theoretical design was added to the process. Other cities in the United States have benefited from Chicago's experimentation in adapting PB to the ward/council level. These changes have been integrated into subsequent implementations throughout America.

Neighborhood Assemblies

From November to December 2009, nine neighborhood assemblies convened throughout the ward, including one in Spanish,[13] in community areas accessible to residents that included fieldhouses, churches, and schools. The alderman's office paid canvassers to post fliers and also sent e-mail fliers, stating: "You have a date with democracy."[14] At the meetings participants were given an agenda, a map of the ward, a brochure on the PB process and the roles for community representatives, a list of previous "menu money" expenditures, and a survey to complete at the end of the meeting. Attendance varied with approximately thirty individuals at each meeting.

Community Representative Budget Committees

Following the neighborhood assemblies, those who signed up to be community representatives were contacted with information about attending budget committee meetings. Over sixty out of the eighty people who signed up showed up at the next meeting and participated as representatives.[15] The PB coordinator gave a presentation, outlining the roles and responsibilities of the community representatives, and residents broke into groups, which quickly became the budget committees.

Ideas from the neighborhood assemblies were compiled, sorted into committees, and designated "eligible," "maybe eligible," and "ineligible or unnecessary."[16]

13. Summers (2011).
14. See "You Have a Date with Democracy—Decide How Your Tax Dollars Will Be Spent in the Ward," *Rogerspark.com*, October 28, 2009 (http://rogerspark.com/rp/news_articles/view/you_have_a_date_with_democracy—decide_how_your_tax_dollars_will_be_spent_i/).
15. See Summers (2011).
16. Gilman (2012).

The designation criteria were largely based on which projects would be eligible for "menu money," funds that were restricted to infrastructure projects. The steering committee had decided that each budget committee should have a committee chair and vice chair as well as a "mentor" from the steering committee.

Each of the six committees had five pre-planned meetings already scheduled. Some committees held additional meetings; all meetings took place at the ward office on different evenings. After the initial meeting of all the community representatives, committees were given a great deal of discretion regarding how to make decisions, organize their process, and facilitate discussions. The committees were told to provide rationale for ideas suggested at the neighborhood assemblies.

Although they shared an organizational framework, each committee had different relationships with the process and with the specific agencies with which they interacted while drafting proposals.[17] Some, like the transportation committee, broke up into subcommittees, such as "sidewalk repairs," "bike transportation," and "public transportation." Varying levels of bureaucracy interacted in the different thematic governance areas. Some agencies proved more cumbersome to work with than others. Additionally, some committees conducted more surveys of the areas than others. For example, the streets committee divided up the ward into sections and the members inspected streets in need of repair.

The community was able to keep abreast of projects through a blog, maintained by the ward, on which committees would post updates.[18] Residents of the ward could comment and post ideas for projects on the blog. The "art and other projects" committee posted a survey on the blog that roughly 350 people filled out. In the weeks before the vote, a sample ballot was posted on the blog.

The Second Round of Neighborhood Assemblies

Though not part of the original rulebook, a second round of neighborhood assemblies was added a month before the final vote. The alderman felt that a second round of neighborhood assemblies would enable more citizen feedback in the process—and indeed, citizens frequently requested additional ways to be involved in the process outside of simply voting or being a community representative. The second round of assemblies was publicized through ward e-mails and fliers. Outreach to the Hispanic community was given particular attention and achieved primarily through existing church networks.

For the second round of neighborhood assemblies each committee was instructed to label their projects as either "recommended"—meaning the project

17. See Summers (2011).
18. Gilman (2012).

would probably be put on the final ballot—or as "other suggested" for projects that were deemed likely to be culled. Three second-round neighborhood assemblies were held, including one for Spanish-speaking residents. Approximately two hundred people attended these two-hour meetings.

Each meeting began with committee presentations followed by a structured question-and-answer session led by community representatives; each also included a science fair format for displaying information about the projects. Committees laid out tables with visual presentations. After the initial discussion, attendees were able to walk around and visit the different committee booths and ask questions about the projects. The committees were not given specific guidelines about presenting their work. As a result, some committees, such as the "art and other projects" committee, used PowerPoint, while the streets committee made a color-coded map to show their recommendations.

After the second round of neighborhood assemblies, scheduled a month before the vote, committees had a limited amount of time to discuss the suggestions from the assemblies and to try to incorporate them in the final proposals. Much of the feedback from ward residents could not be integrated in time. The second round of assemblies primarily provided residents with information about the PB process and the upcoming vote. It successfully educated residents but was less successful as a method of marshaling another layer of citizen input into the project proposals. Residents were unaware of the bureaucratic requirements for projects, such as the limitation of scope to infrastructural matters, and this further diminished the value of the feedback. Additionally, a tight timeframe was in place to implement feedback.

Elections

Ward residents had to meet several criteria to vote. These included being at least sixteen years of age and able to show proof of residency (or signing an affidavit affirming it) and provide photo identification. Residents could vote regardless of formal citizenship status. Sample ballots were produced and distributed before the vote. The official ballot was a two-page folded booklet listing the ballot options, project titles, cost estimates, and a brief description for each project, limited to one or two sentences. Projects were listed in alphabetical order and grouped by committee.

A "get out the vote" (GOTV) campaign was conducted for about three weeks before the elections. Strategy sessions for the GOTV effort included steering committee members and community representatives brainstorming creative ideas—like creating signs to encourage voting, reaching out to local civil society organizations (CSOs), standing in front of trains during rush hour to give out fliers, and putting up window signs in local businesses. The ward office created fliers, posters, yard signs, window signs, and palm cards, and it paid for a canvasser. Committee members also made their own fliers and signs to promote their individual projects. The community representatives and the ward office made a Facebook page. The alderman wrote and placed an op-ed piece about the process in the *Chicago Tribune* and posted it on the Huffington Post. The office also reached out to major news organizations, such CBS, WTTW, Fox News, and Univision, as well as several local university newspapers.

The election was scheduled at a local school on a Saturday afternoon, with an option for early voting at the ward office Monday through Friday of the preceding week. At the school site, citizens could vote anywhere in the cafeteria, including in a private voting booth. They were asked to place their completed ballots in a homemade "voting box." Steering committee members and ward volunteers staffed the voting locations. Each committee was given a poster board they could use to present their projects at the site. In addition, a PowerPoint presentation featuring all of the projects ran continuously throughout the voting assembly. Each committee was given five minutes to give oral presentations at different points throughout the day. Four hundred people voted early at the ward office, while roughly twelve hundred voted on the official voting day. A total of 1,652 people voted in the election, the first participatory budgeting election in the United States.[19]

The Projects

Comparing infrastructure projects in the ward before and after the implementation of PB shows that when citizens are empowered to make decisions as to where and how to allocate funds, they prioritize community needs.

I have created the following typology to distinguish the nature of the projects:[20]

1. **"Conventional"** (C) projects maintain the form of typical "menu money" funding. As discussed below, however, PB has enabled a more locally driven process to target projects that meet equitable community needs.

2. **"Innovative"** (I) projects depart from typical projects funded through "menu money" allocations the previous year. Beyond simply meeting traditional forms of local infrastructure needs, these projects also incorporate communal

19. Josh Lerner and Megan Wade Antieau, "Chicago's $1.3 Million Experiment in Democracy," *Yes! Magazine*, April 20, 2010 (www.yesmagazine.org/people-power/chicagos-1.3-million-experiment-in-democracy); Lerner (2014).

20. This typology is based on my qualitative data and is limited to a difference-in-difference approach to only one year before and after the treatment of PB.

ingenuity, for example, the insights that arise when citizens deliberate that might not be immediately apparent in the previous appropriations process.

These categories are not intended as a hard binary distinction—in fact, there is a great deal of gray area. Rather, they are intended to serve as a useful typology for thinking about the role of civic creativity in PB. This typology, schematic instead of exhaustive, illustrates that when citizens are empowered as decision-makers they can both pragmatically determine where to spend funds and effectively tap into their communal creativity.

Comparing projects directly illustrates the typology.

Pre-PB Projects (2009)
—Street resurfacing: $937,278
—Street lighting: $325,000
—Sidewalk repairs: $92,889
—Avenue design: $65,000
—Curbs and gutters: $60,143
—Alley resurfacing: $48,596
—Alley speed humps: $8,225
—Street speed humps: $3,500

PB Projects (2010)
—Sidewalk repairs: $188,292
—Bike lanes: $100,000
—Dog-friendly area at a park: $110,000
—Community gardens in two parks: $33,000
—Underpass murals: $84,000
—Traffic/pedestrian signal: $230,000
— Artistic multifunctional bike racks: $105,000
—Additional benches and shelters on Chicago Transit Authority "El" platforms: $84,000
—Street resurfacing: $102,000
—Solar-powered garbage containers: $41,000
—Convenience showers at park beach: $50,000
—Completion of path in park: $25,000
—Historical signs in park: $42,000
—Residential street lighting: $130,000

Out of the fourteen projects, I categorize seven as innovative and seven as conventional. As discussed later, 38 percent of the projects in the PBNYC pilot year were innovative, while 62 percent were conventional. PB in Chicago produced a higher proportion of innovative projects in its pilot year than PBNYC. The even split in Chicago suggests this implementation was effective both at bringing new ideas to fruition as well as showing that citizens can address standard community needs via rational proposals.

Studying the conventional projects that emerge from PB is particularly informative because these PB efforts take on tasks (such as sidewalk repair) that would be addressed normally through capital funds, and they focus them on a specific need (such as a particular street) determined by citizens. These more standard projects suggest that citizens based in their own local communities are best able to assess need.

The innovative projects were effective at bringing the community together in new ways. They not only effectively addressed community needs, but also reimagined those needs. Without PB these projects would not have happened. As one transportation committee member told me: "There was a tension for people living a car-based lifestyle with focus on a bike lifestyle. Ultimately, the bike people were able to convince many people to join their cause."

The creation of bike lanes, dog parks, and underpass murals demonstrate projects that would not have happened without PB and also exemplify participants forming a new understanding of what they might be able to accomplish together through the PB process itself. Projects such as solar-powered garbage cans, community gardens, and historical signs represent commitments to specific ideals and values. All of these projects favor policy solutions that extend civic involvement into spaces typically not opened to the community.

Chicago's PB projects suggest that fears of including citizens in the budgeting process are unwarranted. Residents were able to effectively isolate district needs and create projects to address them, showing innovation and creativity in the process.

Lessons Learned

Engaging citizens who live in local areas provides opportunity for policymakers to understand not only *what* a given community needs, but also precisely *where* and *how* to deliver it. People who spend their lives in a given location can identify precisely where an additional bench is needed. Chicago's experience with PB offers a model for assessing challenges and opportunities for other implementations; indeed, it has acted as a paradigm, informing PB's expansion throughout the United States.

While many embraced the pilot process in Chicago, it was not without its critics. As I heard in conversations with participants and others, some community members raised concerns that the alderman's office had too strictly imposed top-down control in the process, without allowing for community input. Some were concerned that it was driven more by his reelection desires than a desire for genuine community engagement. Faced with the particular composition of the steering committee, people asked why certain community members were invited to participate over others. Some became disillusioned with what they perceived as patronage and lack of transparency.

By its very design, participatory budgeting will be vulnerable to such critiques. Electoral ambitions can be understood as a necessary component of the process, creating an incentive for elected officials to devolve some of their power back to citizens. Electoral ambitions alone do not delegitimize the process if the result is significant increases in citizen engagement. Disentangling electoral considerations from process implementation will remain difficult. Therefore, if PB is to be considered an impactful and legitimate democratic innovation, it must genuinely encourage and rely on citizen participation at every step. As the process brings citizens in, part of the way they may exercise their newfound authority is by criticizing the process itself, which inevitably has its own winners and losers. Throughout the process, citizens will also need accurate and timely information to ensure that the process is fully transparent.

Aftermath

Participatory budgeting is still expanding in Chicago. Four wards implemented PB during 2012–13.[21] In 2013, Mayor Rahm Emanuel created a citywide staff position to support Chicago wards in PB efforts, tasking this office with "providing technical support to any alderman who wants to utilize participatory budgeting in local menu fund spending decisions."[22]

However, one Chicago ward decided after a year's trial that the process was too time intensive and that the turnout was too low to justify continuation.[23] Although enthusiasm for the process was cited, the ward decided to implement a type of "PB lite" titled an "infrastructure improvement program."[24] This in-

21. Ellyn Fortino, "The Votes Are In: A Look at Participatory Budgeting in Chicago," *Progress Illinois,* May 10, 2013 (http://progressillinois.com/posts/content/2013/05/10/votes-are-look-participatory -budgeting-chicago).

22. Mayor's Press Office (Chicago), "Mayor Rahm Emanuel Announces New Support to Aldermen Who Use Participatory Budgeting for Local Investments," October 23, 2013 (www.cityofchicago.org /city/en/depts/mayor/press_room/press_releases/2013/october_2013/mayor_rahm_emanuelannounces newsupporttoaldermenwhouseparticipato.html).

23. Bishku-Aykul (2014).

24. John Greenfield, "No 5th Ward PB Election This Year, But Residents Still Have Input on Budget," *Streetsblog Chicago,* April 17, 2014 (http://chi.streetsblog.org/2014/04/17/no-5th-ward-pb-election -this-year-but-residents-still-have-some-say/).

volved representatives from four neighborhoods organized into four committees to make recommendations for how the ward should spend $250,000 on infrastructure improvement. In April 2014, the committees offered their budget recommendations to the ward office.[25] For the fiscal year 2014–15, one ward set aside $2 million for a park district, using tax increment financing (TIFs).[26] After recent municipal elections, the process in 2015–16 includes five new wards in Chicago.[27]

The slower adoption rate for PB in Chicago, especially when compared with current efforts in New York City, deserves closer attention. I explore below how the process has rapidly unfolded in New York. Structural differences alone cannot explain the discrepancy. Despite concerns and challenges in scaling the process, it was the overall success of the PB pilot in Chicago that prompted other cities to take notice. Joe Moore, the alderman who initiated PB, spoke about it across the country, sparking interest among practitioners and researchers alike.[28] Just two years after Chicago's pilot, New York embarked on the largest PB experiment in the United States. To date, New York City continues to run the largest implementation of PB in the United States. Mayor Bill de Blasio, who won election in 2013, included a campaign proposal to bring PB efforts to greater use in the city.

From Brazil to the Big Apple

In his 1949 work, *Here Is New York,* E. B. White wrote:

> By rights New York should have destroyed itself long ago, from panic or fire or rioting or failure of some vital supply line in its circulatory system or from some deep labyrinthine short circuit.[29]

Thankfully, E. B. White's predictions have yet to come true—far from it. And today, New York has emerged as a petri dish for a new kind of democratic experiment: a participatory budgeting process on a scale previously unheard of in the United States. It was first implemented as a pilot from 2011 to 2012 with

25. Ellyn Fortino, "The Votes Are In: A Look at Chicago's 2014 Participatory Budgeting Cycle," *Progress Illinois,* May 12, 2014 (http://progressillinois.com/posts/content/2014/05/12/votes-are-look -2014-participatory-budgeting-cycle-chicago).

26. Great Cities Institute, University of Illinois at Chicago, "Participatory Budgeting" (https:// greatcities.uic.edu/uic-neighborhoods-initiative/participatory-budgeting/).

27. See www.pbchicago.org for more information on the Chicago expansion.

28. In fact, it was at a dinner with Alderman Moore in Cambridge, Massachusetts, that the author first learned about this process.

29. White as quoted in Mollenkopf (1992, p. 12).

four members of the New York City Council. These members included three Democrats and one Republican, here listed anonymously "A, B, C, and D." Notably, the PB process in New York City spanned partisan and ideological divides. The *New York Times* noted: "participatory budgeting, which has sprung up in cities around the world, is the ultimate inclusive party."[30] Even though the four districts that implemented the PBNYC pilot have the ordinary characteristics of many New York City Council districts, by instituting PBNYC they chose to do something extraordinary.

For decades, the discretionary funding system employed by the New York City Council had been criticized for its lack of formulaic decisionmaking tied directly to need. Many viewed the speaker of the city council as the arbiter of dispensed funds. Below, I outline existing budget politics of the New York City Council, relevant city council history, and the trajectory that brought PB to the city. Within this particular political ecosystem, PBNYC emerged as an alternative model to traditional city council discretionary funds, yielding major changes in both process and outputs.

In examining the initial PBNYC pilot, I apply the typology of "innovative" and "conventional" projects in evaluating Chicago's PB projects. I classified 62 percent of the projects voted upon in the PBNYC pilot year as conventional. These projects directly challenge critics who contend that citizens cannot make rational, pragmatic, and informed public policy decisions. The PB process allowed these projects to be more fair and accurate in assessing district needs than those resulting from traditional nontransparent budget processes. Further, PB offers more opportunities for civic creativity than the traditional budget process.

The projects selected through PBNYC suggest that when citizens are offered tools for empowerment, they use them pragmatically and are able to isolate hyperlocal needs more effectively than the traditional, or status quo, budget process. More creative PB projects disprove critics who contend that ordinary citizens are not able to effectively understand the intricacies of city budgets and put forth viable proposals distinct from those that came before. In several cases, in the view of this author, the projects chosen via PB assessed and addressed community needs more creatively and effectively. The PB process offers residents a legitimate way to propose and enact new kinds of projects. In turn, the viability of the resultant projects confers legitimacy on the PB process itself.

By detailing empirical findings, with a focus on participation, deliberation, and institutionalization, I aim to assess the full outputs of the PBNYC pilot project

---

30. Ginia Bellafante, "Participatory Budgeting Opens up Voting to the Disenfranchised and Denied," *New York Times*, April 17, 2015 (www.nytimes.com/2015/04/19/nyregion/participatory-budget ing-opens-up-voting-to-the-disenfranchised-and-denied.html).

as an alternative to the status quo ante that carried important lessons for democratic innovation. New York City offers an illustrative paradigm for PB's expansion in the United States. A project that began in four districts expanded, in the fall of 2014, to encompass nearly half of the city's districts. In 2015, PBNYC operated on a scale that represented nearly 4.5 million residents and allocated roughly $32 million in funds.[31] In her "State of the City" address in early 2015, New York City Council Speaker Melissa Mark-Viverito called for PB to be applied to parts of the Tenant Participation Activity (TPA) funds within New York City Housing Authority (NYCHA) funds for public housing.[32]

New York City Council History

> The City Council has not usually used its institutional potential offensively and extensively to represent the diversity of New York City residents, and has not served as an arena of consequential public discussion, and controversy, even less as an instrument of control of the executive.[33]

New York City displays a strong mayor–weak council leadership system, as described by James Svara.[34] Historically, the role of the New York City Council has been a limited one, with the mayor of New York wielding nearly complete power over the budgeting process in particular. For a long time, the New York City Council was "ignored and by-passed by the non-government groups, by bureaucrats, and by governmental leaders of the City and other jurisdictions."[35] Under the reforms to the city charter initiated in 1989, however, the balance of power began to shift.

The new charter expanded the number of city council members from thirty-five to fifty-one and enhanced their roles by adding to their powers.[36] It also abolished the city's Board of Estimate, which had been in charge of decisions pertaining to the budget and land use. That same year, the U.S. Supreme Court had deemed the body unconstitutional in the case *Board of Estimate of City of*

31. New York City Council, "Participatory Budgeting" (http://council.nyc.gov/html/pb/home.shtml).

32. Council of the City of New York, Office of Communications, "Speaker Melissa Mark-Viverito Delivers 2015 State of the City Address," press release, February 11, 2015 (http://council.nyc.gov/html /pr/021115soc.shtml); Sondra Youdelman, "NYC Speaker Melissa Mark-Viverito Announces New Resources and New Decision-Making Power for NYC Housing Authority Residents," Community Voices Heard (website), February 14, 2015 (www.cvhaction.org/node/654).

33. Windhoff-Héritier (1992, p. 54).

34. Svara (1990).

35. Sayre and Kaufman (1960, p. 622).

36. By contrast, Chicago, a city with roughly a third of the population of New York City, has fifty aldermen, who serve as the rough equivalent of New York City Council members.

New York v. Morris. Under the revised charter most of the Board of Estimate's former powers were given to the city council, with the council specifically given power over land-use decisions such as zoning changes, housing and urban renewal plans, and community development.[37] The expanded and empowered city council was intended to more directly represent each district's constituencies.

These reforms also had an impact on New York City's fifty-nine community boards (CBs). Each board has a membership of fifty members who must reside in or be stakeholders in the community, and who are appointed by borough presidents or city council members for two-year terms without term limits.[38] In 1989 the roles and responsibilities of community boards were expanded under the new charter to include a provision for each community board to hold an annual open meeting on its budget. Yet no mechanisms for accountability were stipulated within any provisions for community boards. As a result, some budget meetings have become "nothing but pro forma."[39] According to some CB members interviewed for this book, some community boards have stopped holding them without any consequences.

The relationship between the city council and community boards is complex. While the reforms of 1989 aimed to increase the representativeness of the community boards, by the middle of the 1990s community boards were acknowledged to be less inclusive than they either could or should have been.[40] The lack of diverse representation on community boards is largely due to their structure, wherein members are appointed rather than elected. As scholar Roger Sanjek noted: "Particularly in racially and ethnically diverse community districts they did not fully 'look like New York City.'"[41]

The revised charter and other reforms of the 1980s aimed to increase the power of the city council. In 1986, the leader of the majority party in the city council

37. New York City Council, "About the Council" (http://council.nyc.gov/html/about/about.shtml).

38. Residents can also apply directly to community boards for appointment as "public members," who may serve on CB committees but not as full members. See for example, City of New York Manhattan Community Board 3, "Public Member Application," July 2012 (http://www.nyc.gov/html/mancb3 /downloads/cb3docs/public_membership.pdf).

39. As told by one longstanding community board member. See also Fainstein (2009).

40. Sanjek (1998, p. 375). Both a descriptive and a normative argument can be made. The former contends that community boards should reflect the demographics of New York City, while the latter champions the normative imperative that calls for greater inclusion and diverse representation on the community boards. In Sanjek's account, the community boards were able to accomplish neither the representative nor the normative goals.

41. Sanjek (1998, p. 375). In his in-depth study of CB4, Roger Sanjek shows that the transition to making community board appointments led to greater inclusion but did not lead to full representation or a board that "looks like Elmhurst-Corona" (Sanjek 1998, p. 376). Elmhurst-Corona, where the population was at least one-third Latin American at the time, had only six Latin Americans on its community board (CB4) out of thirty-nine members.

was elevated to the role of speaker, retaining power for this leader in making budgetary decisions. According to an article in the *New York Times* from May 1985, "[City] Council is not the most politically powerful institution in city government, but whatever power it has is concentrated in the office of the majority leader."[42] Members of the majority party now elect the speaker in a closed vote that involves internal coalition building.

The Democratic Party has had a stronghold on New York City politics, especially in the City Council, for an extended period of time, with the infamous Tammany Hall as its emblem of corruption.[43] In the 1990s, Adrienne Windhoff-Héritier argued that one of the principal reasons the city council had not reflected the diversity of New York City was the dominance of the Democratic Party, which historically was a noninclusive party.[44]

The city council's discretionary funds provide evidence for the small role it plays in city budget making. These funds have traditionally been determined by the speaker in a process that has created a meaningful role for the city council, despite the fact that these funds combined amount to less than 1 percent of the city's annual budget. The city council has two types of funds at its discretion, capital and expense funds. Expense funds totaled $150 million in FY 2012.[45] These monies must be used within one fiscal year.[46] Capital funds totaled $428 million in FY 2012 and they can be used for infrastructure projects, such as building parks and renovating schools.[47] This money can be allocated for spending that stretches over several years. Capital projects must cost at least $35,000 and have a projected use for at least five years from the date of completion or installation.[48]

Further complicating the budgeting process are overlapping layers of jurisdiction for many projects involving the state and the city. For example, a project to fix a sidewalk may fall under both state and city jurisdictions, leaving significant discretion to individual agencies for timelines for project implementation and responsibility. Straightforward capital projects involving only one agency are

42. Joyce Purnick, "Cuite Retiring after 16 Years as Council's Majority Leader,"*New York Times,* May 25, 1985 (www.nytimes.com/1985/05/25/nyregion/cuite-retiring-after-16-years-as-council-s-majority-leader.html).

43. Tammany Hall was the Democratic Party organization of Manhattan that, with the exception during a reform period, dominated the city's politics until the middle of the 1960s. See also *Encyclopedia Britannica,* online ed., s.v. "Tammany Hall" (www.britannica.com/EBchecked/topic/582027/Tammany-Hall).

44. Windhoff-Héritier (1992, p. 55).

45. Fauss (2012, p. 1).

46. New York City's fiscal year runs from July 1 to June 30.

47. Fauss (2012, p. 1).

48. Fauss (2012, p. 18).

typically able to get projects completed in one year, while capital projects involving multiple agencies may take years to implement.

Criticism about lack of transparency and corruption in the use of the city council's discretionary funds has been widespread.[49] To address these concerns, then speaker Christine Quinn enacted a series of reforms starting in 2006 aimed at rendering the process more transparent and credible.[50] In 2006 the city council made the list of all programs or organizations receiving funding—also known as "Schedule C"—available online.[51] Yet this list covered only those organizations receiving expense funding, not capital funds. In 2007 the council began using "transparency resolutions"—public documents available on the council's website, outlining changes to discretionary funds that occurred outside of the traditional budget process.[52]

Yet these reforms did not go far enough. In 2008 a citywide scandal erupted that revealed that city council members had used fictional names for organizations to serve as erroneous placeholders, and that the funding thus obscured totaled $17.4 million of taxpayer money since 2001.[53] The result was a new series of reforms aimed at increasing transparency and accountability, this time including preclearance requirements for organizations, an online database of discretionary funds, limits to the ability of members of the city council to sublet office space, and limits on hiring outside consultants.[54] Reforms to the nature of discretionary spending have also accelerated since the participatory budgeting pilot took place in 2011.

49. Fauss (2012).

50. Mark Berkey-Gerard, "Reforming—and Not Reforming—the Budget Process," *Gotham Gazette,* July 10, 2006 (www.gothamgazette.com/article/iotw/20060710/200/1904).

51. For example, see the current disclosure. Latonia McKinney, "Fiscal Year 2015 Adopted Expense Budget Adjustment Summary / Schedule C," New York City Council Finance Division, June 25, 2014 (http://council.nyc.gov/downloads/pdf/budget/2015/FY15%20Schedule%20C%20Template%20-%20Final.pdf).

52. Fauss (2012). In FY 2010, the city council voted on twelve transparency resolutions. New York City Council, "Fiscal Year 2010," website (http://council.nyc.gov/html/budget/fy2010.shtml).

53. Sara Kugler, "NYC Pol Caught in Slush Fund Probe," Associated Press, April 5, 2008 (http://usatoday30.usatoday.com/news/nation/2008-04-04-4271129950_x.htm); "Councilman Martinez Resigns as Feds Close In," *NBC New York,* July 16, 2009 (www.nbcnewyork.com/news/local/Councilman-Martinez-Set-to-Resign-.html); Ray Rivera and Russ Buettner, "Phony Allocations by City Council Reported," *New York Times,* April 4, 2008 (www.nytimes.com/2008/04/04/nyregion/04quinn.html); New York City Council Office of Communications, "Speaker Quinn, Council Budget Team Present Best Practices for Budget Allocation Process," May 7, 2008 (http://council.nyc.gov/html/pr/039_050708_BudgetBestPractices.shtml).

54. Preston Niblack, "City Council Fiscal Year 2010 Adopted Expense Budget: Adjustments Summary/Schedule C," Council of the City of New York, Finance Division (http://council.nyc.gov/downloads/pdf/fy_2010_sched_c_final.pdf); New York City Council, Office of Communications, "Further Protecting the Integrity of the Use of Public Funds, Speaker Quinn Announces Budget Reforms," April 30, 2010 (http://council.nyc.gov/html/pr/discretionary_04_30_10.shtml).

Nonetheless, a report from Citizens Union in 2012 stated: "The current discretionary funding process, while improved from a decade ago, remains flawed and needs additional reform."[55] This report outlined why the recent reforms, although a step in the right direction, were insufficient to make the system more transparent. The amount of discretionary funds each council member received varied widely: the smallest amount of discretionary fund received by a city council member was $2,490,321 and the largest was $12,532,564 for FY 2012.[56] If funds were distributed equally, each council member would have received roughly $8.3 million in FY 2012.[57] While that would not have been equitable according to need, it would have been equal, akin to the distribution of "menu money" allocations in Chicago's wards.

The Citizens Union report charged that discretionary funds do not correlate with the needs of a neighborhood, as might be determined by such measures as median household income, unemployment, size of particularly needy populations (of youth and the elderly), number of recipients of food stamps, or number of persons living below the poverty line. Instead, the relationships between council members and the speaker seemed determinative. The report pointed to the fact that three of the ten districts with the highest median incomes received the most discretionary funds, while two of the three districts with the lowest median incomes received the least amount of discretionary funds.[58] It ended with a call for greater innovation in the budget process, including "greater use of pilot programs to improve the current system such as the participatory budgeting project taking place in four council districts during the current FY 2012 budget cycle."[59] The report attached a caveat: "Citizens Union, however, withholds judgment on the expansion of this particular pilot program citywide until greater data is available regarding its effectiveness."[60]

Updates to New York Discretionary Funding

A few important reforms have occurred since the 2011 PBNYC pilot. First, one of the four council members to bring participatory budgeting to New York was elected speaker. This also elevated several other council members, part of the original PBNYC coalition, to more powerful leadership positions. Second, PB has expanded dramatically in the city—from four council districts in 2011 to twenty-four

55. Fauss (2012, p. 4).
56. Fauss (2012, p. 26).
57. Fauss (2012, p. 4).
58. Fauss (2012, p. 31).
59. Fauss (2012, pp. 10, 41).
60. Fauss (2012, pp. 10, 41).

in 2014. Finally, and perhaps most critically, in 2014 the speaker and the city council helped usher in a series of reforms to the city council's discretionary spending regime.[61] Instead of the ad hoc discretionary system described earlier in the chapter, the council proposed a more objective model based on needs.[62] The goal is to create a more transparent and equitable needs-based funding system.

The FY 2015 proposed reforms include:

—**Expense funds:** Equal distribution with a needs-based increase to members, using a formula based on poverty in districts.

—**Capital funds:** Equal distribution with a ±5 percent allowance from the average amount, since capital funds are allocated in one lump sum.

This action accompanies an effort to make the database of where and how money is spent more accessible and comprehensive.

These are significant reforms.[63] Citizens Union and others noted the importance of these reforms in securing more transparent and accountable spending. Citizens Union also pushed for Schedule C spending disclosures to be provided in a format that is more easily machine readable, as opposed to use of a PDF.[64] One council member reflected on the change in policy, citing the pre-reform environment: "[The speaker used] public tax dollars to be vindictive and to ultimately punish communities because she didn't get along with a particular council member, or they didn't always do what the speaker had wanted them to do. . . . I was absolutely punished. . . . Now that's not happening anymore."[65]

What is the relationship between these reforms and participatory budgeting? They are intertwined as part of a good governance agenda that brings mechanisms of greater transparency, participation, and accountability to government. They may also be mutually reinforcing—with PB bringing pressure for reform and the reform pressure offering an incentive for PB. PB has brought greater public

61. Council of the City of New York, Office of Communications, "Council to Vote on Landmark Rules Reform Package," press release, May 14, 2014 (http://council.nyc.gov/html/pr/051414stated .shtml).

62. Citizens Union, "New Council Member Items Uphold Promise of More Equality for Districts," press release, June 24, 2014 (http://us3.campaign-archive2.com/?u=ca0fb41d668202ba6cc542ca8&id =11237b6cbb&e=%5bUNIQID).

63. Ross Barkan, "City Council Rejects Quinn Era with Rules Reform," *New York Observer*, April 29, 2014 (http://observer.com/2014/04/city-council-rejects-quinn-era-with-rules-reform/).

64. Kristen Meriweather, "City Council Member Discretionary Fund Allocation Shows Far Greater Equity," *Gotham Gazette*, June 25, 2014 (www.gothamgazette.com/index.php/government/5126-city -council-member-items-discretionary-funds-greater-equity).

65. Michael Howard Saul, "New York City Council Divvies Up $50 Million in Discretionary Funds," *Wall Street Journal*, June 24, 2014 (www.wsj.com/articles/new-york-city-council-divvies-up-50 -million-in-discretionary-funds-1403661246).

attention and scrutiny to the discretionary funding process, while the prior scandals help to justify its use. A single causal relationship, therefore, is difficult to isolate.

The reforms make planning for PB easier. If city council members know they have a set discretionary budget, they can more easily plan to implement PB. This is especially important as the fiscal year in New York City government runs from July to June, whereas a PB cycle typically runs from September to April. Prior to these reforms, the varying amounts of discretionary funds, fluctuating from one year to another, made it difficult to plan for PB or to allocate large funds to the process. PB requires advance planning and, ideally, a pooling of resources. Tracking the impact of these reforms and other transparency efforts on future PB implementation in New York City will prove valuable.

PB Arrives in New York City

The Participatory Budgeting Project (PBP) and Community Voices Heard (CVH), a nonprofit organization located in one of the implementing districts, were integral to launching PBNYC. CVH is a membership multiracial organization that organizes low-income populations to influence policy change, and PBP is a nonprofit organization that seeks to support the implementation of PB in the United States and Canada. In 2010 PBP and CVH held two public events to garner support for PB.[66] CVH served as the community lead and PBP as the technical lead. PBP used its experience in bringing PB to the United States in Chicago to directly inform the structure of the process in New York City. CVH brought their networks and background in organizing low-income populations. A large organizing effort helped bring PB to New York City, as Baez and Hernandez note: "The CMs [Council members] had never heard of PB before being approached by community-based organizations."[67]

In 2011 four city council members—three Democrats and one Republican— decided that they would each put a portion of their discretionary funds into the hands of their constituents to let them decide how to allocate the monies. The four council members each opted to put at least $1 million of their capital discretionary funds into the process, with the option to add additional monies to fund other projects. There were three main reasons the council members decided to restrict the project to capital funds: (1) there are stricter and clearer guidelines for capital funds, (2) capital funds are less likely to be co-opted by special interests or lobby-

---

66. See Lerner (2014) and Baez and Hernandez on "The Long Road from the World Social Forums to NYC" (2012, pp. 319–23).

67. Baez and Hernandez (2012, p. 324).

ing groups, and (3) capital funds pertain to local infrastructure projects in which local residents can offer expertise. City council districts in New York are similar in size and densely populated, with diverse and varied populations. Equal population distribution at the current level would result in approximately 160,710 people in each district, though actual counts vary slightly with redistricting fluctuation.[68]

Capital Funds

The New York City Council has strict guidelines and restrictions for discretionary capital funding. For city council capital projects the norm is for the city agency to be the implementing body. It is rare for nonprofits to get funded through this mechanism, though they do. For projects that are not on city-owned property, all recipients must be legally recognized nonprofits, and the project itself must directly benefit the city. Further, recipients for capital funds relating to property must have a preexisting contract for operating funds with the city.[69] To receive funding, the nonprofit must enter into a legal agreement stating that the capital funds will be used only in a way that enhances the city. Some institutions, such as private schools, are excluded from receiving capital funding.

The strict requirements for capital funds help to create the perception that these projects serve actual needs and are less easily co-opted by individual groups or lobbying. The scale and scope of such projects also convey legitimacy since they involve physical infrastructure (that is, things citizens can see). Programs that are covered by expense funding are often less tangible. Another benefit to capital projects, when viewed from the perspective of their suitability for PB, is that residents already possess the knowledge to decide which parks in their neighborhood need repair. By contrast, it is more difficult for residents to visibly ascertain information about specific programs as they relate to expense funds.

Once council members had decided the types and amounts of funds to put into PB, they worked in conjunction with a steering committee on a host of other issues surrounding the basic structure of the nine-month process. This steering committee was co-chaired by CVH and PBP. Together with the council members, PBP and CVH served as the executive members of the steering committee for Participatory Budgeting in New York City (PBNYC).[70] The

---

68. Calculation based on New York City Districting Commission, "February 6th Plan, Population Statistics," spreadsheet data, 2015 (www.nyc.gov/html/dc/downloads/pdf/Feb6_Population_Statistics .xls).

69. City of New York, "Guidelines for Capital Funding Requests for Not-For-Profit Organizations: Fiscal Year 2016" (www.nyc.gov/html/capgrants/downloads/exhibit1guidelines.pdf).

70. Lerner and Secondo (2012).

steering committee was composed of about forty other CSOs represented on the steering committee. Each district also had a district committee of active citizens, including some community board members and representatives of CSOs, who were invited to serve by the city council members.

The majority of the members of the steering committee came from civic organizations in New York that work to locally empower citizens and build coalitions. Seven community boards were represented on the steering committee, as community board districts and city council districts differ. There were also local academic institutions such as the City University of New York (CUNY), Pratt Institute, and Marymount Manhattan College.

The Community Development Project at the Urban Justice Center (CDP) led the research and evaluation of the process and worked to organize graduate students, professors, and practitioners in the field of participatory budgeting to draft surveys to be administered at different phases of the process—during the neighborhood assemblies, budget delegate committees, and at the vote. The Center for Urban Pedagogy (CUP) received a small grant for the design of the logo, pamphlets, interactive maps, and ballots for the process. The Project for Public Spaces (PPS) created the online interface for project submission. The steering committee agreed upon three basic principles to guide the project: transparency, equality, and inclusion. From its start, the process was focused on engaging those who typically are politically disenfranchised.

While about forty organizations originally signed up to be on the steering committee,[71] it is hard to accurately determine how many organizations stayed involved throughout the process and to what extent. Some organizations were given specific tasks, such as designing a pamphlet, and thus they made more tangible contributions to the process than other organizations. Steering committee meetings were held roughly every other month throughout the process. Fifteen to twenty specific, recurring individuals tended to show up. Some steering committee members stayed active and involved throughout, while other organizations stopped their involvement early on in the process. At these steering committee meetings, at least one representative from each council district attended: typically a staff person, a council member's chief of staff, or active members from the district committees. Citizens were not part of the initial theoretical structure for the steering committee, but some active district committee members ended up at steering committee meetings. They came to express concerns and fill in when offices of city council members lacked staff support.

---

71. Information taken from the PBNYC.org website on May 7, 2012.

While many community boards were supportive, some community board leaders were also skeptical of PB, believing the process was thwarting their own power and "adding just another layer to the already dysfunctional budgeting system without changing the systematic nature of the process," as one person described to the author. The way that these four council members came together to deliberate and decide upon the rules to govern the PBNYC process was striking. The history of the New York City Council has been marked by members sometimes striving for individual power while trying to maintain a strong relationship with the speaker. Nonetheless, these city council members acted independently and collaboratively, agreeing upon rules to govern a common experimental process and formalizing guidelines for the pilot year, with the option to revisit the process in year two.

The most pertinent debates on the guidelines centered on participation eligibility requirements. Questions contested included voting age (sixteen or eighteen?) and legal status (could noncitizens vote?). These were critical questions in districts with large populations of youth and immigrants, many of whom were potentially undocumented residents. The compromise reached was that participants had to be stakeholders in the community, that is, they had to work or live in the community but they did not necessarily have to hold residency or be eighteen years of age to be budget delegates. Budget delegates could be sixteen years of age or older. Voting, however, would require residency, and voters would have to be at least eighteen, regardless of citizenship status.[72] Two of the four council members had separate "youth committees" where youth expressed their preferences and concerns. This may have set the stage for Boston's first ever youth-driven PB in spring 2014, as discussed in chapter 6.

The steering committee decided upon the structure of the process. Its basic principles—equality, transparency, and inclusion—guided the process. With a great deal of assistance from PBP, the structure was largely adapted from the process used in Chicago and incorporated lessons from changes made during the Chicago pilot. In Chicago, the plan originally called for community representatives to be voted upon and only one round of neighborhood assemblies would be held. However, in reality, community representatives—the equivalent of budget delegates in New York—were not voted upon, and there was a second round of neighborhood assemblies. Learning from this, the original guidelines of the PBNYC steering committee stipulated that budget delegates would not be selected through a vote and second rounds of neighborhood assemblies were planned. Yet the process in New York City was not a mere copy of that in Chicago. For example, in Chicago, only residents could participate as community representatives,

---

72. In subsequent years this was amended.

whereas in New York a person only needed to be a "stakeholder" in the community (that is, work or go to school in the district) to be a budget delegate.

This is the process calendar that was set up by PBNYC:[73]

— Planning (May–September)

A citywide steering committee designs the PB process. Project leads develop materials, raise supportive funding, and build relationships with local partners.

— Information Sessions (August–September)

Stakeholders in each district learn about the process of participatory budgeting, what it is, and how they can get involved.

— Neighborhood Assemblies (October–November)

Stakeholders in each neighborhood learn about the available budget funds, brainstorm initial spending ideas, and volunteer to serve as budget delegates.

— Budget Delegate Meetings (November–March)

Budget delegates meet in thematic issue committees (based on proposed ideas) to review project ideas, consult with government experts, fully develop project proposals, and prepare project posters and presentations.

— Second-Round Neighborhood Assemblies (February)

Budget delegates present poster presentations in a science fair format and neighborhood residents walk around, ask questions, and give project feedback. After this, budget delegates have time to incorporate feedback and prepare projects for the ballot.

— Voting (March)

Residents vote for which projects to fund in their districts.

— Evaluation, Implementation, and Monitoring (April and Continuing)

The council members work to implement the projects that receive the most votes. Ideally, citizens and civil society remain involved to evaluate the process and monitor project implementation.

This schema determined the basic framework for the process; however, the actual implementation of its stages sometimes varied in specific districts. The steering committee agreed upon the basic structure of the process, whereby each district would have its own district committee, which would have local ownership over the various stages of the process, such as determining where to hold neighborhood assemblies and how to do outreach and mobilization.

In the Chicago pilot, only one ward participated in PB, so the steering committee was able to closely monitor the process and set broad guidelines, such as having members of the steering committee serve as "mentors" for thematic com-

73. CDP and PBNYC (2012).

mittees. By contrast, in New York City the steering committee instead devolved a great deal of power to the local-level district committees.

Participatory budgeting in New York City has seen a rapid expansion since the initial pilot in 2011. The leading partners on the steering committee offer stable roots: PBP is based out of New York City and CVH has strong community ties. These organizations have helped support the rise of PB.[74] The process has proven to be politically popular—especially with politicians. One of the first implementing council members was subsequently elected speaker of the city council. As PB efforts have grown across the country, New York City has maintained its prime position as the site of the largest experiment. PB in New York City continues to serve as an important petri dish for other cities in the United States that are looking to explore, adopt, and expand their own versions of PB.

The following sections outline the voted projects in the 2011 PBNYC pilot. Subsequent chapters provide an in-depth look at the process itself.

The Voting Sites

In Governor Andrew M. Cuomo's "State of the State" address in 2012, he noted that New York State ranked forty-eighth in voter turnout nationwide.[75] In November 2009 New York City reported its lowest voting numbers in a mayoral race since 1969.[76] Only about 29 percent of New York City's 4.1 million registered voters cast a ballot for mayor in 2009.[77] Instances in which city council elections coincide with mayoral elections typically result in higher voter turnout. Special elections can yield very low draws. Only a few thousand people voted to elect one of the council members who implemented PBNYC's pilot in a special election in February 2009. The member was elected by a number of people only roughly double the amount of people who came out to vote in PB in the same district. The low turnout in some local elections sets the stage for assessing the added value of PB as a vehicle for expressing civic preferences in a vote.

This context is critical for assessing turnout for participatory budgeting in New York City Council districts. Roughly six thousand people voted in the initial PBNYC election (see figure 3-1).[78] While this represents a fraction of the total

---

74. CVH Power (CVH's affiliated sister 501c4) did a considerable amount of work to expand the process and ensure that candidates for Speaker would be supportive of centralized PB infrastructure.

75. Governor Andrew M. Cuomo, "New York State of State Address," Albany, New York, January 4, 2012 (www.governor.ny.gov/sites/governor.ny.gov/files/archive/assets/documents/Building-a-New-New-York-Book.pdf), p. 27.

76. Bardin and others (2012, p. 5).

77. Bardin and others (2012, p. 5).

78. CDP and PBNYC (2012, p. 11).

Figure 3-1. *PB Voters Broken Down by District*

District	PB Voters
A	2,213
B	1,048
C	1,085
D	1,639

Source: CDP and PBNYC, 2012.

residents in each area, it also signals a number of people who were previously not engaged with public decisionmaking in this capacity.

Each district committee picked various voting locations, many where neighborhood assemblies had been held, and allowed voting to stretch over the course of a week. Each city council member's district office also hosted voting throughout that same week. Districts instituted special voting days and times to accommodate distinct populations, such as Sunday voting for Orthodox Jews and early morning voting for the elderly and those with challenging work schedules. Each voting site differed in layout, yet all displayed the posters of the different projects. Some voting spaces were larger than others, enabling larger colored posters. Other smaller sites had smaller eight-by-eleven-inch, black-and-white handouts.

Each voting site was staffed by volunteers—mainly district committee members and budget delegates—who checked people in and handed them both the ballot and a survey compiled by the steering committee's research and evaluation team. The volunteers asked for proof of residency or a sworn affidavit affirming such. Some sites had a computer with a Google document where people could enter in voter information, so as to limit the chance of people voting at multiple locations throughout the district.[79] Yet these rules were not strictly enforced and people were not turned away from voting. On the contrary, people were encouraged to vote—even residents who showed up at voting sites for another purpose and had been unaware of PBNYC.

The ballots featured images depicting the various projects. Each ballot folded open, giving residents a selection of several projects from which to choose. Voters could pick a total of five, with no weighing of votes.[80] Residents were given an

79. These are shared documents run on a Google site that can be updated in real time. Data entered throughout various voting locations could be simultaneously updated.

80. CDP and PBNYC (2012, p. 11).

opportunity to walk around the voting site, to look at posters, and to sit at tables to fill out their ballots and surveys.[81]

The steering committee had instituted rules prohibiting anyone speaking on behalf of a specific project at the voting sites. Organizers of PBNYC placed restrictions on how near to their projects people could stand at the voting sites. There was a fear that project supporters might try to cajole people into voting for their specific projects. Volunteers were allowed to answer questions about translation and some sites had translators available as well.

In the official surveys and in my research, many citizens expressed a desire to vote for pragmatic projects. I attended a vote in every district. When I asked voters which projects they had voted for and why, the preferences they stated were generally the same, supporting projects that served children, helped the elderly, and improved safety. Not a single voter identified creativity or innovation as a reason to choose a project. These preferences present a normative challenge to PB's ethos: Does the proposal of projects by a small, self-selecting group of citizens constitute an imposition of choices onto the larger public?

A criticism of a different variant of PB as practiced elsewhere, including by Kal Masser in Germany, is that the small number of people who come out to vote shows that the process was, or could be, co-opted by those who petitioned their colleagues, neighbors, and friends to support their projects.[82] Important questions arise about the degree to which it is appropriate for participants to mobilize their communities through a kind of lobbying and about how to curb co-option by parties that become overly invested in specific outcomes. Even if PB voters represent a limited sampling of citizens, nonetheless PB amounts to more citizen involvement in budgetary decisions than the prior procedure without PB. Throughout the process, budget delegates were cognizant of the limits to their ability to represent their districts and worked as much as possible to obtain broader district information.

Many of the questions that arise from voting in PB—such as whether a small group of citizens or elites should determine the nature of projects that have an impact on a wider portion of citizenry—manifest tensions that are inherent in a democracy. Many of the critiques of voting in PB can also be applied to voting for city council members and to other elections in the United States. As noted earlier, the voting rate for some city council elections, especially special elections, can at times be comparable to voting rates in PB. The issue of the degree of

81. Voters theoretically had the option of completing their ballots in private, although this option was neither publicized nor utilized.

82. Kal Masser, "Participatory Budgeting as Its Critics See It," *Buergerhaushalt* (website), March 30, 2013 (www.buergerhaushalt.org/en/article/participatory-budgeting-its-critics-see-it).

representation in elections is an important one for democratic theory—but it should not be conflated with critiques of the PB process itself.

Results

This section outlines where capital funds were spent in the four New York City Council districts that implemented the PBNYC pilot. For each district a direct comparison is made between those projects implemented before and those carried out after PB.

As the process unfolded, budget delegates responded to the combination of community needs and their own need to formulate a successful strategy for achieving viable, voter-approved projects. The results suggest that practicality often triumphed. Of a total of thirty-one projects, 62 percent were those that I categorize as conventional and 38 percent were those I label as innovative.

Reasons for putting forth pragmatic proposals included pressure from city agencies and city council member offices to formulate strategic projects that would likely yield the most votes and fit within existing capital funding guidelines. The high number of conventional projects—62 percent—that were in line with typical capital funding in the preceding year without PB suggests that PB is capable of producing funding allocations that are comparable to those produced through traditional decisionmaking by the experts. The 38 percent of projects that I classify as innovative more directly reflect self-expressed community needs. PB enables district need to be assessed fairly, sometimes more creatively and perhaps accurately, than the traditional nontransparent funding process as reflected in both conventional and innovative projects.

What does the nature of the projects reveal about citizen involvement in participatory budgeting? For some participants, the PB process was too narrowly structured, which prevented them from putting forward the inventive proposals they desired to make. The proposals I categorize as creative were those that deviated from the normal pattern of spending for capital funds. Nonetheless, they were still projects centered on pragmatic community needs.

Take, for example, the following sample of innovative projects from each district:

—**D-A:** Planting one hundred new trees on blocks throughout the district with few or no trees **(I)**

—**D-B:** Ultrasound system for hospital **(I)**

—**D-C:** Funding toward the purchase or renovation of space for a proposed community resource center **(I)**

—**D-D:** Gazebo bandstand or outdoor performance space **(I)**

Each one of these projects is vital to community interests. Though none depart radically from capital projects in previous years, they would not have been implemented without PBNYC. These projects offer a unique vision of self-identified community needs while still staying within the tenets of more traditional projects.

As in Chicago, the innovative projects in New York City were imaginative, but they were not so inventive or focused on a particular area as to be out of sync with the needs of the community. Because these innovative projects are the byproducts of a citizen-led initiative, they are granted legitimacy. If city council members were to institute these kinds of projects in their respective districts without using PB, questions might arise surrounding their validity. Since these projects were selected through the PB process, however, they were imbued with legitimacy—people had multiple opportunities to engage in decisionmaking. PB opens up important space for projects that tap into people's creativity. It enables new ideas to gain legitimacy. In turn, viable innovative projects confer legitimacy onto the PB process itself by demonstrating that the process is not co-opted by elected officials.

The innovative and the conventional projects highlight disparate aspects of the PBNYC process. The conventional projects show that citizens are able to identify standard community needs, perhaps more effectively than city council members, as evidenced by the following sample:

—**D-A:** New technology for two public schools **(C)**
—**D-B:** Playground improvements at two public housing complexes **(C)**
—**D-C:** The installation of floodlights in each park in the district **(C)**
—**D-D:** Pagers for four volunteer fire departments **(C)**

I categorize these projects as conventional because they take a traditional capital project and give it a specific dimension—typically by focusing on a particular geographic location though sometimes via a tool or usage, such as "pagers for volunteer fire departments."

These more standard projects confer legitimacy on the entire PB process, illustrating that when citizens are given the opportunity and means to influence budgetary decisions they are able to accurately reflect need, while also adding a critical local perspective. Conventional projects, like innovative projects, directly challenge critics who contend that citizens cannot make rational, pragmatic, and informed public policy decisions.

Chicago versus New York

Many structural, institutional, and political differences exist between Chicago and New York that inform each city's unique adoption and implementation of participatory budgeting. The PB pilot in Chicago differs from that in New York City in that, in Chicago, only one alderman instituted the process, while four city council members came together across party lines to take it on in New York. Having only one alderman institute PB opened up the process to personalized critiques. The structure of PBNYC's pilot implementation was more diversified.

The first years of PB in Chicago and New York differed in three important respects: (1) the number of politicians participating, (2) the size of representative districts, and (3) the existing budget process in each respective city. These structural differences are instructive for other cities in the United States exploring whether to adopt participatory budgeting. As discussed in subsequent chapters, cities may want to consider these institutional factors in considering process implementation and execution. Yet these structural differences do not fully account for the different process trajectories. Idiosyncratic factors relating to individual personalities and politics do influence perceptions of the process.

The first major difference between PB in Chicago and in New York City is the number of politicians involved. The Chicago process began with one alderman. In contrast, the process in New York City began with four city council members. The fact that PBNYC began as a bipartisan effort afforded a degree of legitimacy to the process. This made it more focused on good governance and reduced criticism of the process as a whole based on individual council members.

District size was another difference. The wards in Chicago are much smaller than council districts in New York City. There are fifty aldermen for Chicago's roughly 2.7 million residents. In contrast, New York City has fifty-one city council members for roughly 8.4 million residents.[83] The structure of wards in Chicago may encourage a closer relationship between citizens and their alderman, on the one hand, while, on the other, it may enable more opportunities for patronage—or at least the perception of patronage.[84] New York City's districts, meanwhile, are so large it is difficult for personal relationships between constituents and elected officials to develop. This may also prevent the perception of personal patronage that is common in smaller localities.

The challenges of getting elected officials to sign on to PB include the existing structures of funding that could be tapped (e.g., discretionary, capital, etc.) and the fiscal calendar year. Many fiscal budgets are decided in the late spring

83. Population data for both cities via the United States Census Bureau website, Census.gov.
84. See also Lessig (2011).

and early summer and require at least a year of advance planning. Thus, if elected officials see that PB is successful in neighboring districts, it can still take two years to begin the process in their own districts. Yet funding structures alone, divorced from political ecosystems, cannot explain variance in the adoption of participatory budgeting. In 2013 one ward in St. Louis put $100,000 into PB.[85] PB has come to St. Louis at a time when alterations to the city's institutional design are under consideration, as its city council weighs ward redistricting and other changes that could have an impact on funding.[86]

In New York City, participatory budgeting has benefited from strong civil society groups, particularly PBP and CVH, advocating for expansion. Distinctively, CVH is a membership organization, which helped garner grassroots legitimacy and support. One of the founding PBNYC council members became speaker of the city council—a powerful position. Political contingencies contribute to an elected official's decisions regarding whether to adopt PB. They range from electoral demographics to social and political realities. Political ecosystems will vary. Instead of trying to isolate and identify them, I have focused on the structural conditions and their import.

Conclusion

Participatory budgeting's arrival in the United States began in one ward in one city. Ever since, it has been picking up momentum. Chicago and New York City have served as instructive paragons for how PB can be implemented. The evolution of the PB process in Chicago—from the original rulebook to modified practice—directly influenced the design and implementation of PB in New York and elsewhere in the United States. Elements of the Chicago model were directly incorporated into PBNYC's structure and are now common in American iterations of PB, including not having community representatives elected, holding a second forum to view projects, and grouping participants into flexible thematic committees. Cities across the country that are looking to try PB are learning directly from the experience of Chicago and New York. As PB continues to grow, there is variance in how PB gets off the ground. For example, in some places PB starts with council members voting to approve the process (for example,

85. See the official website for participatory budgeting in St. Louis (http://pbstl.com/) and Jessica Lussenhop, "Participatory Budgeting—St. Louis Launches Pilot Project in 6th Ward," *River Front Times,* April 3, 2013 (http://blogs.riverfronttimes.com/dailyrft/2013/04/participatory_budgeting_can_th.php); Gordon (2014).

86. David Hunn, "St. Louis Board of Alderman Votes to Reduce Itself," *St. Louis Post-Dispatch,* July 7, 2012 (www.stltoday.com/news/local/govt-and-politics/st-louis-board-of-aldermen-votes-to-reduce-itself/article_f6e12c38-b48e-5832-8170-f13fca13c94d.html).

Buffalo). In other places the mayor's office is the instigator of the process (for example, Boston). PB in both Chicago and New York City began with small amounts of money that were already at the discretion of individual elected officials.

Process governance is critical when starting PB. Who is eligible to participate? How will voters be determined? In both Chicago and New York City these decisions were decided in conjunction with civil society. As the process continues to expand, citizens have been given more opportunities for meaningful participation. What is the nature of this participation and engagement? The following chapters provide an in-depth exploration of participation and deliberation in the PBNYC pilot.

The differences in the structure of PB in Chicago and in New York City suggest institutional design is critical for evaluation.[87] Another critical aspect for localities to consider is the role of community-based organizations in the origins and development of the process itself and holding public officials accountable. Institutional design alone cannot fully account for the different experiences of the participants or for the differences encountered in achieving civic rewards in the process. Idiosyncratic factors relating to individual personalities and politics influence how the process is perceived. The dynamics influencing which council members did or did not implement PB in New York City are imprecise. At the time of the pilot, the power and reputation of the existing speaker of the city council meant that implementing PBNYC carried a potential political risk for these members. Nonetheless, they chose to devolve some of their elected power back to citizens. This proved to be politically rewarding: one implementing council member was elected the next speaker of the city council by her party.

The opportunities and challenges in expanding implementation of PB beyond its pilot year offer instructive examples with respect to scale and institutionalization. After an initial pilot year an innovative process must acquire additional political support to ensure participation continues and to avoid process fatigue. Innovations in process can be subject to politics. Insofar as is possible, focusing PB on effective governance over politics and partisanship can help catalyze innovation. These themes are explored in subsequent chapters.

---

87. Again, these differences are (1) the number of politicians participating, (2) the size of representative districts, and (3) the budget structure at the time of respective pilots.

4

The Nature of Participation

I joined PB to change our democracy—not to work on toilets and trees.[1]

These are the remarks a budget delegate uttered after the project on which she had spent the last several months working failed to be voted on. Her frustration points to a central question: why do people participate in participatory budgeting? Another question is closely connected: what does that participation entail? The process offers several unique and meaningful opportunities for participation. Some opportunities are more time and resource intensive than others. This book's introduction puts forward substantive participation alongside deliberation and institutionalization as three criteria for assessing PB in action. This chapter offers a definition of substantive participation and illustrates the way in which some of the most rewarding opportunities to participate are also the most challenging.

Theories abound about why people choose to be active in their communities. Some scholars posit that people engage in participatory budgeting in particular due to its perceived effectiveness.[2] In contrast, I argue that many citizens found satisfaction in this form of sustained participation not necessarily because of its effectiveness in terms such as material service delivery improvement or putting forth a specific proposal but rather because of PB's civic rewards.[3] Participants routinely cite the number of opportunities for knowledge transfer and direct

---

1. All quotes are transcribed from my research.
2. Avritzer (2006).
3. Again, I use the term "citizen" to refer to people engaged in civic processes, including especially participants in PB. I am not referring to formal citizenship status.

contact with government officials and agencies as the primary reasons the process constitutes a uniquely engaging civic activity.

This chapter uses data on participation and engagement in the PBNYC pilot year (2011–12)[4] to articulate a civic typology for understanding who participates in democratic innovations. I engaged with three key emerging groups: "usual suspects," "active citizens," and "new citizens." These groups are characterized primarily by how they engage with the process. It is not a comprehensive data assessment but rather a stylized account that illustrates an opportunity for multilevel civic engagement to empower those beyond the usual civic suspects.

The full typology suggests there are many dimensions along which to assess diversity in civic participation. Traditional indicators, such as economic, gender, and racial diversity, are included in the analysis, but they do not tell the whole story. There are also several ways to participate. Participants demonstrate different engagement preferences. I argue that democratic innovations should enable multiple entry points for different styles of citizen participation in addition to seeking to reflect diversity as measured by more traditional indicators. Ensuring diverse participation throughout may also necessitate additional resources to provide support, such as childcare, food, or transportation reimbursement. Empirical results from PBNYC showed that the less demanding forms of participation, such as the final vote, often had the most diverse participants.[5] In fact, some districts saw a higher share of minorities and low-income residents vote in PB than in the 2009 New York City Council elections.[6]

This chapter assesses when and how PBNYC offered opportunities for engagement, looking especially at the volume of such opportunities over time. Throughout the process, PB offered innovative participation opportunities for all types of participants—all groups in the typology. Citizens experienced frustration but nonetheless continued with PB in order to gain lasting civic rewards from participating.

The process can be resource and time intensive. Even accounting for these considerable barriers to entry, participation can result in frustration and disillusionment, in part because PB's inherent winnowing involves eliminating many projects. Some of the tensions arising from, and potential threats to, substantive participation in PBNYC were linked to structural conditions, such as government capacity and the specific bureaucracy of New York City, which influenced how the pilot worked. Challenges to participation were varied, though they were consistently high.

4. Demographic data on who participates comes from the Community Development Project at the Urban Justice Center with the PBNYC Research Team, published in CDP and PBNYC (2012).
5. CDP and PBNYC (2012, p. 20).
6. CDP and PBNYC (2012, p. 20).

While obstacles frustrated many citizens, nonetheless quite a number stayed engaged in PB. The civic rewards it offers—greater civic knowledge, strengthened relationships with elected officials, enhanced community inclusion, and leadership development—may not conform to typical behavioral accounts offering reasons for political or civic participation, yet they are rational incentives. This chapter concludes with policy and process recommendations exploring the implications of participation and civic rewards.

Norms Regarding Participation

Participation is the necessary condition of participatory budgeting. Furthermore, this participation must be sustained. To understand what this means, empirical findings should be grounded in theoretical framing.

From a normative perspective, participation by individual citizens serves the dual purpose of both educating these citizens and empowering them to serve as a check on elected representatives and governmental bureaucracy.[7] The act of participation allows residents the opportunity to establish self-worth in their identities as citizens.[8] Scholars have shown that citizens who become skilled in democracy build social capital.[9] This includes strong networks of trust and information sharing. Participation that includes a deliberative component has been shown to both increase democratic legitimacy and foster deliberative political culture.[10]

Some scholars argue that establishing a more participatory and deliberative political culture has become increasingly important. One reason is that, as government bureaucracy has expanded, it has been unable to foster inclusive and robust relationships between citizens and their elected officials.[11] The low level of citizens' trust in government is but one indicator of the dysfunctional relationships between those tasked with authority and those they are intended to represent.[12] Given the current dynamics, some scholars posit that participation can undermine institutions of representative government.[13] Yet there are varying degrees of civic participation, including some that are more and some that are less robust and therefore more or less disruptive of existing governmental procedure.[14]

---

7. Wampler (2002); Barber (1984).
8. Kweit and Kweit (1981); King and Stivers (1998).
9. Putnam (2001).
10. Habermas (1996b).
11. Zajac and Bruhn (1999).
12. Edelman, "Trust around the World," 2015 Edelman Trust Barometer (www.edelman.com /2015-edelman-trust-barometer/trust-around-world/).
13. Lynn (2002).
14. See Sirianni on collaborative governance (2009, pp. 39–65).

To better understand the nature of participation in PB, I offer a definition of substantive participation: those affected by the decision must be included,[15] the participation is sustained and has a genuine impact on public decisions,[16] and officials take the input of citizens seriously.[17] I argue that PB offers opportunities for substantive participation and that this is a critical dimension to its civic rewards.

This chapter outlines modes of participation in practice. The challenges to these modes include the time commitments involved and the resulting representativeness of the participating group. Voter inclusion and mobilization serve as the mechanisms by which public officials substantiate participation in the process.

Modes of Participation

Opportunities for citizen engagement extend beyond those originally conceived of, such as having some citizens involved with citywide governance-level decisions about process. These modes of citizen engagement supplement opportunities for participation. The next chapter discusses the ways in which deliberation and decisionmaking took root in the PBNYC process.

A variety of opportunities emerged for citizens to join in the PBNYC process, reflecting its commitment to improving both short-term service delivery and long-term civic engagement. Broadly speaking, participants fell into two general categories—those on their district committee and those not on the committee.

Each New York City Council member's office assembled its district committee by inviting local organizations and people to be engaged with PB process governance for the district.[18] District committee members could influence everything from which meeting rooms to secure to how to conduct communications and outreach to the wider district community. Expectations for the district committees included organizing district-level initiatives, such as neighborhood assemblies, budget delegate committees, and the process of vote mobilization and outreach.

In one district, committee members inadvertently ended up involved in citywide governance process decisions made at the steering committee level, as the council office was strapped for official staff to coordinate PB efforts. Across the board, district committee members were empowered with responsibilities that often exceeded original expectations. Some of these obligations included coordinating logistics with both city agencies and council member offices.

15. Habermas (1991).
16. Fox and Miller (1994).
17. Pateman (1989).
18. CDP and PBNYC (2012, p. 12).

For participants who were not on the district committees, three other additional types of participation were available. Two were less substantive forms of participation: attending neighborhood assemblies or voting on projects. The third was a more substantive participatory role: serving as a budget delegate.

In summary, four ways were available to participate in PBNYC, listed in descending order of time commitment: as a member of a district committee, as a budget delegate,[19] by attending a neighborhood assembly, or by voting on projects. Several participants participated in all four levels of engagement.[20]

Civic Typologies

A variety of people took part in PBNYC via these four opportunities for participation. It goes without saying that each participant's contribution is unique, but I found certain common elements. My full typology offers an informal snapshot of participants I witnessed in the parks and recreation budget delegate committees and throughout the pilot process, with three key groups emerging—"usual suspects," "active citizens," and "new citizens."[21]

Civic Typology

—**"Usual suspects"**—These are people already engaged in civic life through established outlets such as community boards, block associations, or tenant associations. Their engagement is often the means by which they self-identify within their community.

—**"Active citizens"**—These are people who are somewhat engaged in civic life, but they are open to more outlets for engagement if they are presented. Their engagement is not a defining feature of their identity within their community.

—**"New citizens"**—These people were not previously engaged. Participation in PBNYC is a marked new step for them. Many are largely unfamiliar with the current civic infrastructure or opportunities to participate in civic life.[22]

---

19. Arguably the time commitments involved in participating on district committees or as budget delegates were sometimes comparable over different time periods.

20. This also raises the question of how to design the process to promote long-term engagement, such as Brazilian PB's thematic regional councils, and to foster improved community inclusion and mobilization. Some people also volunteered to help with outreach and voter engagement, including some CVH members.

21. This snapshot is based on scores of meetings I have attended. It is meant as a rough approximation across the four districts of the distribution of the typologies of individuals. More detailed district snapshots are also explored in this chapter.

22. See also Ariel Schwartz, "The Interested Bystander Effect: Why Even People Who Care about the World Don't Vote," *Fast Company*, April 10, 2015 (www.fastcoexist.com/3044484/the-interested -bystander-effect-why-even-people-who-care-about-the-world-dont-vote).

There are overlapping traits amongst these participants.[23] PB's ability to draw out people who do not usually participate created important new dynamics. How they take part in deliberation and decisionmaking is outlined in the following chapter.

The existing capacities of city council members and civil society organizations (CSOs) were intermediary factors bringing together these people, as outreach at the district level by council members and CSOs was critical in engaging all three main types of citizens—usual suspects, active citizens, as well as new citizens. Once these citizens were effectively mobilized to participate, the capacities of city council members, civil society, and district committees sustained the relationships among these people for the duration of the PB process. Ideally they continue to sustain this participation after the vote as well, to enable citizen engagement in project implementation and monitoring.

New and dynamic relationships form among these individuals during participatory budgeting. Preexisting urban demographics and the district makeup shape the overall group of people before they enter the process. Each of these districts has its own demographics, in terms of socioeconomic status (SES), race, and education level. Each district's budget committees represent a sampling of such demographics. PB's opportunities to participate in civic governance rupture typical channels for engagement in the city and forge new ties across these demographics. Suddenly, people who have never before interacted are working together closely to make important decisions.

Who were these citizens and how did they get involved with PBNYC? Many of the "usual suspects" were already familiar with one another. They came into the PB process with their own conceptions of where the problems lay in their communities. Some of them were long-standing members of community boards who entered into the process with established viewpoints and existing relationships with the city council members. The majority were personally called by their council member and invited to participate on a district committee. Others opted not to be on their district committee because they were "skeptical of this pilot process and . . . already over committed."[24]

Many remained skeptics on the sidelines, only attending neighborhood assemblies and the final vote. Yet several usual suspects I spoke with shared statements like "PBNYC [wa]s the most fulfilling mode of civic engagement I have ever been part of."[25] When assessing the value of PB, usual suspects cite the number of opportunities for knowledge transfer and for direct contact with council members and city agencies as the primary reasons that PBNYC differs from other

---

23. All estimations are based on my qualitative research.
24. As one long-standing community board member noted.
25. As described by another long-standing community board member.

forms of civic engagement, namely community boards, parent-teacher associations (PTAs), and block associations.

The majority of "active citizens" who participated in PBNYC were looking for new outlets for civic engagement and seized upon those provided by PBNYC. These people were already somewhat involved in their community. They might have sat on a PTA or a neighborhood block association. Yet the level of engagement of an active citizen is less than that of a usual suspect in any given week or month. I found usual suspects more likely to define their identity through civic engagement than active citizens. Many active citizens view their civic engagement as a smaller component of their identity. The involvement of active citizens in PBNYC transforms the hours they spend on civic engagement and enlarges their civic identity. Suddenly, they are spending more time and energy thinking about their community and interacting with public officials—and often with neighbors they had never before met.

"New citizens" who participated in PBNYC found that their involvement constituted a marked departure from their typical lives. These citizens were not previously engaged in civic life beyond elections and not all of them were regular voters. Many new citizens were inspired to get involved by the civic activism of their neighbors. Indeed, several new citizens who engaged with PBNYC heard about the process through a citizen who was more active than they were. Some were also intrigued by an e-mail, or a city council member's newsletter, or a flier. Some active citizens and usual suspects personally brought new citizens to neighborhood assemblies or to vote. This person-to-person mobilization was often conducted through established networks such as churches or schools. For these new citizens, PBNYC has the potential to be the most transformative civic activity in which they take part because, unlike more traditional forms of engagement such as voting, PB also provides opportunities for knowledge transfer and iterative civic participation.

PBNYC faced a challenge to reconcile these disparate types of citizens within a cohesive process. Each phase of PB involved a different level of engagement and required a commitment of time, and each contained different proportions of the three main types of citizens.

Structural barriers to deep civic engagement, such as time commitment, were encountered. Often, inclusivity was inversely proportional to time commitment, that is, the parts of the process that were the least time consuming, such as the vote, were able to draw in the highest volume of new citizens. There was a focus among PB supporters and organizers on diversity and outreach throughout the process, and particularly for the vote—a logical investment within a resource constrained environment with limited funds for process implementation itself. Based on my observations, the most time-consuming parts of the process, such as serving on district committees or as budget delegates, often had a higher proportion of usual suspects. This underscores that diversity of participation can include a variety of factors, such as previous knowledge and experience with civic life.

The district committee members and budget delegates groups, made up of several usual suspects, were tasked with outreach and mobilizing new citizens. These district committee members and budget delegates spent the most hours involved in PBNYC, becoming personally invested in the process while exerting ownership and influence over it. Many district committee members felt an obligation to serve as public trustees and mobilize a diverse range of participants. This illustrated a tension in the role of district committee members: they were simultaneously participating in PB as district residents while also taking on authority roles in district process governance, such as organizing participation.

In terms of outreach, however, this dynamic also sets PB apart. Participatory budgeting is a unique process in that citizens can reach out to fellow citizens. In many typical civic engagement structures, elites engage citizens. In contrast, PB empowers ordinary citizens to decide *how* to engage their fellow community members. This feature creates both opportunities for genuine engagement as well as a new dimension of power politics. PB also enabled community-based organizations—for example, CVH, Flatbush Tenant Coalition, Fifth Avenue Committee, amongst others—to reach out to their constituents and offer them a new engagement opportunity. As noted in chapter 2, implementations of PB in the United States have been less focused on representation than its Brazilian counterparts. For some, district committee members represent another opaque layer obscuring the decisionmaking process—especially when it comes to understanding *who* gets to serve and why. Nonetheless, the district committees were attuned to their communities and worked diligently to genuinely engage them.

Who Participated?

In addition to my civic typologies, other measures of diversity can indicate how representative the participation in the PB process was of these overall districts. As previously discussed, PBNYC offered four specific participation opportunities during the process. I analyze data from the Community Development Project at the Urban Justice Center, which surveyed participants at neighborhood assemblies, budget delegates, and voters, using the results to illustrate the representation levels of PBNYC.[26] The numbers of voters in the following charts reflect voters who filled out surveys—not the total amount of voters within each dis-

26. CDP and PBNYC (2012).

trict. Surveyed participation rates for each district are compared with data from the 2010 census. The surveys were formed using census categorizations to ensure continuity of terminology for race and ethnicity.

Voting data for each district reflect targeted outreach and mobilization that varied by district. The organizing lead partner, Community Voices Heard (CVH), set aside a portion of money for the purpose of implementing the PBNYC process; these funds were used for mobilization and outreach within different communities, with a particular focus on the final vote.[27] Within each district, specifically low-income and typically disenfranchised populations were to be targeted for the vote.[28] Some districts, such as District B, saw a higher share of minority and low-income voters in PB than in the 2009 elections (see table 4-1 and table 4-2).[29]

Comparing District Participation

> I thought all the affluent white people would look down upon me because I live in public housing—in reality they were all understanding and wanted to help.
> —Budget delegate

Based on data on race and income from the Community Development Project at the Urban Justice Center[30] and on my observations, participants exhibited variation along my civic typologies as well as along more traditional indicators of representation. Furthermore, participation by demographics was not static.

The composition of participants varied from district to district.[31] Throughout the process, council members and district committees had agency in determining how to execute outreach and mobilization. Sometimes this appeared to reflect district committee priorities while in other cases it seemed to be broadly

---

27. Monies that CVH used for outreach were foundation resources.

28. The decisions about which sections of the district to target for outreach for the vote were partially based on a needs assessment. Decisionmaking was ultimately up to the council members and district committees and often featured competing priorities. Council members were often eager to reach as many voting constituencies as possible and encouraged wide mobilization, bringing their own biases on mobilization around the vote. In the end, district committees wielded influence over mobilization and over deciding where to do outreach—since they carried out many of the responsibilities associated with outreach.

29. CDP and PBNYC (2012).

30. CDP and PBNYC (2012).

31. Demographic data on who participates is from the Urban Justice Center, published in CDP and PBNYC (2012).

Table 4-1. *Local Election Voters in 2009 versus PBNYC 2011–12 Voters by Race*

	District A		District B		District C		District D	
	Voters 2009 (%)	Voters PB (%)	Voters 2009 (%)	Voters PB (%)	Voters 2009 (%)	Voters PB (%)	Voters 2009 (%)	Voters PB (%)
Black or African American	8	3	31	34	79	87	6	3
Hispanic or Latino	11	6	39	50	4	6	18	4
White	55	87	22	17	11	7	61	89

Source: 2010 Census; CDP and PBNYC (2012).

Table 4-2. *PB Voters and Projects Funded*

	District A	District B	District C	District D
Population (2010)	154,341	162,734	139,731	38,309[a]
PB Voters	2,213	1,048	1,085	1,639
Online Project Submissions	180	40	17	8

Source: 2010 Census; CDP and PBNYC (2012).

[a.] This population is smaller because PB was implemented only in a portion of the district.

consistent with district demographics. Microlevel choices such as when and where to hold neighborhood assemblies invariably had an impact on participation in the process.

One new citizen in District A described his reasons for engagement thus: "I met my community through walking my dog. I wanted to give back to this community that has meant so much to me." District A was able to galvanize active and new citizens to participate in PB, many as budget delegates. These active and new citizens were themselves often white, affluent, well-educated members of the district.

District B effectively mobilized lower-income residents to participate as budget delegates, to attend neighborhood assemblies, and to vote. The district committee chose to mobilize the largest area of lower-income residents, as opposed to a smaller pocket of the district, by focusing outreach attention on a public housing complex managed by the New York City Housing Authority (NYCHA). Within resource constraints, the district chose not to target mobilization efforts for the vote in the portion of the district containing residents who were wealthier and more educated.

District C effectively mobilized those in lower-middle-income brackets. Many new and active citizens participated throughout the process as budget delegates. Several were brought into the process through church networks. Fifty-six percent of PB voters in the district reported they were born outside the United States.[32]

District D mobilized the low-income portion of the district who lived in an NYCHA complex for the vote.[33] The district committee was chaired by a usual suspect—a white woman, self-identified as conservative—who wanted to ensure that people from the housing complex were targeted for the vote. She explained, "I know our district is divided and I want to reach out to people who haven't yet participated in PB to vote."

Districts varied on indicators of diversity. Based on my firsthand observations, some were better at certain aspects of achieving diverse participation and worse at others. District A and District C effectively brought in new and active citizens as engaged participants in PBNYC who attended neighborhood assemblies and served as budget delegates. Several of these new and active citizens came from demographic groups that represented a majority in a given district. District B was able to bring new and active citizens into the entire PB process, including as budget delegates.

Decisions about which pockets of a district to target for mobilization were at times idiosyncratic and did not follow a specific model. Rather, existing political structures, individual preferences, and local politics often influenced mobilization decisions. The process placed a premium on reaching traditionally disenfranchised populations. Resource constraints necessarily meant that all parts of the districts could not be targeted for vote mobilization.

This raises the question of whether a normative obligation exists to mobilize equally all portions of the districts for equitable representation. In its current manifestations in the United States, PB has been restricted due to a limited amount of funds. As decisions on spending funds through PB expand, pressure may grow for equitable representation that includes traditionally marginalized members of the community. This will require dedicated funds for process implementation, mobilization, and outreach.

32. CDP and PBNYC (2012).
33. CDP and PBNYC (2012).

Challenges to Participation

> PB will die of its own weight based on the sheer amount of meetings.
> —District committee member and budget delegate

Even for participants able to navigate the existing bureaucratic structures and politics within districts in New York City, the demands of participation were still high. For the usual suspect quoted above, PB constituted a uniquely cumbersome form of engagement, even though she had served on a community board for decades. In this section, I outline the multifaceted challenges to substantive participation. The next section reaffirms the civic rewards of sustaining consistent participation throughout the demanding process.

Organizers of PBNYC were cognizant of the high costs of participation. In every district someone—either the city council member herself or a member of staff or an organizer—would thank participants at every meeting. One pastor made a point of beginning every meeting in the district by saying: "I really appreciate you taking the time to serve as budget delegates." The number of meetings requiring attendance by budget delegates or district committee members was at times a barrier to entry. Some budget delegates were also district committee members.

Attending a neighborhood assembly or budget delegate meeting takes hours during the week, conflicting with already busy schedules for people who may have to work shifts in the late afternoon, or at night, or take care of children. These meetings implicitly prioritized those who could afford childcare. Likewise, almost all district committee meetings took place during the day, requiring flexible work schedules.[34]

Further dissuading participation, barriers to involvement were coupled with feelings of disillusionment in government. One Caribbean woman noted:

> Black people want to know why white people get government money in their communities—it's because white people participate. I try to tell people in my black church to stop complaining about government and get involved. This is why I participate in PBNYC. We especially need to be here to look out for those who cannot in our community, such as the youth and elderly.

She viscerally understood why members of her church community feel politically ineffectual. Yet she viewed their behavior, coupled with feelings of discontent in

---

34. Some PB advocates, including CVH, have long argued that resources need to be provided at each district-level meeting for translation, interpretation, transportation, childcare, and food.

their resource allotment, as self-defeating. She struggled to encourage new citizens to participate in PBNYC, reflecting:

> I brought a few friends to an initial neighborhood assembly. They signed up to be budget delegates but stopped coming after the first meeting. They wanted to participate but had to take care of their children.

While able to encourage her fellow congregants to attend a PB meeting, resource constraints proved too burdensome to sustain their involvement. Even when participants are able to overcome disbelief in the value of civic engagement, this cannot remove the obstacles that resource constraints present to sustained participation.

Typically when citizens engage in public decisionmaking they serve in a consultative or advisory role. In contrast, participation in PB leads to binding results. Therefore, citizens have a heightened level of responsibility with both positive and negative impacts for participation. For some who become galvanized by PB, the process presents seemingly endless opportunities for participation: attending steering committee sessions, district committee meetings, budget delegate meetings, neighborhood assemblies followed by the vote.

Some usual suspects or active citizens wanted to participate as much as possible while simultaneously feeling overwhelmed. These sentiments were particularly related to the dual roles of district committee members: serving on a governance level of the process as well as serving as active participants in it.[35] One usual suspect with years of community board experience would arrive late to budget delegate meetings, vocally expressing her exhaustion from just having attended another civic meeting. She would sigh, "I can't believe I have to come to yet another meeting," as she entered.

Yet during the process of mobilization for the vote she wrote an angry e-mail to her council member's office expressing her outrage and dismay at how little power the budget delegates were given. On the one hand, she wanted less involvement with the process, while on the other hand she wanted greater autonomy.

Even for participants able to overcome the barriers to entry, including disillusionment with politics and substantial resource costs, participation in PBNYC had inherent tensions. Those who entered the process with a specific proposal sometimes had to face disappointment—at times, more than half of such proposals were not deemed viable and never made the ballot. Given all these obstacles the question emerges: *Why* participate at all?

---

35. How participants experience the process intricately relates to institutional design decisions.

Why Participate?

> MOTHER:[36] We have an obligation to put forth projects to help our portion of the district—we are the people who have put in the time.
>
> DAUGHTER:[37] I disagree. We are public trustees and we have an obligation to put forth projects that will benefit as much of the entire district as possible.
>
> MOTHER: But we are the neediest portion of the district.
>
> DAUGHTER: That is not necessarily true, we have a skewed vantage point.

This conversation, between a mother and daughter taking part in PB, was overheard and loosely transcribed by the author on a car ride home from a budget delegate meeting. The mother was a typical usual suspect who was engaged in many aspects of civic and church life. She had personally brought many participants to PBNYC, including her own daughter. The latter, a new citizen, was familiar with civic life through her mother.

This discussion highlights the dual nature of PBNYC participation: Is it a matter of serving as representatives or of putting forth your own opinions and projects? Especially for budget delegates, there is an inherent tension between two paradigms: individual interests and public trusteeship. If budget delegates are representatives of their districts, by what means are they granted these powers? In contrast to Brazilian PB where representatives were elected, the community did not elect budget delegates for PBNYC. If people are representatives, then are they "representative of the district" as a whole? PBNYC did not aim for representative participation in its process. This is partially due to resource constraints and partially due to an ideological commitment to engage previously marginalized community members.

With self-appointed budget delegates, the question arises: What are the incentives for participation? I identify two broad classes of incentives. One is tied to specific outputs—completed final projects emerging from PB—as material. But there is more that sustains participation beyond a goal of achieving success in the form of a material proposal. Those who participate choose to sacrifice their own resources of time and often money, in the form of donations of food, production of fliers, and transportation costs to meetings—all without being elected and without the incentives that exist for seeking elected office. In my discussions with participants, many expressed an obligation to become active and engaged

---

36. Usual suspect.
37. New citizen.

in their community. This sort of engagement is not a matter of material outputs because it relates to a desire for community and a sense of connection to others.

In the subsequent discussion, I classify these nonmaterial reasons for sustained involvement as civically driven, allowing participants to: (1) gain insight into how city government works, (2) forge connections with city council members, and (3) forge connections with fellow residents. Others described their participation as (4) predicated on a commitment to a more abstract democratic ideal. As one budget delegate noted, "PB should not be the place of basic things like bathrooms. PB should be the place we do progressive democracy."[38]

I refer to achievements in these areas as civic rewards. Incoming participants' reasons for participation varied a great deal, as expressed in conversations with the author and others. Some usual suspects came into the process with specific projects in mind; they often used their knowledge and experience with the system to successfully implement these. Other usual suspects came in looking for more fulfilling forms of civic engagement. Many usual suspects expressed interest in opportunities for knowledge transfer about the New York City budget process. Some active citizens sought to deepen their community involvement or to propose a specific project. Rarely did new citizens express commitment to a specific material project; rather, many new citizens had a more inchoate desire to be engaged. Because these new citizens lacked preexisting information about how the system worked, they were often the least likely to have the information necessary to come into the process with a premeditated project.

The reasons for engagement discussed here are those expressed to the author and to others by the participants themselves. Mapping out these reasons— material or civic—onto citizens' identities is a task that should be approached with humility. It is difficult to categorize reasons for participation through typologies of engagement. Residents often showed a confluence of rationales for engagement, some more explicit than others. Further, the process of PB itself is capable of transforming participants' civic engagement and thereby altering the reasons participants offer for engagement.

It was not uncommon for reasons for participation to evolve for usual suspects during the course of the process. Many became involved in PBNYC because they are the people who *always* get involved. They entered out of a longing to be "a good citizen" in their tight-knit community and to take responsibility for their neighborhood. Many usual suspects expressed feelings of obligation, stating that being a "good citizen" means investing time in one's own community. Many did not come into PB with a set project; rather, they collected one or two

38. See also Fisher, Svendsen, and Connolly (2015).

ideas at the neighborhood assemblies that they then championed. Some became impassioned about specific projects or causes. Many felt both invigorated and exhausted by the end of the process. As PBNYC progressed, the line between material and civic rationales for engagement—never hard and fast in the first place—was often further blurred.

Given that usual suspects typically entered into PB with more information and experience than other types of participants, information asymmetries had the potential to lead to process domination by the usual suspects. I witnessed some, as in District D, assume pragmatic roles and leverage their civic expertise by expediting the formation of realistic projects. Other usual suspects, such as in District C, were impassioned about ideals and expressed their ideologies through conversations about the democratic ideal. Usual suspects sometimes proved a challenge for facilitation. In the following chapter, I explore examples of facilitation and their effects on the conduct of PB.

As frustrations with the process mounted, budget delegates continued to invest time in PBNYC because of connections formed with fellow citizens. Moreover, these new networks of engagement redefined power dynamics—people enjoyed spending time with one another. For those who entered the process to support a specific proposal, at times more than half of their proposals were not viable and never made the ballot. For such delegates, choosing to maintain their involvement—as some but not all did—was a decision made for reasons beyond material interests.

The same cause of frustration—the depth of knowledge normally required in budgetary procedure, such as awareness of cumbersome bureaucratic rules—formed a key part of the reasons citizens stayed involved. Knowledge transfer held significant appeal. I found that many who were involved in PBNYC would rather know about a piece of information, even when the information itself or the process of obtaining it is frustrating, than not know it. For those who opt into PBNYC, being part of a shared experience, however flawed, is paramount.

Implications

Participation in the PBNYC pilot year illustrates the multilevel approach to civic engagement taken in versions of participatory budgeting in the United States. The varying modes of, and rationales for, participation suggest an opportunity for democratic innovations in seeking to find ways to simultaneously accommodate various types of citizens, while keeping in mind their differing civic capacities, previous proclivities, and engagement preferences, in addition to their more traditional demographic profiles or socioeconomic needs.[39] Accounting for a single type of diversity is important but insufficient. Rather, this chapter shows that diversity exists in terms of both traditional indicators as well as civic indicators. Providing accurate information about when and how to participate during the various parts of the PB cycle can maximize several dimensions of diversity.

PB is unique for empowering people not just to participate but to also be architects of their participation. During the pilot year, some citizens were involved in process design of governance at the district level and in decisionmaking. When citizens conduct outreach to other citizens, they deepen relationships with each other and with their communities, creating new process norms and expectations for information flow. As PB continues to expand and grow in the United States, a tension is emerging between pursuing opportunities to reduce barriers to entry, on the one hand, while ensuring, on the other hand, that participation remains substantive. Some of the most rewarding opportunities to participate in PB are also the most time and resource intensive.

Throughout each phase of the process—from project development to the actual vote—information and communications technologies (ICTs) could mitigate barriers to entry and streamline participation. As explored in chapter 7, as PB grows, cities are using online tools to collect project submission ideas. These innovations, more fully explored in the subsequent chapters, are aimed at reducing time commitments and galvanizing diverse participation. Some platforms use geospatial software to help residents more easily identify community locations and needs. In other parts of the world as well as in the United States, PB has experimented with using Short Message Service (SMS) to enable participation—allowing citizens to text their feedback, vote on projects, and receive results information via cell phones and other mobile devices. Subsequent chapters deal with the rise of such innovations, many of which are already taking hold across many cities in the United States.

Understanding the basic types of and rationales offered for participation can inform strategic process decisions. New technologies are usually aimed at new citizens, with the goal of engaging typically marginalized people. For many, PB will be their first civic activity. If their involvement is limited to interacting via new technologies, however, the risk arises that they will have limited opportunities to obtain civic rewards.

Yet these are the very citizens who could most benefit from civic rewards. They typically have limited previous civic engagement—PB can be a radical departure from their status quo. If their involvement is funneled toward ICTs, however,

---

39. See Arnstein (1969); Han (2014); and Sirianni (2009).

this could theoretically reduce their opportunities for face-to-face civic learning. Many of the aforementioned rewards for participation result from in-person experiences. Some come from spending lots of time with new people and learning from one another. Though at times frustrating, this experience is part of what makes PB rewarding.

Questions of access to meaningful participation create an inherent tension in the PB process. While ICTs could engage new citizens to participate at lower costs, the chance exists that their experiences will be shallower and less substantive. This is especially risky for the overall trajectory of PB because, as I argue, citizens primarily sustain their involvement in it because of PB's civic, not material, rewards. They do not engage in PB chiefly because of desires to see particular projects come to fruition. Yet civic rewards are much more difficult to acquire online—especially in condensed engagements. Online tools may be more effective at reducing barriers to entry, but this can come at the expense of, and as a result of, limiting the sometimes painful but fruitful learning process of laborious participation.

The challenge is to find ways to reduce the considerable barriers to entry while also ensuring there are genuine opportunities for in-person engagement. This requires careful judgment about how and when to use new tools. The least resource-intensive forms of participation, such as the vote, may be the most amenable to online tools. A PB strategy should incorporate civic typologies within a broader engagement plan.

Conclusion

Unlike some traditional accounts of material rationales for civic involvement, I argue participation in participatory budgeting is maintained primarily because of transformative civic rewards. Despite considerable barriers to entry and obstacles to participation, citizens remained active participants in the PBNYC pilot. Intangible civic rewards included greater civic knowledge, strengthened relationships with elected officials, greater community inclusion, and both leadership and skill development. Through participating, citizens often learn new skills ranging from how to work in groups to how to budget.

Empirical results from the PBNYC pilot show that some districts, such as District B and District C, mobilized a larger share of minorities and low-income residents to vote in PB than in the 2009 elections.

The reasons why those with fewer resources—such as education and income—would be less likely to participate are interwoven with feelings of citizen efficacy, including perceptions of how effective one's participation might be in projects such as PB.[40] Even for people who may perceive their engagement as efficacious, the PBNYC process itself is resource intensive and frustrating. Demands placed on participants due to existing structural conditions, such as government capacity and bureaucratic design, added to their frustrations.

The skill set required for intensive participation, such as serving as a budget delegate, may be more likely to be found with those who possess higher levels of education or certain types of socialization associated with socioeconomic status. For example, every budget delegate committee used e-mail as a communications tool, creating another barrier to entry. Beyond specific competencies and access to technology, a broader process of socialization plays a role in shaping who participates—one that involves being inquisitive about bureaucratic regulation, feeling comfortable speaking in groups, and feeling efficacious enough to devote this much time to a civic act. The ability to use speech as a communicative tool through reasoned arguments is a learned behavior.[41]

The vote is a portion of the PB process that does not require citizens to speak and appear before one another. Most important, the vote also involves the briefest time commitment of any aspect of the process. The vote is suited to attract the largest numbers of participants due to its more private nature, lack of required public deliberation, and limited time commitment. The vote requires the fewest skills of prior socialization, such as using reasoned arguments or assessing complex bureaucratic codes. These aspects of the vote may make it more appealing as an entry point for civic engagement for people who are typically disenfranchised.

Although all forms of participation were ostensibly aimed at reflecting the diversity of the council districts, many obstacles to diverse and broad participation were encountered throughout each phase of the process.[42] For citizens able to bypass the considerable barriers to entry, participation itself resulted in frustration and disillusionment. Nonetheless, people sustained their involvement due to the transformative effects of participation.

Through the act of participating, people formed new relationships with their elected officials, neighbors, and even the physical spaces of their community. The high demands of participation resulted in high levels of knowledge transfer; citizens left with a unique civic education in politics. Citizens were forging a communal identity—albeit frustrating, a collective identity that sustained their involvement. This collective identity is the by-product of authentic and binding

40. See Warren (2001).
41. Habermas (1991).
42. The four levels of participation include: (1) membership on the district committee, (2) service as a budget delegate, (3) attendance at a neighborhood assembly, and (4) voting.

substantive participation. Despite the varying rationales offered by citizens who entered into the process, civic rewards sustained their involvement.

This chapter suggests that democratic innovations could potentially reduce barriers to access for civic participation by offering multiple channels for diverse citizen engagement that also enhances civic rewards. Creating the space for substantive participation is an important criterion for PB and other civic innovations. It is not simply enough to tack on civic engagement to a civic experiment. Rather, for a process to truly be participatory, it must engage diverse citizenry with intentionality and purpose.

5

Engagement: Deliberation and Decisionmaking

As participatory budgeting (PB) continues to spread from its origins in the Global South throughout the United States, many have suggested that it will have to change radically to adapt to its new environment. Some argue Americans are too busy or disaffected to be actively engaged in making policy decisions.[1] A few go so far as to posit that citizens simply do not want to be engaged in day-to-day political decisions.[2] The previous chapter explored participation in PB. This chapter considers deliberation—another critical dimension in assessing PB. It draws on field research—qualitative and quantitative surveys of New York City's pilot PB program (PBNYC) in 2011–12, process tracing of the parks and recreation budget committees in four districts, and in-depth interviews—to explore deliberation and decisionmaking in participatory budgeting.[3]

I chose the parks and recreation committees because they allowed for natural project variation and were uniquely suited to the small capital projects that PBNYC seeks to create. This setting served as a useful petri dish for democratic innovation. Rodrigo Davies outlines that parks and gardens are the most common, and least controversial, proposals for civic crowdfunding projects.[4]

I immersed myself in all four committees, attending meetings of these groups, observing site visits, and reading some group e-mail discussions. In addition, I conducted separate conversations with delegates in both the parks and recreation

---

1. Schudson (2010).

2. Hibbing and Theiss-Morse (2002).

3. Survey data are from the Community Development Project at the Urban Justice Center with the PBNYC Research Team, published in CDP and PBNYC (2012).

4. These are civic projects in which citizens themselves provide funds; Davies (2014).

committees and other budget committees before, during, and after they served as budget delegates.

The chapter ends with policy implications to address challenges for deliberation posed by information and communications technologies (ICTs), which extend the reach of citizen deliberation even as they potentially weaken the commitment to face-to-face engagement that makes deliberative exercises worthwhile. In this context, technology enables a dynamic that allows for rapid-fire communication without providing the same opportunities for face-to-face exchanges. This fact has ramifications for a process that hinges on small-group dialogue and deliberation.

Norms of Deliberation

When properly conducted, then, democratic politics involves public deliberation focused on the common good, requires some form of manifest equality among citizens, and shapes the identity and interests of citizens in ways that contribute to the formation of a public conception of the common good.[5]

These principles outlined by Joshua Cohen underpin a modern conception of deliberative democracy. The field observations presented in this chapter illustrate that two norms of deliberation—efficiency and inclusiveness—can manifest in differing approaches to deliberation, with most PB deliberations existing on a continuum between the two.

Deliberative democracy begins with the assumption that we live in pluralist democratic societies.[6] Such societies are characterized by conflicts driven by political and moral differences. Deliberative democracy aims to find new ways to understand and address such conflicts without sacrificing the ideal of pluralism. As an ideal of political practice, deliberation rests on the assumption that rational discussion and exchange of reasons will enable a wider array of considerations to be taken into account, resulting in both the triumph of the better argument and a continually revitalized sense of civic identity.[7] In the process of deliberation citizens should be civic minded and ready to evince reciprocity in their conversations in being open to the arguments of their fellow citizens.[8]

---

5. Cohen (1989, p. 19).
6. Gutmann and Thompson (2004); Weinstock and Kahane (2010).
7. Gutmann and Thompson (2004); Cohen (1989).
8. Gutmann and Thompson (1998); Weinstock and Kahane (2010).

Some critics fear that the process of deliberation will lead to problematic outcomes. Others posit that the deliberative process itself magnifies and reifies hegemonic norms such as white supremacy or male domination.[9] Beliefs can be manipulated and induced through the process of deliberation, vitiating the "democratic" aims of the project.[10] In the end, citizens may be further alienated from one another as participants become more attached to their initial views and as divisions widen.[11]

Other critics contend that when citizens are not empowered to make consequential decisions, deliberation may amount to little more than uninformed conversations.[12] Even when they are given real responsibilities, these critics continue, most citizens will lack the knowledge or understanding to make binding and authoritative decisions.[13] Some go so far as to suggest that advocates of deliberative democracy do not actually believe that large groups of citizens should be empowered; rather, they hold that these new forms of deliberative democracy will consolidate elite control.[14] Modeling democracy on a "faculty workshop" stifles the range of available options as it implies that political influence will go to the most learned and skilled rhetoricians.[15]

Participatory Budgeting as Efficacious Deliberation

Participatory budgeting programs in the United States have two goals that can sometimes lead to differing approaches: improving service delivery and deepening democratic engagement. Each goal can lead to different focuses within the conduct of deliberative engagement. To the extent that the goal of PB is the improvement of government service delivery, participants may be encouraged to arrive in a timely manner at concrete, practical proposals. By contrast, a focus on improving and sustaining civic engagement emphasizes robust participation by a wide and diverse range of citizens. In theory—and sometimes in practice—these two goals can overlap when an effective process leads to more inclusive dialogue that yields both more projects likely to be voted upon and representative projects. A challenge for the first wave of PB in the United States has been to find a way to achieve the goals of results-driven efficiency and inclusiveness in ways that are mutually reinforcing.

9. Young (2000); Mouffe (2000).
10. Stokes (1998). See also Olken (2010). Olken finds direct citizen participation can lead to higher levels of satisfaction.
11. Sunstein (2009).
12. See discussions in Richardson (2002).
13. Walzer (1999).
14. Posner (2003).
15. Sanders (1997).

Unlike the famous case of participatory budgeting in Porto Alegre in Brazil, which divided deliberation into "thematic" and "pragmatic" assemblies, implementations in the United States seek to reconcile PB's dual goals in one set of citizen deliberations. Deliberators and facilitators put forth projects for the community to vote on, with some participants more focused on forming projects likely to "win" than others. To accommodate PB's competing goals, I observed individual facilitators and deliberators working to reconcile competing norms of results-driven efficiency and process-driven inclusiveness. Conditions varied district by district with distinguishing features that included bureaucratic capacity, composition of each budget committee, and especially facilitation technique.

My definition of deliberation includes the concepts of (1) dynamic and iterative process,[16] (2) rational discourse,[17] and (3) an emphasis on the publicity of discourse to promote public spirit.[18] It is critical that decisions are made through an ongoing process, with rational policy constraints guiding discussion in public.

Decisionmaking is more complex than simply achieving a consensus. Reaching a policy decision in a deliberative setting requires accurate information, communication between participants, and an ability to prioritize the most salient issues. I argue that deliberation and dialogue should be viewed as important factors in evaluating the efficacy of various civic innovations. Deliberation is multifaceted. Those who wish to spur democratic innovation ought to plan accordingly.

To assess local deliberations in committees, I traced the budget delegate processes of thematic committees on parks and recreation within each of the four districts in the PBNYC pilot year (2011–12). This constituted a four-step process:[19]

1. *Neighborhood assemblies*
   Residents identified community needs and some signed up to be budget delegates. Budget delegates had to be at least sixteen years old and have a strong connection to the district, such as living, working, or attending school in the district, or having a child attending school in the district.
2. *Budget delegate committees*
   Delegates worked closely with city agencies for months to create viable projects for the community to vote upon.
3. *Second-round neighborhood assemblies*
   Delegates presented projects to the wider community for feedback.

16. Gutmann and Thompson (2004).
17. Habermas (1996a).
18. Chambers (2005).
19. CDP and PBNYC (2012).

4. *Voting*

Community residents, at least eighteen years of age, voted on which projects to fund. Elected officials who sponsored the entire process pledged to
implement the winners.

Budget delegates divided into thematic groups reflecting the initial ideas presented
at neighborhood assemblies, as compiled by the offices of city council members.
Thematic groups included transportation; schools and education; parks and
recreation; public safety; housing; public health and environment; community
facilities; and transit, streets, and sidewalks. Facilitators ran these budget committee groups. They received varying degrees of leadership training.

The outcomes of budget proposals in PB are more constrained than the outcomes of some other prominent deliberative exercises. Instead of focusing solely on
moral agreement in concept, deliberations in PB are also concerned with policy
limitations in practice. Some of the normative pressures of deliberation, such as
morally justified decisionmaking, are therefore reduced. According to Dennis
F. Thompson, "legitimacy prescribes the process by which, under these circumstances, collective decisions can be morally justified to those who are bound
by them."[20] Many theorists posit that a decision is legitimate if it responds to reasons identified to justify a decision.[21] PB generally focuses on viable project proposals aimed toward achieving equity and the public good.

How to Deliberate?

Although arriving at viable final proposals was a predetermined end of the deliberations I observed, wide disagreement emerged about *how* to decide on projects.
Were the goals to craft the most innovative proposals or those that accurately assessed
tactical district needs? What was the best way to determine district need? Should committees put forward the proposals most likely to garner votes? These are some of
the many questions that emerged in the course of these deliberations.

PBNYC devolved power to individual budget committees to come up with
their own solutions. Some facilitators and deliberators privileged putting forth
"winning" projects that they thought were likely to be selected by residents at
the final vote. Other groups were less concerned about putting forth projects likely
to win and were instead more invested in open-ended discussions and engagement with their neighbors. Since the predetermined goal of PBNYC's deliberations was set as coming up with viable projects, without strictly delineating how

---

20. Thompson (2008, p. 502).
21. Cohen (1989, 1997); Gutmann and Thompson (2004); Mendelberg (2002).

this should be achieved, these deliberations consequently showed a great deal of variance in approach across committees. Ultimately individual facilitators and in-group deliberation dynamics shaped how various districts balanced these competing norms.

Districts also put in place mechanisms designed to focus on youths and seniors. In addition to the thematic budget committees in each district, District B had a youth committee and a senior committee, each focused specifically on these issues and comprised of people from these respective demographics.[22] District C, which included a youth committee, faced a challenge: while the rules allowed participation of those sixteen years or older, voting was restricted to those eighteen or older. This resulted in the youth participants spending months as budget delegates without being allowed to vote for the projects they had worked to fashion. "I loved participating, I wish I could have voted—maybe one day," noted a youth budget delegate.[23]

Deliberation in Action

Residents attended neighborhood assemblies to brainstorm ideas and potential projects. Some signed up to be budget delegates.[24] These delegates opted to work with city agencies over the course of several months to craft viable budget proposals for residents to vote upon. After city council district offices compiled the ideas generated at the neighborhood assemblies into categories, individuals volunteered for thematic committees. These committees met regularly over several months, engaging in small-group dialogue and deliberation. Budget committees often were diverse, with some delegates who had never before been active civically working alongside some who were long-standing community leaders.

As discussed in the previous chapter, levels of involvement by city council members differed across districts and budget delegate committees. In all districts except District A, the council member's office set specific dates and a centralized location for budget delegate meetings. District A had twice as many people sign up to be budget delegates—roughly one hundred people—as the other districts, each of which had approximately fifty budget delegates. With so many budget

22. As outlined in chapter 4, districts have been anonymized as Districts A, B, C, and D to protect the privacy of participants.

23. All quotes from PB participants are from my research transcriptions. These youth committees may have set the stage for the first youth-driven PB in Boston, as explored in the next chapter.

24. Originally, in Chicago, the process was designed to have an elected set of delegates or "community representatives." In practice they ended up being self-selected. Perhaps learning from Chicago, in other instances of PB in the United States it has not been stipulated that budget delegates should be elected. In Boston's youth-driven PB these deliberators were called "change agents."

delegates, District A allowed each thematic group to determine its own meeting times and locations. The district was also forced to subdivide its budget delegate committees on issues such as transportation into subcommittees focused on specific issues such as subways and buses.

Every budget delegate committee, regardless of configuration, inevitably experienced significant attrition in membership and attendance. This was especially true in District C. Here the city council member's office was understaffed, meaning that the district committee members were forced to handle the additional tasks of running and planning the budget delegate meetings. In the ensuing confusion, many who initially signed up lost interest, and District C saw the largest reduction in its number of budget delegates.

At the initial budget delegate meeting each committee sifted through proposals put forth in each neighborhood assembly to assess their feasibility. The goals of the committees were to (1) sift through the ideas presented at the neighborhood assemblies, (2) assess needs in the district through site visits, (3) deliberate on new projects, (4) work directly with city agencies, and (5) develop project ideas for the community-wide vote. Budget delegates were instructed to identify projects that would have a broad physical impact on the district for five years and cost at least $35,000.[25]

Some ideas were ineligible for reasons of cost or because they involved expense funds rather than capital funds. Capital funds are used to pay for brick-and-mortar projects, such as building a community garden. Expense funds, by contrast, are designated for projects involving people and services, such as teacher training programs.[26] Other ideas were eligible only with modifications, such as a proposal for replacing a stop sign, which was initially too inexpensive to qualify. This project was combined with other additions to the streetscape, including a countdown bus clock, in order to meet the cost threshold.

Once eligible projects were identified, groups discussed how best to assess the relative need for each project. Budget delegates wanted to ensure that projects accurately reflected district needs—not just the preferences of those who attended a neighborhood assembly. Therefore, committees often conducted site visits to assess district need. This included, for example, spending afternoons visiting every park or school in a district.

25. CDP and PBNYC (2012, p. 8).

26. For more information see Participatory Budgeting in New York City, "About the New York City Process" (http://pbnyc.org/content/about-new-york-city-process).

Variation among Districts

Training was one of the major factors that influenced how facilitators oversaw and helped to coordinate PB deliberations. The quality of that training depended, in turn, on the structure and organization of the city council member's office and the resources each devoted to training. These training efforts were often supplemented by the work of the district committees, groups of citizens who took a leadership role in the organization of PB assemblies in each district. CVH and PBP also did a citywide training. In districts where council members had staff devoted to PB, there were fewer burdens on district committee members.

Council member staffing and district committee capacity greatly shaped the training of facilitators. In District C, many facilitators dropped out during the process and were replaced by people who had received no training, due to capacity limits and time constraints. District B, meanwhile, had a training process with weekly check-in calls for facilitators run by the council member's staff.

Bureaucratic constraints often affected how participants assessed needs and fulfilled deliberative goals across all budget committees. Individual bureaucrats working in city agencies were responsible for providing necessary information to budget delegates. Differences among the city government agency officials interfacing with the four districts influenced how each committee was able to acquire information useful to projects. This factor—the availability of bureaucratic time and attention—was difficult to anticipate, control for, and design into the PB process. Some agency officials were intrigued by the process and devoted time to attend budget delegate meetings. Others were frustrated by the process and sent e-mails to the staff of council members requesting that budget delegates stop contacting them. This variation affected the flow of information to budget delegates and subsequently the quality of the process.

The policy recommendations in chapter 7 include developing a more centralized information database to reduce this variance. In the current model, PB often hinges on the goodwill and volunteer time of agency officials. This uncontrolled variable does not maximize accuracy or efficiency in the distribution of city information to budget delegates.

Facilitators

If the participants are mostly like-minded or hold the same views before they enter into the discussion, they are not situated in the circumstances of deliberation. They do not confront the problem that deliberation is intended to address.[27]

Facilitators were sometimes also members of the district committee. During my year of intensive study of the PBNYC pilot and other pilots, I observed some facilitators oriented toward more efficiently reaching agreement on viable projects, whereas others prized free and inclusive discussion even when it became digressive or unfocused. The difference was a matter of emphasis: it goes without saying that all worked to run an inclusive process and to reach optimal results.

It is the opinion of this author, after intensive study of the four districts, that the role of the facilitator was critical. Disparate methods of facilitation played an important role in creating widely varying forms of deliberative discourse. The importance of facilitators is sometimes underappreciated in the current literature.

In committees with thicker preexisting networks of activism, facilitators faced challenges in keeping delegates on task. The facilitator in District A's parks and recreation committee was a well-educated, white professional overseeing a predominantly well-educated, white professional committee, which included one Asian American woman, one black woman, and one Orthodox Jewish man. The facilitator ensured that projects were debated in a timely fashion while making every effort to give all participants a chance to comment. When voting neared, the facilitator had participants e-mail the committee updated versions of their proposed projects prior to the meeting. The facilitator came to the meeting with extensive notes that systemically covered each project. Rather than open-ended deliberation, this meeting was highly focused on efficiently reaching a viable result.

Some were disappointed by this. "I've been working on this project for the last five months and now it is dead," one budget delegate lamented, shortly after her project was voted down. Yet the majority of people were glad the meeting was brief and efficient. Another member of the committee praised the process, noting that: "Everyone came prepared, did their homework, and our facilitator made tough calls based on agencies rules—we have to do what we have to do."

The facilitator was technocratic. While stern, this individual did not put forth preferences. Instead, the facilitator conveyed information and rules according to instructions from the city council member's office. The majority of budget delegates at the final meeting responded favorably to the facilitator's approach. But disagreement lingered as well as hurt feelings.

One middle-aged woman whose project had been voted down the previous week absented herself, voicing her frustration about the process:

27. Thompson (2008, p. 502).

I've made a board of projects for next year. I am hopeful that it will get chosen next year, I was sad it didn't get chosen because I am skeptical of politicians in general—was this process really up to the people?

Next to her board of projects for the following year, she placed a board for people to write criticisms and complaints of the process. By the end of the meeting, the two boards were entirely filled with comments. Examples of suggested process improvements included "more outlets for citizen engagement" and "finding ways to improve democracy beyond just PB."

The failure of this delegate's project to make the final ballot underlines the ways in which a focus on efficiently reaching viable projects can be in tension with a desire to tap participants' creativity. While her project was highly innovative, it would have required navigating a thicket of different city bureaucracies that had little or no history of—or capacity for—collaborating with each other.[28] But her frustrations went beyond the limitations of the city bureaucracy to encompass the style of the facilitator as well. The city council member and the district committee had the capacity and organization for facilitation training, including clear protocols for assessing the feasibility of projects. As a result, the facilitator did not necessarily encourage freeform deliberation that might lead to projects ineligible for funding. Part of this delegate's frustration was simply that "no one gave my project a chance because it wasn't a cookie-cutter project."

Other budget delegates were interested in her idea and expressed discontent at being forced to work on small-bore projects, derisively called "sidewalk repairs" by one participant. As another budget delegate stressed, "I am here to do big projects to strengthen our troubled democracy." Facilitation focused more on efficiently arriving at viable projects, however, also had a degree of success in bringing together disparate viewpoints, personalities, and project ideas in other committees where delegates were less familiar with one another.

By contrast, in District C, the understaffing of the city council member's office created a leadership vacuum that was filled by the district committee. Robust church networks would often ensure that food was provided at meetings. The facilitator, who did not receive training from the city council office, was tasked with managing a diverse assortment of citizens, ranging from a Caribbean woman with a white-collar job to a British man living in a homeless shelter, many of whom were meeting each other for the first time.

The facilitator was already burdened with community commitments and missed half the meetings. As a result, the facilitator's roles and responsibilities were

---

28. See Sirianni (2009, pp. 58–61) on transforming institutional culture.

often distributed between two other members of the group. One, an older woman, pressed the group to embrace creative proposals; the other, a younger woman, urged the group to focus on pragmatic proposals with a higher likelihood of success. The facilitator, when present in person or via e-mail, tended to offer personal opinions in lieu of providing neutral arbitration between the various positions.

One meeting that started forty-five minutes late was typical in the peripatetic course that it followed:

> PARTICIPANT A: When you reach out to the agencies you realize they have thought of these things but they don't have the resources, funding or otherwise.
> PARTICIPANT B: When the parks guy came, everything is so expensive, and overhead costs are ridiculous.
> FACILITATOR: Want to disband politics and start over?
> [Laughter]

Discussion continued, with people outlining opinions and ideas for proposals covering an expansive range of projects. The facilitator ensured that everyone's opinion and voice were heard. The District C facilitator's approach to facilitation appeared to emphasize creating an environment in which everyone felt that his or her opinion was valued, adding views where necessary to move the discussion along. Yet the meeting did not reach consensus and no clear next steps by which to turn these ideas into action were evident.

At a final meeting before the vote, city council staff and organizers tried to explain to budget delegates why a particular creative proposal would neither be viable nor have a high probability of being approved by many voters. The facilitator was absent at that meeting, so the group was left to organize the debate without a leader.

They were starkly informed that their creative project, involving arts and community heritage, would be impossible to realize largely due to the complex agency coordination required. Nonetheless, they did not begin to frame the discussion in terms of results; rather, the four participants who attended the last meeting continued to speak in favor of the project. Even when given the option to make a more "realistic" decision, they continued to prize deliberation above all. Ultimately, their project was put on the ballot, but it received far too few votes to advance. Yet the participants remained confident in their decisions.

"Even though our project was not chosen, we began the process to put forth the type of proposal we want to better our neighborhood. This is just the beginning," one delegate recounted. Though their project did not win, these delegates, in their discussions with the author, remained energized by the inclusive process.

Deliberative Lessons

> There is wide variation along every single dimension of the PBNYC process. But that is ok. If the purpose is civic engagement and encouraging participation, we do not need perfect uniformity across every committee.
> —PBNYC budget committee facilitator

Varying structural local conditions influenced deliberations, including bureaucratic constraint and committee composition—suggesting that PBNYC need not require perfect uniformity among districts. This on-the-ground variation and structural creativity allowed budget delegates to use their disparate backgrounds. Greater uniformity could have provided a measure of quality control, but it would also have meant imposing a top-down structure, stifling the creative democratic energies PB purports to foster. In theory, greater top-down control of the deliberative structure could have been more efficient. In practice, implementing deliberation and decisionmaking processes was highly dependent upon the makeup of the committees as well as individual facilitators, which would have varied regardless. Committees were beholden to facilitators with wide variance in background, organization, and time commitment to PBNYC.

The dual goals of PB—short-term service delivery and long-term civic engagement—require structured deliberations that offer opportunities for long-term knowledge transfer on the basis of specific information conveyed in a manner conducive to forming relationships.

Effective and meaningful deliberation is also critical to ensure that the community's projects are not simply dictated by one or more specific organizations. I witnessed people who came to PB originally as representatives for a specific project emerge from the process with an understanding acquired via deliberation that a wider range of concerns, needs, and proposals required their attention. As PB expands, deliberation will be an essential safeguard for avoiding process co-option by special interests. In face-to-face deliberations, people defend their projects and engage in a dialogue about community needs.

Information and Communications Technologies

Some scholars suggest that "network effects" brought about by the mass proliferation of information and communications technologies (ICTs) will necessarily

Figure 5-1. *Levels of Online Tool Adoption by Districts*

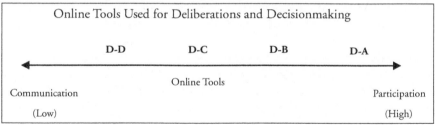

bring about more democratic social conditions.[29] Yet in this section I show that, although online tools can enable more rapid communication, in democratic innovations this comes at the cost of the civic benefits derived from face-to-face and in-person deliberation.[30]

Even accounting for local contexts and bureaucratic constraints, human idiosyncrasies in facilitation and deliberation will affect the expression of these values. What if this variance could be reduced? Online tools and mediums provide a plausible alternative to the idiosyncratic personalities of facilitators and others engaged in dialogue. In most districts these tools served as conduits for discussion and decisionmaking (see figure 5-1). Based on my observations, they were used most heavily in District A and they were used least in District D.

District composition, particularly in terms of age, was a determining factor in how readily a district adopted online tools. The least "tech savvy" districts were District D and District C. A binary measure of "online" or "not online" does not tell the whole story. For example, an e-mail list offers one-way communication whereas multifaceted tools can enable two-way participation. This section seeks to describe that varied texture.

Communication

One committee facilitator in District D, a younger woman, created an e-mail list for the committee and sent out e-mails regularly. The median age of parks and recreation committee budget delegates in this district was older than the participants in the corresponding committees in the other three districts. Thus there was a larger "digital divide" to overcome in District D. The majority of delegates appeared to be uncomfortable with ICTs. Many participants were frustrated by and did not use the online tools.

29. See Benkler (2006); Shirky (2008).
30. See also Leighninger (2011).

District D used e-mail minimally only to communicate meeting times and locations. Further, committee meetings generally took place at the same time at the same location—in the district office. Thus there was less dependence on e-mails as an information source for meeting times, locations, and dates. District D was the only district that did not keep a blog or use any form of social media. The most popular ICT used in the district was the telephone.

District D's largely older, white, Irish Catholic constituency did not put pressure on the office for more online tools, in part because many participants would not have been able to use them. When online tools were used in District D, they were employed purely for communication rather than to foster additional channels for participation.

Participation

In District A, various online tools were used throughout the process. This included an online interface for project idea submission, Google groups for committees, and Facebook groups. The high penetration rate of online tools in District A raised questions of how online tools alter the processes of deliberative democracy. For example, do people behave differently over a listserv than when deliberating face-to-face? The immediacy of e-mail correspondence coupled with the distancing veil of the Internet created unique dynamics of deliberation and decisionmaking.

The following story is illustrative of these dynamics and questions. The facilitator of the parks and recreation committee in District A sent an e-mail prior to the second-round neighborhood assembly, asking people to vote online about whether to put a somewhat controversial proposal for a dog run on the ballot. The committee had a vocal contingent in favor. However, while the proposal was approved by the city's Department of Parks and Recreation, local associations of dog owners did not support it. Further, it was slated to be expensive. As a result, the facilitator's e-mail questioned whether the project should go on the ballot, asking delegates to vote on the matter online:

> Ah, democracy! In that spirit, please cast your vote by midnight tonight—we have to know by tomorrow so that ballots can be designed and printed in time. Please use this form to vote. Please feel free to reply and discuss, but definitely vote whether or not to keep the Dog Run proposal on the ballot.

This prompted a rapid exchange of fourteen e-mails between budget delegates. Delegates were trying to balance competing interests; they were sympathetic to the work put into the proposal and wanted to be supportive of fellow delegates, but also they recognized that less expensive projects would be more likely to win votes. Below is a truncated snapshot of these fourteen e-mails.

> PARTICIPANT C: Our group worked extremely hard on this! To see no proposal for our cause is disappointing. We need to give people a chance to vote . . . wasn't this the premise of creating this process in the first place?
>
> PARTICIPANT D: Even though I was a dog owner until my 15 year old black lab passed recently, I support the decision not to put so much of our limited funds on this one single project. It's a big district with many needs.
>
> FACILITATOR: Parks approved that idea, but unfortunately it's too expensive—$650k. The Council member's office has set the maximum at $500k per project.
>
> At this point, it's not the Council member's decision—it's yours (all of yours). The decision to limit the maximum amount per project was done out of fairness to ensure that multiple projects would be funded, and at this point it can't be changed. So given what we've got, it's up to the committee to decide whether or not to put the current Dog Run proposal on the ballot, and if it does go on the ballot, it's then up to the community to decide whether or not to fund it.
>
> [After people had filled out the survey and more e-mails opposing the dog run were sent . . .]
>
> FACILITATOR: Thank you for your quick response on the dog run issue. The committee voted 6–3 to take the proposal off the ballot. I know this is a disappointment to everyone—people worked really hard on the proposal, and obviously lots of folks in the community want dog run improvements. However, given the cost and complications with the local Dog Owners Association, I think this is probably the right decision. But still, what a bummer!

These fourteen e-mails were all sent within a few minutes of one another and provided an opportunity for discussion without the pressure and tension of a face-to-face argument.

The facilitator in District A was focused on efficiency using online tools; targeted questions were presented via e-mail, with deadlines and an online poll. Yet without the intervening face-to-face interaction, online tools create the risk of diminishing participation. E-mail provides a short timeframe for decisionmaking sometimes at odds with a process of deliberation aimed at maximizing discourse and dialogue. These technologies enabled a dynamic that transcended the traditional economy of moral disagreement: rapid-fire e-mails conveyed brief commentary without providing opportunities for deliberation.

The introduction of these distancing, impersonal components in the PB process has implications for technology's role in deliberation and decisionmaking. The nature of e-mail alters the substance and style of deliberation. Are people hiding behind technology? Are they able to speak in ways they would not if they were looking into the eyes of another person?

Anonymity can be seen as a virtue at times, opening up a space for criticism or for a voice that can potentially escape some of the hegemonic factors that shape in-person rhetorical exercises. An anonymous digital poll reduces the costs of public disagreement by creating a form of secret ballot. While names are attached to a personal e-mail, nonetheless a named e-mail address and a physical presence lead to two very different dynamics. The costs of certain kinds of speech are reduced when discourse is not conducted in person. However, this can run counter to the ideal of democratic deliberation by offering opportunities for voice without fostering a situation of pluralistic equality via such discourse. Further, face-to-face communication has a far greater potential to mitigate the rigidity of results-oriented deliberations.

Online tools will continue to be integrated into participatory budgeting. Some have argued that ICTs will not just shape behavior in interactions like these, but also lead to a broader transformation of identity for actors in politics.[31] The next chapters explore the role of innovation and institutionalization in the continued expansion of PB. Given these trends, it will be critical to understand the nature of deliberation and decisionmaking in the process so as to best deploy tools that can enhance rather than mitigate PB's positive features.

Making online deliberation a more pervasive part of participatory budgeting requires developing unique online norms and facilitation guidelines in order to understand and compensate for how the Internet reduces some social barriers while creating others. Unlike more utopian views of the effects of online networks on engaging citizens in politics, this section and the following chapter illustrate both the opportunities and the challenges provided by online tools.[32]

Policy Implications

What is the relationship between how information is communicated and how decisions are made in deliberation? On first glance, it may seem that if more in-

---

31. Singh (2013).
32. Benkler (2006); Shirky (2008).

formation is communicated, the level of citizen engagement and dialogue will inevitably rise. This chapter describes a more complex dynamic at work.

Information shared via PBNYC empowered a broad set of actors and interests. The capacity of individual city council members and their staff to convey information to district committees and facilitators influenced how budget delegates, in turn, experienced the PB process. Similarly, how this information flowed directly related to how facilitators interacted with budget delegates. Some facilitators, such as those in District B, were equipped with lots of information. Others, such as in District C, at times lacked basic information about process requirements and deadlines. Not only did this district see a drop-off in budget delegates, it also had far fewer project proposals than other districts.

In examining the processes of the budget committees, facilitators emerge as critical conduits between budget delegates and council member offices. This affects both individuals participating in PB as well as broader process decisions. Ensuring that facilitators are equipped with necessary opportunities for two-way information flow will positively shape the conditions under which the PB process arrives at critical decisions. In addition to equipping facilitators with information, centralized district-level support throughout PB can also foster improvement.

As more PB activity takes place online, understanding these variations in information access and delivery will become even more critical. It is not enough that citizens simply receive more information. Rather, the ways in which they interact with it and how it is conveyed also matter. Choices between different communication mediums, tools, and processes all matter. Communicating via online tools provides varied ways for how citizens process information, leading to changes in dialogue and deliberation that must be considered.

Conclusion

Deliberation and decisionmaking in the PBNYC pilot took on a multiplicity of forms. The question of how to structure these processes remains more complex than choosing the easiest options. People expend time and energy to engage in dialogue and deliberation. I observed conditions, such as facilitator style as well as bureaucratic constraints and varying demographic and socioeconomic compositions among the districts, that influence decisionmaking processes and outcomes.

Tension lingers between the desire both for the most efficient process and for ensuring participants have the time and space to forge meaningful connections. There are also trade-offs between top-down processes and bottom-up modifications. Facilitators varied widely in their backgrounds, levels of organization, and time commitments to participatory budgeting. This enabled opportunities for on-the-ground variation and creativity and gave budget delegates the ability to use their unique backgrounds to inform projects. Meanwhile, greater process-level control would have created more uniformity and consistency in decisionmaking across budget delegate committees. The tension between top-down quality control and creativity remains unresolved.

I have shown that PB's goals of deliberation will be fulfilled neither monolithically nor easily. But it may still be true that PB can be a viable model for deepening democracy in the United States while at the same time producing "winning" projects. Understanding the nuances of facilitation and deliberation is especially important for civic innovations aiming to engage citizens through dialogue and bring them into the decisionmaking processes. Online tools add further opportunities and challenges. Further study of the varying approaches to deliberation put forth in this chapter could serve as critical frameworks for integrating technology into the process of decisionmaking, as further explored in subsequent chapters.

6

Innovation and Permutations: Boston's Youth PB

Youth are not the problem, they are the solution.
—PB youth organizer

The nation's first youth-driven participatory budgeting project was initiated in Boston in 2014 and continues to date. It offers important lessons for PB's continued growth in the United States. Involving young people between the ages of twelve and twenty-five, it represents an innovation within an innovation—providing a unique lens for examining iteration in PB and containing lessons for future civic experimentation.[1]

I present an in-depth case study of the first youth-driven participatory budgeting effort in the United States, which Boston staged in 2014. I embedded myself in this process, contributing to the overall research design, methodology, and implementation led by the Harvard Kennedy School's Ash Center for Democratic Innovation and Governance. I conducted interviews with officials and participants. An outline in this chapter of several salient aspects of the youth participatory budgeting program in Boston informs the guidelines for further innovation and institutionalization.

A goal of focusing on Boston's first youth PB program is to highlight an innovation on PB's path from experiment to institutionalization. Approaches to expanding PB will inevitably shape how it is practiced across the United States. These choices will also necessarily involve adaptation and experimentation.

---

1. In 2015 the municipality of Cambridge, Massachusetts, launched a version of PB that allowed voting by those aged twelve and up. In 2016 Seattle, Washington, is slated to introduce a youth PB (Office of the Mayor, 2015).

Future innovation in PB could come in several areas, including its geographic reach, monies, techniques, participants, or impact evaluation. Within each of these elements, opportunities exist for experimentation and learning. While PB constitutes democratic innovation in itself, it also offers multiple opportunities for process alteration.

Boston

Boston has proved itself to be a hotbed of civic engagement and experimentation. Under Mayor Thomas Menino Boston created the first Mayor's Office of New Urban Mechanics (MONUM), which was tasked with using technology to drive participatory reform. This office has created tools that connect citizens more directly with government officials and more robustly engage citizens in decisionmaking. For example, this office created a mobile application, Citizens Connect, that enables constituents to directly report nonemergency public problems to the city and track the city's response. People can see other reported cases and are informed when a case has been resolved. It has served as a national and international model for engaging citizens in urban governance.[2]

Boston has also been an urban leader in youth engagement. The Mayor's Youth Council was started over twenty years ago and has served as an example for other cities. Additionally, the Boston Centers for Youth and Families are a network of facilities run by the city with a wide range of programmatic activities.

Efforts to bring PB to Boston arose within the context of a willingness on the part of city government, in partnership with PBP, to explore new strategies and approaches for citizen engagement.[3] Though initial forays began under the Menino administration, it was not until late 2013—under Mayor Martin Walsh—that the process planning truly started. Truncated due to the mayoral transition, the PB pilot's public timeline began in January 2014. Boston put $1 million of capital funds into it. To qualify for PB, projects had to cost at least $25,000, have a lifespan of at least five years post-implementation, and involve physical infrastructure (including technology) on city-owned property.[4]

The pilot's truncated timeline became an overarching theme for participants who felt like there was "never enough time" for the process.[5] The city forged an oversight committee, which included staff from the Office of Budget Management

2. See Puttick, Baeck, and Colligan (2014).
3. See "City Moves Forward with Youth Participatory Budgeting Process: Mayor Menino Announces Partnership with the Participatory Budgeting Project, Search for Youth Organizer Underway," City of Boston.gov, November 14, 2013 (www.cityofboston.gov/news/default.aspx?id=6408).
4. YLC (2014); Gordon (2014).
5. A common refrain from participants.

(OBM), the Mayor's Office of New Urban Mechanics (MONUM), Boston Centers for Youth and Families, the Mayor's Youth Council, and the Department of Youth Engagement & Employment. PBP provided organizational support and hired two organizers based in Boston who ran most of the day-to-day operations. These organizers were deeply embedded within Boston's youth communities.[6]

Consistent with PB's focus on citizen engagement in all aspects of the process, in addition to the oversight committee, a steering committee was formed through outreach to Boston's robust network of youth-focused civil society organizations (CSOs). After applying to serve on the steering committee, each organization was asked to select two representatives—at least one youth—to serve on the committee. From this group, co-chairs from the Mayor's Youth Council, the City School (a collaborative program aimed at developing youth leadership in issues of social justice), and Youth on Board (a nonprofit dedicated to youth organizing) were selected to organize meeting logistics and outreach.

The steering committee designed the process governance, including voting rules and requirements. They determined that the process would be called "Youth Lead the Change" and that budget delegates would be called "change agents" (this book adopts this term, their chosen nomenclature, to describe youth who signed up to shape project proposals). The process structure is outlined in figure 6-1.

They decided that residents of Boston aged twelve to twenty-five would be permitted to vote. This last decision came after a fraught and heated debate. Greater Boston is made up of several small and widely spread out municipalities: it is not uncommon for someone to work in one municipality, such as Brookline, and live in another, such as Cambridge. After several rounds of deliberation, it was determined that only residents of Boston could participate.

The steering committee subdivided into various groups, such as social media and outreach. As a whole group, however, they decided upon common goals and core principles: increase youth power; allow all voices to be heard; build stronger, safer, and healthier communities: strengthen a citywide sense of pride, solidarity, and equality.[7]

The principles established by the steering committee were less clearly elaborated but nonetheless concrete. They consisted of youth power, solidarity, transparency, inclusion, equality, respect, courage, boldness, and innovation. These principles became organizing themes rather than specific targets. The theme of "youth power" was especially salient with young participants. The refrain that

6. See Department of Youth Engagement and Employment, "Youth Lead the Change: Committee Members," Department of Youth Engagement & Employment (http://youth.boston.gov/youth-lead -the-change/about/committee-members-2/).

7. List of goals according to the 2014 rulebook for Youth Lead the Change: YLC (2014).

Figure 6-1. *Roles and Responsibilities, Youth Lead the Change*

Boston youth	• Brainstorm ideas at public meeting • Volunteer to become change agents • Vote on projects
Change agents	• Turn the brainstormed ideas into viable project proposals
Steering committee	• Design overall PB process and make decisions
Steering committee co-chairs	• Assist in facilitation of steering committee • Review materials • Promote PB
Participatory budgeting project (PBP)	• Provide technical expertise • Share knowledge based on other PB processes globally
City departments (staff and experts)	• Give feedback on project feasibility and cost
PB oversight committee	• Appoints steering committee • Assists in event planning • Provides background for participants and connection to city staff • Oversees PBP

Source: Youth Lead the Change rulebook 2014.

this PB process involved "REAL money and REAL power" was a strong and important selling point for participants.[8]

Idea Assemblies

The resultant processes in Boston took on a similar form and structure to those in Chicago and New York City. A series of idea assemblies—to inform people about the process and generate ideas—took place at Boston Centers for Youth and Families facilities across Boston, including in Dorchester, East Boston, Mattapan, Roslindale, Roxbury, and South Boston. At many, a jovial atmosphere prevailed; participants were offered pizza, and some assemblies even began with spoken word poetry. *These assemblies generated 473 proposals.*[9]

8. YLC (2014).
9. Grillos (2014).

It was at these gatherings where youth signed up to be change agents, though it is worth noting that the assemblies themselves also provided opportunities for small-group dialogue and deliberation. Young people paired off to generate ideas, trying to balance their desires with communal needs when coming up with projects to suggest. Based on the ideas generated at these assemblies, six thematic committees were formed: (1) food, health, and environment; (2) community centers; (3) libraries, arts, and culture; (4) parks; (5) schools and education; and (6) streets, transit, and safety. Each committee received roughly fifty to one hundred suggested projects compiled from these assemblies, based on committee themes.

Youth delegates cited as a top priority technology improvements, such as lightweight Google laptops known as Chromebooks. Approximately 20 percent of the original proposed projects were not eligible for capital funds, while roughly 30 percent were "maybe eligible."[10] Additionally, Citizinvestor, a civic crowdfunding platform, launched a custom-made platform for Youth Lead the Change, where people could suggest new projects, "like" others, and vote.[11] Yet only nine additional eligible proposals were submitted by the deadline. The online proposals were offered in similar categories to those generated at the idea assemblies. Examples of project proposals included installing security cameras and creating designated "free wall spaces" for local visual artists.

Some common themes emerged at the idea assemblies. One was the high level of violence in many communities. Others included the need for improved parks and safety. Several young people told stories about knowing someone who had died. Violence was a top-cited problem for both assembly participants and PB voters.

The committees of "change agents" met weekly for about eight weeks and also held separate meetings with relevant representatives from city departments. Ultimately, they prepared fourteen final proposals for the ballot. This winnowing process—from more than four hundred ideas to fourteen final proposals—is laid out in table 6-1.

While the number of projects decreased over time, the number of participants increased. There were roughly 300 attendees at the budget assemblies and 1,531 voters. Voters in the pilot could choose up to four projects to support. After the youth participants had finalized their budget proposals, voting took place throughout the city for one week. Sites included six high schools, five community centers, four "T" stops,[12] and the offices of five collaborating organizations.

10. Grillos (2014, p. 17).
11. This platform is still available online (http://boston.citizinvestor.com/).
12. The "T" is the name of the light-rail transit line in the public transportation system in Boston.

Table 6-1. *Number of Project Ideas over Time*

	Arts and libraries	Community centers	Environment and health	Parks	Schools and education	Streets and safety	Total
Initial proposals	52	111	47	108	71	84	473
Capital eligible (may be eligible)	18 (29)	44 (45)	17 (14)	93 (11)	33 (17)	43 (16)	248 (132)
Proposals on PB ballot	1	2	1	2	4	4	14
Winners of PB vote	1	0	1	2	1	2	7

Source: Grillos (2014).

The Vote

The results of the vote showed that the winning projects were broadly representative of the same concerns as the initial proposals. With the exception of community centers, every other issue area was represented in the vote outcomes.

The winning projects were:

Park playground and picnic area upgrade	($400,000)
Boston "Art Walls"—public spaces for local artists to showcase their work	($60,000)
Chromebook laptops for classrooms in three area high schools	($90,000)
Skatepark feasibility study	($50,000)
Security cameras	($105,000)
Street playground makeover	($100,000)
Renovated sidewalks and lighting around two Boston parks	($110,000)[13]

When compared to projects in Boston's FY15–FY19 capital plan, a few differences emerge. PB participants emphasized certain neighborhoods, including Dorchester, East Boston, Jamaica Plain, and Mission Hill, over others, while the largest portion of spending went to parks. The city's capital plan allocated the

13. City of Boston, "Mayor Walsh Announces Results of the Nation's First-Ever Youth Participatory Budgeting Initiative," City of Boston.gov, June 30, 2014 (www.cityofboston.gov/news/Default .aspx?id=12695).

most funding to streets and transportation and to schools and education. The geographic focus of the winning projects can be partially explained by the chosen sites for assemblies and the fact that Dorchester and East Boston were also the neighborhoods where many participants lived. However, because comparing a four-year budget with one year of allocations is imprecise at best, this data should not be seen as conclusive of broader trends or disparities.[14]

Implications and Civic Rewards

> I wish people would remember this is a pilot year—it's a first year process and we are all learning.
> —Steering committee member, Youth Lead the Change, Boston

Boston has a robust network of youth-focused organizations as well as city staff dedicated to engaging with youth. This infrastructure laid the foundation for implementing Youth Lead the Change, but also heightened expectations. Some participants wished there was a greater willingness to experiment and perhaps even accept instructive failure. For some youth, the steering committee process was cumbersome and not nearly as exciting as making decisions involving where to spend "real money." Adults typically view engagement with process governance as providing legitimacy. In contrast, some youth grew frustrated with what they viewed as lots of discussion without tangible results.

The desire to get away from decisions about rules and focus on making "real decisions with actual money" was a constant refrain. Attendance at steering committee meetings waned. Participants' response to what they considered onerous deliberations pointed back to the overarching theme of money, which was equated with power. Several frustrated participants at idea assemblies simply did not believe there was real money on the table. Some young people went so far as to argue directly with city officials, incredulously insisting, "This money is fake."

Even though turnout increased for the vote, each phase of the process faced attrition. Originally, sixty-one young people signed up as participants. However, only thirty-one change agents were left by the end of the process. Much of the attrition was immediate. The idea assemblies were designed to encourage youths to volunteer, but their roles and responsibilities had not yet been clearly or entirely delineated. Some change agents complained about not understanding the full extent of their commitment.

---

14. Unlike in Chicago and New York, the money for Youth Lead the Change came from the mayor's office. As a result, direct comparisons to pre-PB allocations are less viable, and I do not apply the "conventional/innovative" typology.

Nonetheless, the majority of change agents cited the experience as creating important social benefits, what I call civic rewards—the nonmaterial benefits from civic engagement, including enhanced learning and transformed relationships. Change agents appreciated having a space to work closely with other youth, where they could make new friends and share opinions. Many described feelings of empowerment; for example one participant noted: "We have power now, so they want to hear our voices instead, so that's why I liked to do it."

Commuting distances to attend meetings contributed to attrition rates. As the meetings for change agents were organized into citywide thematic committees, coordination was more difficult than for meetings at the district or ward level in New York City or Chicago. One of the unique challenges of a citywide process is in finding convenient geographic meeting points. The distance to meetings proved to be a hindrance to participation. Some change agents complained about having commutes that took an hour or longer. "The T took forever" was a constant refrain. As a result, many were late to meetings or not able to attend at all. This fact played a role in declining retention rates.

Change agents faced a tension between putting forth specific projects in their communities and thinking about needs throughout Boston. One change agent noted: "Education in my school is being deprived and I want to do something to change it . . . education is a big factor that affects poverty."

This change agent was working to find an issue that had both specific and broader appeal. To turn ideas into viable projects, change agents tried to connect their local-level needs to larger community concerns. For many, hands-on education in policymaking from elected officials was a highlight of the process. In special sessions, elected officials generously donated their time to engage directly with youth. Many officials enjoyed learning from the actual young people who were the intended beneficiaries of their policies. Sessions were not prescripted. Rather, elected officials appeared to engage spontaneously and enjoy the experience.

Youth left these sessions with a nuanced understanding of the opportunities and challenges involved in governance. Implementing projects in practice is far more difficult than it might seem in theory. In my conversations, youth expressed appreciation for the opportunity to learn through practice. Change agents asked tough questions and, most important, received answers in return. Watching young people engage directly with government agency officials underscored PB's transformative potential. For the youth, this experience proved to be second to none. They could speak with and be heard by public officials. The officials, in turn, got the opportunity to directly engage with the constituents whom they aim to serve. The relatively small size of the group enabled dialogue instead of the traditional presentation paradigm.

The sessions with government officials were among the most resource-intensive aspects of the process. They required high levels of coordination to ensure that meeting times and locations would be mutually convenient for all. A few of these sessions started late, attendees having to wait for people having transportation difficulties. Though among the most rewarding aspects of the process, these sessions may also be among the most difficult to expand to a larger scale.

Lessons Learned

> It definitely honed a lot of skills that I already had, like for instance . . .
> communication skills. . . . And it made me more aware that you gotta pay
> attention to how people react in certain situations. Like, some people work
> good in big groups, some people work good in small groups.
> —Participant, Youth Lead the Change, Boston

While the youth participants in Boston's PB pilot reported that sessions with public officials were some of the most rewarding parts of the process, at the same time, some youth felt that the process was co-opted by adults. Adults sometimes dominated steering committee meetings. Additionally, many of the small-group facilitators at idea assemblies were adults. These process tensions could become magnified if youth-driven PB continues to grow and scale.

Yet where adults did not play as active a role, other difficulties emerged. One group of youth on the steering committee was tasked with publicity and outreach—including with social media. For some, this was their first experience with using social media for engagement. In theory it makes sense for youth to be engaged, driving all aspects of the process. In reality, not having trained professionals in these areas hindered dissemination of information about the process on social media. This presents just one trade-off between the need to meet expanding youth roles and ensure basic competencies.

Choosing to pursue a version of PB driven by youth presents unique questions, including regarding the proper role for delegates as young as fourteen years old in addressing civic needs alongside adults. If the process had involved greater sums of money, there could have been pushback from older community residents fearing that youth could not adequately represent their needs. Community stakeholders might call for other eligibility measures besides age and Boston residency.

Boston's trial of the first youth-driven version of PB in the United States contains valuable lessons for further implementations of PB. Boston was successful at bringing new voices to the political process. The 1,531 people who voted on Youth Lead the Change's proposals are people who did not previously have other opportunities to vote on budget priorities, as many were too young to vote or not previously civically engaged. The process was effective at reaching traditionally marginalized communities, including people of color from low-income neighborhoods. For those under eighteen, this was their first vote. For younger people, especially those between twelve and sixteen, it provided an important opportunity to flex their civic muscles and experience civic rewards from voting.

Youth Lead the Change also suggests an opportunity for youth, particularly in public schools, to engage in governance and decisionmaking. Of the voters who answered the survey question about "school attendance," nearly 80 percent were students at Boston public schools. Schools provide a community anchor institution for hosting neighborhood assemblies, outreach, and voting sites. The hands-on civic education of change agents could transform their civic lives. It is difficult to know how participating in Youth Lead the Change will translate into other forms of civic engagement. Roughly 80 percent of voters who filled out the survey, 780 people, said they would vote in PB again.[15] However, a great deal can happen in a year—including disillusionment when implementing projects takes longer than expected.[16]

Young people may also discover other forms of civic activity that interest them. This may be especially true for a new generation with unprecedented technological tools with which to express themselves. Current indicators are not sufficient to understand future forms of engagement when tracking the civic activity of the young people who participated. As explored in chapter 8, PB represents just one new civic innovation among many. Taken together, these new approaches demand more expansive thinking about democratic processes that look beyond traditional forms of participation, such as serving on a community board or voting.

Conclusion

Discussions of innovation are too often limited to tools and technologies. Boston's youth PB pilot program shows that innovation can come in many different forms, including in the makeup of the participants and in the process structure. I use the term "innovation" expansively to include both new techniques and new tools, as further explored in the next chapter. In evaluating various innovations, I privilege the importance of civic rewards and face-to-face opportunities for civic engagement, evidenced in Boston, over process improvements that do not enhance these.

---

15. Grillos (2014).
16. In 2015, Boston continued to implement Youth Lead the Change.

Youth Lead the Change sets the stage for thinking more expansively about experimentation in implementing PB. I have shown that innovations in PB can have a wide scope and take on a variety of meanings—from who can participate to how people access information.[17] Eligibility requirements, design of ballots, and amount of funds available are all potential areas of adaptation. Innovation in PB is not limited to technology alone.

In Boston some of the most meaningful opportunities for civic engagement occurred during face-to-face meetings with elected officials. Similar encounters will be some of the hardest to scale. In the previous chapter, I illustrated dialogue and deliberation driven by both results and by process. By design, ICTs tend toward expediency over deliberative dialogue. Further integration of ICTs will need to address this potential imbalance.

What will be the next innovations and evolutions within PB? How can PB be placed within a broader ecosystem of more inclusive governance? In the next chapter I outline a schema of key issues and actors involved in PB and pose questions I consider ripe for further consideration by researchers and practitioners. Each is an area where future innovations are possible as PB continues to expand and work toward institutionalization.

---

17. See also PB in schools, "Learning Democracy by Doing Participatory Budgeting in Schools," *The Participatory Budgeting Project*, March 17, 2015 (www.participatorybudgeting.org/blog/learning -democracy-by-doing-participatory-budgeting-in-schools/).

7

Institutionalizing Innovations

The preceding chapters discussed participation and deliberation. These activities are essential criteria for understanding each individual instance of participatory budgeting (PB). The previous chapter also discussed an innovation to the process during Boston's first youth-driven PB. However, to realize its potential, and advance its legitimacy in the process, PB in the United States will need to evolve from an ad hoc civic experiment to become simply the way things get done in communities across the United States. In this chapter, I posit that institutionalization—PB's ability to evolve from civic experiment into routinized practice—represents a third criteria, alongside participation (chapter 4) and deliberation (chapter 5), for understanding PB and potentially other civic innovations in the United States.

In this chapter, I discuss what it means to institutionalize a civic innovation. In particular, I discuss the opportunities and challenges for using information and communications technologies (ICTs) as one set of available tools. This chapter offers policy recommendations for effective use of ICTs that, with the aim of maintaining PB's civic rewards—including participation and deliberation—can be applied toward informing a critical understanding of PB as well as other democratic and civic experiments in governance and public policy.

Why Institutionalize Innovation?

A more innovative system of governance is, among other things, premised on leveraging the expertise, opinions and abilities of the public. While increased transparency and accountability are also open government goals, the involvement of citizens is not simply a one-way street, in which government pulls back the curtain and allows citizens to more closely scrutinize its doings. Rather, an innovative government calls on its citizens to participate in improving governance itself.[1]

Why should people who are interested in civic improvement care about institutionalizing innovations? In fact, a given innovation's ability to be "institutionalized"—transformed from experiment into routine practice—need not always be a concern for process design at the outset of civic innovations. As I discuss in the next chapter, some hyperlocal experiments may lose their ingenuity if they focus on it too heavily. In fact, several types of civic experiments must remain agile and resist institutionalization.

Nonetheless, I argue that for the type of process change PB seeks—changing the relationship of citizens to governmental decisionmaking—working toward institutionalizing it within civic practice is critical. It confers legitimacy and creates lasting incentives that support the change. As I will explain further, when an innovation requires interaction with entrenched actors, institutionalization can be a key ingredient in garnering sustained support.

Institutionalizing a civic innovation means moving from sporadic, episodic experiments toward embedded and routinized easily replicable structures within government that last beyond initial enthusiasm and continue to engage citizens over the course of time.[2] When an innovation crosses this threshold, it can serve as a reliable template for other communities across the country and the world. As an innovation moves from pilot projects to embedded processes, however, challenges to ensuring sustained momentum can arise. As PB extends its reach, it faces not only these hurdles, but also several opportunities for experimentation and variation, highly driven by local contexts, needs, and institutional and political constraints, that hold the promise of further civic innovations within PB.

An inventive process like PB naturally raises questions about why certain adaptations take root while others do not. These questions include: Why is a given experiment adopted? When is one more or less likely to achieve impact than another? What are the criteria for impact? I have articulated participation, deliberation, and institutionalization as important criteria for understanding PB as a democratic innovation. Others may point to different criteria.

Defining impact becomes especially important in adjudicating which criteria deserve the most attention while scaling up processes. For example, at multiple

1. Young and others (2013).
2. To institutionalize not just one innovation but processes of continual change, learning, and innovation more generally, further mechanisms to support research, process review, and experimental development must also become normative and routine.

points in the PB process digital technologies can be added in, each of which will require value-driven decisionmaking. Should organizers place a premium on ensuring that digital technologies reduce barriers to entry or, instead, encourage face-to-face participation? Should those seeking to expand PB focus on increasing the amount of money decided through PB—a wide expansion—or on more substantive participation for all residents—a deep expansion? Should PB in the United States focus primarily on good governance or on empowering traditionally marginalized communities? Some of these may prove to be false choices, but policymakers seeking to expand PB are likely to confront these trade-offs and many others.

Their choices will be consequential. For a democratic innovation such as PB, which aims to enable more citizens to participate in governance, moving beyond one-time-only or ad hoc experimentation is critical. It is the view of this author that civic experimentations pursuing this larger goal can seek to develop, at minimum, a viable plan for broader deployment and sustained engagement. Achieving long-term institutionalization will help translate PB's promise of civic rewards into lasting political results.

One downstream effect of institutionalizing an innovation can be reducing barriers to entry for any group or community that wishes to adopt and implement it—thereby facilitating its practice by greater numbers of citizens. As a democratic innovation like PB expands beyond pilot projects and becomes institutionalized, its widespread practice can lend credibility and momentum to those advocating for its adoption. Constituents can more effectively put pressure on their elected officials to adopt it while convincing those responsible for overseeing its implementation that their efforts can yield a lasting practice rather more than a one-time experiment. Political pressure within a political ecosystem is a useful catalyst for PB.

Each category listed in box 7-1 contains various opportunities to innovate. Information and communications technologies (ICTs) can play a role across these various dimensions. Almost all PB implementations in the United States have online websites that convey information. To date, ICTs have been used primarily for communication rather than participation, where integration has been more limited. In part, this is because the suite of nonprofit, nonproprietary digital tools currently available for fostering meaningful participation is limited.

Information and Communications Technologies (ICTs) in Participatory Budgeting

This section showcases where ICTs have already been used in PB, demonstrating how these can then be applied across the various dimensions of future innovation.

BOX 7-1
Critical Questions for Institutionalizing PB

1. **Institutional Actors:** In the United States elected officials ranging from leaders of local council districts or wards to city mayors have executed PB, often devoting significant time by staff before, during, and after the process. During the process, city agency officials have worked directly with participants to explain procedural rules.

   Questions for Further Study: Who supports the significant staff time PB requires? What are the trade-offs between implementing PB and offering other government services? At what other types of institutions (e.g., academic institutions, housing authorities, municipal utilities, etc.) can PB effectively be applied?

2. **Amount of Money:** What is the amount of money being decided through PB? What are the legal requirements concerning how that money is distributed?

   Questions for Further Study: Can PB, especially in the United States, be applied to larger amounts of public money? As monies increase, so too will opportunities for process co-option. How can the process ensure greater accountability if given more responsibility? If PB in the United States were to handle expense funds, how could the process ensure citizens are equipped with the necessary information to make choices in this arena that are both informed and viewed as legitimate?

3. **Civil society leaders:** CSOs and NGOs typically lead or participate in PB. This includes providing technical support for implementations, such as is offered by the World Bank Institute (internationally) and the Participatory Budgeting Project (in the United States).

   Questions for Further Study: How can PB be incorporated with existing community-based initiatives? What are the pros and cons for a given CSO/NGO, as it decides whether to support PB, in terms of resources diverted from other initiatives? Can PB work with existing CSO strategies in a given context? Should a CSO implement PB from parts of its own operational resources?

4. **Participants:** A group of stakeholders who have been given authority over a set of public monies. Participation requirements are typically decided through a joint governance structure including citizens.

   Questions for Further Study: What are the benefits of a targeted approach (e.g., focusing on a specific population subset)? How important is accurate representation? How likely are participants to engage in other forms of civic activity? What are the best ways to measure sustained engagement after PB?

5. **Funders:** The PB process requires funding to execute and monitor.

   Questions for Further Study: What is the necessary continued revenue stream to fund the process? What is the role of private philanthropy (versus government), and how does this relate to both pilots and embedded structures?[a] What are necessary short-term indicators of impact in order to maintain and increase investment in the process? What is the accurate "rate of return" for funders? What other methods for fundraising (such as crowdfunding) could support process implementation?

6. **Research, Evaluation, and Monitoring:** PB requires research and evaluation in order for policymakers and participants to effectively understand the process and recognize its impact. This includes monitoring and assurance of project implementation.[b]

Questions for Further Study: How can generalizable metrics and criteria be developed for a highly context-specific process? How can short-term impact be assessed, given a process with more likely long-term effects? How can bias in the research and evaluation process be minimized, given that vested parties are sometimes the ones interested in and able to conduct research?

---

[a]For example, in some instances private philanthropy can be an engine to bring about a pilot in a given locality. Afterward, a government can fund institutionalization.
[b]See also Participatory Budgeting Project, "New Research Board to Evaluate PB," October 16, 2014 (www.participatorybudgeting.org/blog/new-research-board-to-evaluate-pb/).

ICTs have the potential to do much more than ease communication—they can enable more interactive, two-way engagement for participants. ICTs can be used throughout, including in: (1) outreach and information dissemination, (2) idea generation and collection, (3) project formation and idea development, (4) voting and weighting of ideas, and, (5) monitoring. Digital deployments can raise the question of how to ensure the diversity and representativeness of participants.

Implementations of PB in the United States are relatively nascent compared with examples of its use in other countries. Therefore it is also true that other nations have more deeply explored the opportunities for bringing ICTs into the PB process. Enabling the online submission of proposals constituted the first use of ICTs in PB, launched in Brazil in Ipatinga and Porto Alegre in 2001.[3] Since 2005 Germany has provided an online platform where citizens can discuss and prepare proposals as well as prioritize them.[4] Later, this same platform incorporated visualizations simulating budgets. Similar experiments have been tried in Belo Horizonte, Brazil.[5] In Peru, the Miraflores district of Lima has a website with training material about the PB process and opportunities for people to cast their votes to prioritize works online.

Short Message Service (SMS) has been used to mobilize and galvanize people in the PB process. The first use of SMS was in 2004 in Ipatinga, Brazil.[6] A

---

3. Sampaio and Peixoto (2014).
4. Caddy, Peixoto, and Mcneil (2007); Sampaio and Peixoto (2014).
5. Sampaio and Peixoto (2014).
6. See Tiago Peixoto, "Multi-channel Citizen Engagement: The Ipatinga PB Experience (PB part 3)," *Democracy Spot*, September 10, 2008 (http://democracyspot.net/2008/09/10/multi-channel-citizen-engagement-the-ipatinga-pb-experience-pb-part-3/).

World Bank pilot in the city of Jarabacoa, in the Dominican Republic, used SMS to encourage face-to-face participation, using a message targeted specifically at women.[7] In districts that used SMS, 32.2 percent of the PB process participants were new, compared with a rate of 20.9 percent for new participants in districts that did not.[8] A survey also showed that 78 percent of all participants identified SMS as a very useful mechanism for obtaining information; 62 percent of new participants and 54 percent of returning participants cited SMS as their information source.[9] Additionally, just over half (55 percent) of participants cited SMS as their primary reason for attendance at in-person meetings.[10]

Online voting is becoming a popular arena for applying ICTs within the PB process in other countries.[11] According to Rafael Cardoso Sampaio and Tiago Peixoto:

> Moreover, online voting can be seen as the gateway for politically inactive or less active citizens. The fact that online participation is generally more affordable can certainly be an extra attraction.[12]

Survey results tied to an implementation of PB in Rio Grande do Sul in Brazil in 2012 that included an online component, in addition to more standard offline PB, found that online voting led to an 8.2 percent increase in total turnout. Online voting was especially popular for new participants.[13]

Recife, Brazil, offers a paradigmatic example of online voting following in-person meetings. Participation there has grown since an online component was introduced in 2007;[14] however, some civil society leaders have been concerned that online voting could decrease mobilization of citizens in specific regions.[15] Similar concerns may be particularly relevant for the United States.

In the United States, implementations of PB have experimented with digital tools for idea generation, outreach, and even voting.[16] Examples include using SMS notifications, online submissions, and computerized voting as well as leveraging

---

7. Sampaio and Peixoto (2014).

8. Sampaio and Peixoto (2014, p. 416).

9. Sampaio and Peixoto (2014, p. 416).

10. Sampaio and Peixoto (2014, p. 416). Many different international case studies are also profiled at Participedia.net.

11. Tiago Peixoto's blog Democracyspot.net offers many resources and thoughtful reflections.

12. Sampaio and Peixoto (2014, p. 423).

13. Spada and others (2015).

14. Best and others (2011).

15. Ferreira (2012); Sampaio and Peixoto (2014, p. 419).

16. Participatory Budgeting Project, "PB Buzz: Improving Participatory Democracy with New Technology," August 4, 2015 (www.participatorybudgeting.org/blog/pb-buzz-improving-participatory -democracy-with-new-technology//).

social media. In 2015 several cities across the United States experimented with adding digital voting (in person) and other digital tools, such as SMS reminders, open source voter check-in, and open source project mapping, to their implementations of PB.[17] For example, Cambridge, Massachusetts, experimented with online voting with SMS authentication.[18] In 2015 New York City and PBP led much of this experimentation, including electronic ballot counting and a partnership with Textizen, which started as a Code for America project.[19] In 2014 Chicago ran a test pilot in which voters used electronic terminals to vote in person, in partnership with Stanford University's Crowdsourced Democracy Team.[20] The city of Vallejo, California, has experimented with MindMixer, a platform where citizens can post ideas, gather feedback, and measure the impact of projects.

Many more international experiments in enhancing PB with technology can be cited. Box 7-2 shows two key examples that demonstrate important innovations in the use of ICTs in PB. These examples illustrate the potential for ICTs to be used to bring in new citizens rather than simply to replace the face-to-face experience of those already likely to participate, such as usual suspects. In the DRC, mobile SMS messages were used to encourage people to participate in person. In Belo Horizonte, people were able to vote online. These two snapshots evince possibilities for ICT use in multiple aspects of the PB process.

What's on the Horizon

Concrete ways are available in which ICTs could be adopted to streamline the PB process. Each opportunity also contains critical pitfalls to be addressed, especially as PB continues to spread and grow in scope. As PB continues to incorporate ICTs

17. Participatory Budgeting Project, "PB Conference, Digital Voting, Annual Benefit, PB in Schools!" March 20, 2015 (www.participatorybudgeting.org/blog/pb-conference-digital-voting-annual-benefit-pb-in-schools/); Participatory Budgeting Project, "New Open-Source Tool for Mapping Community Needs," November 3, 2014 (www.participatorybudgeting.org/blog/new-open-source-tool-for-mapping-community-needs/); Gordon (2014).

18. See City of Cambridge, "Participatory Budgeting" (http://pb.cambridgema.gov/); Derek Pham, "Cambridge Continues Its Inaugural Participatory Budgeting Effort," June 17, 2015, Harvard Kennedy School Challenges to Democracy (www.challengestodemocracy.us/home/cambridge-concludes-its-inaugural-participatory-budgeting-effort/#sthash.m2fNV5z6.dpbs).

19. Alex Yule, "New York City Brings Budgeting to the People," The Textizen Blog, May 5, 2015 (http://blog.textizen.com/nyc-participatory-budgeting-20150505/); Aseem Mulji, "Participation Lab: Developing New Engagement Tools for Transformative Democratic Participation," submitted as the Participatory Budgeting Project's entry to the Knight News Challenge, "How Might We Better Inform Voters and Increase Civic Participation Before, During and After Elections?" March 19, 2015 (www.newschallenge.org/challenge/elections/entries/participation-lab).

20. The Stanford Crowdsourced Democracy Team (http://voxpopuli.stanford.edu/).

BOX 7-2
Digital PB Examples

Example 1: Mobile Enhanced PB
- World Bank Institute Pilot, South Kivu, Democratic Republic of the Congo (DRC)[a] 2011–12 mobile pilot targeted for a country with high mobile penetration rate.[b]
- Outreach: Citizens were invited to PB assemblies via geo-targeted SMS messages.
- Voting: Citizens identified community priorities via mobile phones.
- Information: Mobile phones announced voted decisions.
- Monitoring: Mobile phones asked citizens about their chosen projects; citizens could offer feedback and monitor projects.

Example 2: Online Voting
- Digital Participatory Budget, Belo Horizonte, Brazil.[c] Three rounds of PB in 2006, 2008, and 2011, conducted solely online.[d]
- Roughly 8 to 10 percent of the city's eligible voters participated (roughly 172,000 and 123,000 people in 2006 and 2008, respectively).[e]
- Online participation was between three and five times higher than participation rates in face-to-face rounds of PB occurring within the same years.[f]

---

[a]Felip Estefan and Boris Weber, "Mobile-Enhanced Participatory Budgeting in the DRC," *Information and Communications for Development* (IC4D), blog, February 13, 2012 (http://blogs.worldbank.org/ic4d /mobile-enhanced-participatory-budgeting-in-the-drc). See also Dias (2014).
[b]Ranging from 16 percent to an estimated 47 percent in 2013.
[c]Dias (2014); Leighninger (2011, p. 36).
[d]Wampler and Sampaio (2010).
[e]Wampler and Sampaio (2010, p. 14); Sampaio and Peixoto (2014, p. 419).
[f]See Peixoto (2009); Sampaio and Peixoto (2014, p. 419–22) note that in 2008 the three districts with the most online voters were considered poor in comparison to average city incomes and wealth.

to streamline the process, it will be important for policymakers to work to prevent the emergence of digital divides, ensure privacy, prevent process co-option, find adequate funding for new tools, and ensure that these new tools do not prevent participants from developing or accessing civic rewards.

Several particularly salient questions for thinking about ICTs and PB are outlined here. An underlying principle is to try to use ICTs to supplement, not replace, face-to-face engagements. Much of this work is already underway across America, often led by PBP.

1. Using ICTs to Streamline the Process

ICTs could generate more easily accessible and centralized information to inform the PB process itself.[21] This could include information about current budget

---

21. See also Leighninger (2011).

laws, projects in the city's current funding pipeline, and past PB projects. A centralized PB database could also provide transparency in all aspects of funding, including funds used to implement PB as well as when and how projects are implemented. This is already occurring. New York City has worked to centralize PB out of the speaker's office and create much more centralized data.

Open source tools could leverage open data about the PB process to create useful interactive tools, visualizations, and resources. All the data about PB could be publicly available—for example, data about how much PB costs to implement in different localities, tracking specifically how public funds allocated through PB are spent, and any costs for research, evaluation, or monitoring.

A dedicated group of technologists interested in creating civic and public value via open data produced by governments is already available. Open PB data could enable the civic technology community to build applications via application programming interfaces (APIs), which allow automated export and reuse of datasets in real time, to creatively connect data to different constituencies.[22] An annual "hackathon" or creative awards could be held to spur unique data uses.

Information about common pitfalls across districts and cities could also help support a more streamlined process. Similarly, centralized voter databases could inform how voter outreach and mobilization occur. Accurate information on such voter bases is especially challenging to obtain in places where nonstandard voters participate, such as the undocumented and youth under eighteen.

Many youth in Boston suggested using data from the Boston Public Schools to create a more centralized voter database for Youth Lead the Change. Challenges with this type of database include the requirement for value-driven judgments. For example, would using data from the public schools privilege engaging only those participants rather than similar constituencies enrolled in other schools or no longer connected to the educational system? Youth Lead the Change was open to participation up to the age of twenty-five, long after many residents would have had any connection to the public school system. Relying only on school data could have precluded efforts to engage these young adults in the process.

Choosing how to organize, classify, and select relevant datasets involves critical decisions that require contemplation with careful intention and caution—for example, a database that ensures it does not exclude certain populations (e.g., new citizens) or put a premium on others (e.g., usual suspects). If a PB dataset contains information only about people who have previously participated, greater

---

22. See for example the National Day of Civic Hacking (http://hackforchange.org/).

resources might be spent on mobilizing this group rather than people who have never participated and therefore have less of a footprint in the process.

It is important that databases can be read and shared across districts. This poses both a technical and a political challenge. Many governments currently do not provide data that can be easily shared and that span districts or agencies. Making sure that data can talk to each other, or be interoperable, may also be at odds with some of the more territorial aspects of municipalities. Path dependency, as explored in the following chapter, makes government institutions particularly disinclined to undertake this kind of sharing. Efforts to centralize PB out of a mayor's office, such as in Boston, Chicago, and New York City, offer a promising step toward more easily accessible, centralized data. For example, the New York City Council has an elegant website for its PB process on which people can see a map of participating districts, submit ideas, and comment on proposals.[23]

2. Preventing Digital Divides

Deploying ICTs in more aspects of PB, including for two-way participation, requires extra care to ensure that digital tools do not further stratify communities by creating digital divides within PB.[24] Throughout my observations of participatory budgeting meetings, I witnessed steep learning curves for people unfamiliar with electronic documents or listservs. Even simple tools, such as Google Documents, can be complicated for people who lack related experience or access to reliable high-speed Internet. I have seen participants frustrated by unsuccessful attempts to master and use these tools. Requiring the adoption of new technological skills typically slows down the progress of other elements of PB and can create a new power dynamic between those who can use technology easily and those who cannot.[25] However, learning to use these tools could ultimately be an additional component of PB's civic rewards if the necessary capacity exists to incorporate them into the process.

Preventing the emergence of new digital divides is especially important in traditionally marginalized communities and low-resource communities, where they may be magnified. The experience of the PBNYC pilot in committees with different age groups shows that steep divides can emerge along these lines, especially between more digitally literate young people and their older counterparts.

23. New York City Council, "Participatory Budgeting: Suggest a Project Idea," (http://council.nyc .gov/html/pb/ideas.shtml).

24. See also Leighninger (2011).

25. If properly funded and executed, teaching digital literacy could become a civic reward of the PB process. See also Gordon (2014, p. 27).

In such situations, facilitators can work to be sensitive to these particular disparities—while not neglecting the other demands placed on them, such as ensuring all voices are heard while coming up with viable proposals. Thus ICTs add yet another complex dimension to facilitation.

The increasing use of mobile devices offers particular opportunities for participatory budgeting. A mobile strategy may range from developing mobile adaptive interfaces to using SMS within a multifaceted approach. It will require deliberate intent and execution as well as a unique set of considerations to ensure equitable access. Doing so will raise a host of questions, including: who will be the service provider for these platforms? There are both open source and proprietary providers. An ideal strategy would provide open source tools that could be used across cities with opportunities for iteration. Using such tools in this way would help ensure that applications do not privilege some operating systems over others.

The question of digital literacy is a subsidiary consideration that ties into the basic issue of digital divides.[26] Even when people have access to the hardware, such as smartphones or the Internet, they may lack the skillset to effectively use these devices within the PB process. Using a cellphone for phone calls or simply to check e-mail may be quite different from using the device to engage with democracy. As PB implementations introduce ICTs, they will need to add in digital learning and training components. ICTs will be most effective if they are integrated throughout the process. Therefore, training will need to be a serious consideration and include a deployment strategy for the entire process. It would not be enough to simply train people in online voting at the end of the process. Every new use of ICTs often requires significant additional staff time and support in order to accommodate learning and training to prevent digital divides that could distort the PB process.

3. Ensuring Privacy and Preventing Co-option

As new iterations of PB continue to explore different uses of ICTs, a greater push for online- and SMS-voting options may arise. Voting is the least costly form of engagement in the PB process. The vote can engage the most diverse types of people. Yet because the vote involves a minimal commitment of time, it is critical to ensure that voters receive accurate information. Online voting has not taken root in the United States more generally, as even electronic voting machines continue to raise legitimacy concerns.[27] Worries about voter fraud and maintaining ballot

---

26. See data from Belo Horizonte's online PB in 2008 as discussed in Sampaio and Peixoto (2014); Wampler and Sampaio (2010); and Peixoto (2009).

27. See Benkler's discussion of eletronic voting machines (2006, pp. 225–32).

secrecy—as well as other qualms about new forms of co-option they may enable—are continuing causes for concern with regard to these online mechanisms.

Any type of technology used for voting will also need to effectively address the aforementioned concerns regarding digital literacy and equitable access. In the still nascent days of voting via ICTs, it will remain critical that PB uses these tools in a way that is viewed as legitimate. PB, especially as it expands, will need to safeguard its process against critics. There will naturally be critics of PB—anything "new" can draw criticism. Yet the process ought to avoid needlessly attracting critics of digital tools. Online voting brings with it its own share of legitimacy critiques that advocates of PB would then need to address as well.

4. Funding Challenges

Effective digital tools are costly. Currently funding for open source, nonprofit, and public sector ICTs is limited. How can new PB processes create necessary tools within a context of rising fiscal deficits and budget constraints? Governments face a challenge allocating sizable amounts toward supporting the process itself—its backend costs. This can include leaving aside the question of funds for process research or development of new technologies.

Meanwhile, profit-driven models of technology development will not necessarily support the civic ends of PB. Perhaps civic-minded developers could donate their skills toward generating open source, nonproprietary tools. Yet PB needs more than just new ICTs. It also needs information technology (IT) support throughout the process to troubleshoot, fix, iterate, and adapt such tools as necessary. Just as the PB process itself requires funding, ICT tools also require investment. ICTs, in particular, can have steep upfront costs, while also needing (sometimes overlooked) maintenance funds.

5. Maintaining Civic Rewards

Finally, out of all of these concerns regarding the use of ICTs, the question of how to maintain the civic rewards of PB is perhaps the most pertinent to the goals set forth in this book. Increased use of ICTs in PB raises critical questions. How can organizers lower barriers to entry so that more diverse types of people can engage with the process? How can advocates of PB ensure a smooth process while also maintaining its opportunities for civic rewards? Many of the civic rewards of substantive participation and deliberation are the result of face-to-face engagement. ICTs can in fact enhance in-person engagement if they are used to more widely disseminate information about meeting times and locations. Opportunities for ICTs to be used in physical meetings must also be considered.

As discussed in chapter 5, ICTs can be both assets and liabilities for dialogue and deliberation. Their rapid-fire pace can sometimes prevent the necessary economy of moral disagreement, in which citizens seek common ground based on mutual respect and understanding.[28] For some participants, learning to navigate the economy of moral disagreement is a critical educational component of deliberation. This includes feeling comfortable with contestation. In face-to-face disagreement, arguments can be softened through extraverbal communication, such as expression, tone, and body language. Online media are inherently more conducive for efficiency without necessarily putting a premium on inclusive deliberation.[29] People use these tools to reduce communication time. Yet there is a cost to using these technologies. They can increase misunderstandings, which can in turn create even more obstacles to a satisfactory participatory process. For PB, where significant value lies in the creation of civic rewards, these challenges are especially problematic.

As previously discussed, PB has dual goals—to create viable funding proposals that improve public services as well as to enhance and transform civic relationships among citizens and between citizens and their elected officials and governance institutions. Building civic capacity via PB and its civic rewards requires that people speak and listen to one another. ICTs have the potential to help PB participants create viable funding proposals. They might also be effective at engaging a larger swath of citizens. Yet their ability to help transform traditional political relationships is debatable. If ICTs can help publicize face-to-face opportunities for deliberation and participation to a wider audience, they may be useful in this regard as well. I caution against using ICTs to replace the critical learning opportunities available via in-person discussion with peers and public servants.

Policy Recommendations

I argue that institutionalization, while not critical for all forms of civic innovation, is critical for PB. It will prove to be the lynchpin for whether PB can achieve its maximum impact as an effective tool of civic engagement in governmental decisionmaking.

Institutionalizing innovation includes expanding where a process is enacted and who can participate, as well as the types of monies decided through it. Pilots across the country—from Cambridge, San Francisco, and St. Louis, to name but a few—show that PB is increasing its geographic reach. Meanwhile, Council

28. See Gutmann and Thompson (1998).

29. This is broadly indicated in data and experiences with the current suite of available online tools. Online tools that are more effective at dialogue and deliberation may yet become more widely disseminated. For example, Loomio.org is one such tool working toward this end. Other less frequently used ICTs, such as video livestreams, may also support deliberation. See also the Participatory Politics Foundation (www.participatorypolitics.org).

Speaker Melissa Mark-Viverito called for PB to be applied to parts of the Tenant Participation Activity (TPA) funds within New York City Housing Authority (NYCHA) dollars in her "State of the City" address in early 2015.

If the process remains limited, the benefits of deliberation and participation will remain limited as well. It is important to study PB as an experiment in part because it combines three key elements of innovation in civic governance: deliberation, participation, and institutionalization. The third of these, making PB a regular feature of the governmental process, ensures that substantive citizen participation and deliberation will be incorporated into the structure of public decisionmaking.

While critical, institutionalization and scale also pose challenges for the practice of PB. As discussed, PB is time- and resource-intensive. Because PB creates more entry points for citizens to engage with government, it necessarily requires public officials to spend more time directly engaged with constituents. Some in government complain that it wastes time they could use for other pressing tasks. Implementing PB means that other projects will not be pursued. Elected officials fear the potential electoral costs. There are also barriers to entry for participants who find the process overly cumbersome.

Moving a process from a pilot to an institutionalized norm brings its own challenges. Part of the reason that PB has generated considerable attention in the United States is because it is "new." If budget makers integrate more participatory approaches into their daily operations, a new challenge will emerge—that of maintaining the excitement, devoting the necessary resources, and sustaining participation.

I view the civic rewards of participatory budgeting as the most critical dimension of the process. Yet the conditions that generate robust civic rewards are some of the most difficult to scale. For example, for Boston youth, it was engaging directly with city officials that led to hands-on civic education. Agency officials as well as youth found the experience meaningful, informative, and inspiring. This scenario is quite difficult to replicate and expand.

In current models, PB implementation in the United States presupposes that civic engagement can be deepened through the same mechanisms that generate the project proposals. One strategy to succeed in that equation is to intertwine PB within a broader good-governance strategy developed in conjunction with existing civil society to deepen democracy. This can provide opportunities to channel deliberations around specific proposals into deeper conversations about democratic engagement.

While there are natural limitations, PB continues to grow. I have shown throughout this book that PB is an effective way to engage citizens. In box 7-3 I outline a series of questions that inform my policy recommendations on how it could grow to become institutionalized. The overarching goal is to streamline

BOX 7-3
Issues to Address for Practitioners and Researchers

1. Scale
   How could PB be brought to scale in order to achieve greater reach and impact?
   —Greater diversity of participants (in terms of gender, age, income, education, engagement preferences, civic typologies, etc.)
   —Larger amounts of funding
   —Greater diversity of revenue streams and budgetary responsibilities (public housing, public schools, etc.)
2. Electoral concerns
   How best can elected officials collaborate within a competitive environment?
   —How can elected officials work together while also reaching their specific constituents?
   —How can advocates of PB ensure it remains constant despite changing elected representatives?
3. Process costs
   How can implementing actors be adequately compensated for their time?[a] Could scale help reduce costs?
4. Community engagement
   Who is included in the given community? Who are the necessary stakeholders? Does this change through different cycles or stages of the process? How can the community ensure that it is genuinely empowered and engaged in the process?
5. Reducing barriers to entry
   How can advocates of PB make it easier for diverse populations to participate in the process without sacrificing substance?
   —What online options could reduce barriers while also mitigating new barriers created by such technologies?
6. Stakeholder engagement
   How can the process ensure sustained participation through many cycles, including changes in elected officials? How can advocates ensure citizens remain interested in PB after its novelty wears off?
7. Deepening democracy[b]
   Can PB lead to other forms of civic engagement? What are the opportunities for PB to foster and encourage other forms of democratic engagement?
8. Evaluation
   How can implementers work to ensure that the process remains subject and open to research and evaluation?
9. Communication
   How can PB receive wider attention in order to reach a broader group of stakeholders?
10. Iteration
    How can mechanisms to refine and adapt PB be built into the process, while maintaining both continuity and longevity? How can the process incorporate mechanisms for growth, learning, and change?

---

[a] This includes elected and agency officials, civil society practitioners, and academic researchers.
[b] See also Baiocchi (2005).

the process while ensuring it engages citizens at every step. These questions drive my concrete policy recommendations for how participatory budgeting can be expanded in the United States, so that it is able to grow while maintaining its unique value when it comes to deepening democracy.

In box 7-4 I provide policy recommendations to work toward institutionalizing innovation. They are meant to provide normative contours, not to serve as prescriptive absolutes—recognizing that PB is highly context specific and some of this work may or may not be already under way for a variety of social, political, and institutional reasons. Additionally, these recommendations are designed to be broad enough for the entire set of stakeholders involved. These policy recommendations could reduce barriers to entry, limit chances for process exhaustion, and minimize deleterious political competition. Integrated within these recommendations are more opportunities to widen the support base of PB, so that it will include a wider sampling of citizens, civil society organizations (CSOs), political leaders, and governmental entities. The sustained involvement of these groups of stakeholders will be essential for institutionalizing PB. Advocates of the process could work to find more opportunities for engagement and safeguard it against critiques of co-option, parochialism, and being simply a tool for electoral gain.

Steering committees could work more closely with a broader sampling of CSOs and tie into the programmatic values of these organizations when designing implementations of PB. By tying PB more closely into broader policy issues and debates, such as those surrounding transparency of public funds, practitioners will deepen the democracy-enhancing aspects of the process and offer other avenues for civic engagement.

Research and Evaluation

Research examining the impact of participatory budgeting faces many challenges. The process is relatively nascent in the United States. It is highly context specific but needs uniform metrics and criteria to determine what works and necessary investment. Isolating its causal outcomes is difficult, while some of the terms of its impact, such as feeling efficacious in political life, are difficult to demonstrate. The nonprofit organizations Public Agenda and PBP are working on a coordinated research agenda, which includes a toolkit for evaluators and implementers.[30] PB may have long-term effects—such as greater turnout in general elections or increased community involvement—that could take years to manifest

30. Participatory Budgeting Project, "New Research Board to Evaluate PB," October 16, 2014 (www.participatorybudgeting.org/blog/new-research-board-to-evaluate-pb/); Lerner (2014); Public Agenda, "A Toolkit for Evaluators and Implementers" (http://publicagenda.org/pages/participatory -budgeting-research-and-evaluation).

BOX 7-4
Policy Recommendations

1. Reduce the number of participant meetings:
   —Streamline the process so that budget delegates have the option to meet less frequently to craft proposals.
   —Host in-person and online training sessions and follow-up meetings via ICTs.
   —Coordinate more closely with city agencies—providing agency-specific information sessions and briefing material.[a]
2. Limit competition between elected officials:
   —Steering committees could centrally control participant inclusion and work across localities to share mobilization and "Get Out the Vote" (GOTV) strategies.
   —Enforce voting rules to limit campaigning and ensure voting is not co-opted by special interests.
   —Work closely with mayors and relevant elected officials to gain a broader base of support for PB. Have these supporters provide their own external information about PB to increase awareness.
   —Work toward incorporating PB into operating budgets, making it less subject to electoral changes.
3. Centralized year-round process support:
   —Central city staff dedicated to PB with year-to-year continuity and a knowledge repository with sharable documents and presentations to be customized. For example, the centralization out of the New York City Speaker's office providing support.
   —Available resources to ensure districts can accommodate diverse participation. For example, providing childcare, transportation, or food, etc.
4. Provide incentives to deepen the involvement of civil society organizations (CSOs):
   —Clearly delineate expected roles and responsibilities on steering committees. Map out clear and enforceable expectations and timetables.
   —Ensure meeting times of steering committees accommodate those working in CSOs and citizens working full-time.
   —Work to incorporate PB into existing civil society strategies.
   —Position PB toward strengthening the overall capacity of civil society toward more inclusive and participatory governance.
5. Link PB to other instances at government reform:
   —Research into the impact of PB on other democratic experiments. This could include sharable lessons for localities.
   —Further research and experimentation to understand if and how government can improve how it engages its constituents.
   —Find ways to lift up the success of PB to strengthen and galvanize future civic innovations. For example, as part of the inclusive governance commitments within the sustainable development goals (SDGs).[b]
6. Increase civic awareness about status quo budget models:
   —Short-term improvements in service delivery joined with long-term discussions on thematic issues. For example, structured deliberative open forums during

the process, connecting PB with other community-driven opportunities for deepening civic engagement.

—Couple PB with a civic-awareness campaign to shed light on the nontransparent, inequitable, and unequal nature of discretionary funds, where applicable.

—Hold a deliberative and structured open town hall during PB. It would be open to all in order to discuss the status quo budget process and transparency.

7. Encourage transparency and accountability:

—Incorporate transparent accountability mechanisms to showcase precisely where and how monies allocated through PB result in tangible projects (including signage featuring in-progress and completed works).

—Engage citizens to monitor the process after the PB vote.

8. Engage the civic technology community:

—Creation of a centralized public website, similar to Recovery.gov, with an API for all open data produced via PB.

—Including anonymized information about participants of different stages of the process (attendees of neighborhood assemblies, budget delegates, voters), diverse stakeholders, and project implementation.

—Create an annual "PB Hackathon," building off the National Day of Civic Hacking, and give awards to the most creative use of PB data.[c]

9. Research and evaluation:[d]

—Maintain research and evaluation with its own independent revenue stream that is not dependent on "success."

—Criteria, metrics, and indicators that enable short-, medium-, and long-term assessment.

—Quantitative and qualitative indicators that account for context.

---

[a] That way these agencies can better understand PB and, in turn, provide more accurate information to participants.

[b] SDG, 16.7, calls on signatories to "ensure responsive, inclusive, participatory and representative decision-making at all levels." See United Nations, Sustainable Development Knowledge Platform, "Open Working Group Proposal for Sustainable Development Goals" (https://sustainabledevelopment.un.org/sdgsproposal).

[c] See the website of the National Day of Civic Hacking (http://hackforchange.org/).

[d] Much of this is already underway. Public Agenda, "Research and Evaluation of Participatory Budgeting in the U.S. and Canada" (http://publicagenda.org/pages/research-and-evaluation-of-participatory-budgeting-in-the-us-and-canada).

---

and be difficult to correlate with a given implementation of PB. The process may inspire types of civic engagement we cannot begin to imagine. Yet in order to achieve these returns on investment, PB needs flexibility to grow.

Participatory budgeting, like other forms of democratic innovation, challenges common conceptions of the social sciences and their experiments in the public sector. Typical experiments take a long time to move from concept to improved outcomes. First, a rigorous experiment is designed, funded, and executed.[31] The most rigorous results will be published some time after experimentation. Ideally, these results will translate into improved policy outcomes. Yet the link between institutional change and experimental research can be several layers removed. PB can model a different type of experimental research that works in conjunction with institutions ready to adapt lessons learned.

Participatory budgeting can begin to deploy and demonstrate more rapid, agile experimentation without reinventing the wheel. The ability to do so will be important to provide a rapid response from social scientists as people across communities, cities, and countries work to reengage citizens in democracy. As further explored in the following chapter, PB is one example of civic innovation. It is not the only one. It can work to broaden and deepen civil society capacity toward more inclusive and participatory governance.

In several countries, over decades, participatory budgeting has already shown its potential as a viable model. Its record in the United States suggests that it can mature to help build more long-term capacity for civic innovation. Research on civic innovation need not shy away from discussing its challenges and shortcomings as well. Those who implement PB understand it is time- and resource-intensive, for example. Research on PB could identify more precisely *where* and *how* it can be most effective. This type of research could inform researchers and practitioners alike. It could try to isolate the effects of PB not only on participants, but also on city officials, civil society, and institutional structures. Does the process transform city staff? What are concrete measures that constitute the opportunity costs of implementation? To what extent are citizens more likely to remain engaged in civic life after participating? These are questions that will remain critical as PB continues to grow in the United States.

The Future of Participatory Budgeting in the United States

PB, in recent years, has won support from the White House, which included participatory budgeting among its international commitments to the Open Government Partnership. The United States helped to launch this international multistakeholder partnership in 2011 together with seven other countries (Brazil, Indonesia, Mexico, Norway, the Philippines, South Africa, the United Kingdom). The group has since grown to sixty-six. The member countries pledge themselves to work toward greater government transparency and accountability as well as increased citizen participation. Each member country puts forth a

---

31. Barnett, Dembo, and Verhulst (2013).

National Action Plan (NAP) listing its open government pledges to these core principles. Importantly, the Open Government Partnership is also a pact between civil society and government—it empowers civil society as co-producers of the agenda.

As open government and innovation adviser in the White House Office of Science and Technology Policy, I worked on the National Action Plan of the United States developed for the Open Government Partnership during the Obama administration's second term. This involved, in part, working closely with federal agencies to integrate participatory budgeting into the U.S. National Action Plan and then helping to coordinate government efforts to implement these commitments.

The "Second Open Government National Action Plan for the United States of America" includes a participatory budgeting commitment:

> In 2014, the Administration will work in collaboration with the Strong Cities, Strong Communities initiative (SC2), the National League of Cities, non-profit organizations, philanthropies, and interested cities to: create tools and best practices that communities can use to implement projects; raise awareness among other American communities that participatory budgeting can be used to help determine local investment priorities; and help educate communities on participatory budgeting and its benefits.[32]

This commitment capitalizes on work that is already being done in communities across the country and is supported through community development grant programs. The goal is to provide support for the work being done in localities without adding bureaucratic constraints. The United States Department of Housing and Urban Development (HUD) has put up a resource page on PB on its website.[33] American cities, such as Buffalo, New York, are already exploring the possibilities for using community development grants from HUD to fund PB.[34]

The inclusion of participatory budgeting in Open Government Partnership commitments illustrates the transnational nature of democratic innovation. Brazil, one of the founding member countries, is also the birthplace of participatory budgeting. Adoption of PB in other countries, especially as supported through the multinational partnerships, can help galvanize and mobilize regional implementations.[35] PB efforts in the United States can learn lessons from

32. Obama White House (2013, p. 10).
33. United States Department of Housing and Urban Development (HUD), "Participatory Budgeting," HUD Exchange (www.hudexchange.info/resource/3907/participatory-budgeting/).
34. See the website of Participatory Budgeting in Buffalo (www.pbbuffalo.org/).
35. Keck and Sikkink (2002).

experiences in other countries while at the same time conveying greater legitimacy on those implemented here.

Conclusion

I have outlined some of the challenges associated with greater use of ICTs in the process. Three categories of concern can be identified. The first set of issues surrounds privacy, equitable access, and digital literacy. The second consists of questions about how ICTs could alter the character of deliberation and substantive participation within PB. Finally, as discussed in chapter 8, the question of how digital technologies can help address the broader goals that PB seeks to advance must be addressed.

As the process works toward institutionalization, the long-term future of PB in the United States may be impacted by:

—**Funding:** Securing a sustainable funding stream. Covering both the funds at stake in PB as well as funds to support the process itself.

—**Transparency:** Both in local budget decisions and in the PB process itself. Includes a centralized website with free, open, and usable data such as an application programming interface (API) for all PB data. This centralized open database would have information about discretionary funds in the United States as well as open data about how and where PB money is spent.[36]

—**Community-driven approaches:** Combining PB with other strategies and existing methods for community-driven and inclusive governance, domestically and internationally.

—**Reducing barriers to entry:** The process requires the intensive use of resources and time. This can prove an obstacle to development of and participation in PB projects. The process could work to become more streamlined, while still ensuring more rather than fewer opportunities for genuine citizen engagement.

—**Leveraging technology:** In addition to an open database, leverage information and communications technologies (ICTs) to supplement (but not replace) face-to-face engagement.[37]

36. New York City is taking steps in the right direction with a centralized PB website produced by the city council. New York City Council, "Participatory Budgeting FAQ" (http://council.nyc.gov/html /pb/faq.shtml), for example, is a particularly helpful resource.

37. Examples that range from Boston's custom-made Citizinvestor.com to the use of geotargeted Short Message Service (SMS) texts to spread the word about in-person meetings in South Kivu in the Democratic Republic of the Congo demonstrate potential avenues for increasing effective participation. See Felipe Estefan and Boris Weber, "Mobile-Enhanced Participatory Budgeting in the DRC," Information and Communications for Development (IC4D), blog, February 13, 2012 (http://blogs .worldbank.org/ic4d/mobile-enhanced-participatory-budgeting-in-the-drc).

Working to institutionalize innovation will benefit from continued independent research and evaluation. Monitoring project implementation could become a more robust part of the process. This will require that citizens continue to be engaged with the process after projects are chosen at the vote so as to hold elected officials accountable for delivery and continuation of approved projects.

A complementary publicity campaign could promote the tangible community results of PB. It will be vital to ensure that PB translates into concrete community improvements. This includes conveying successes to a wider group of stakeholders. Such a campaign could also bring about greater transparency and encourage more accountable governance.

Participatory budgeting is not about one group of stakeholders; rather, it is a complex ecosystem, with many different actors and vested interests. Working toward institutionalizing innovation can ensure that PB becomes an integral part of decisionmaking. Incorporating it into the operating budget procedure will make the process less exposed to electoral changes. This suggests that it will be critical to streamline PB with an eye toward institutionalizing it as a part of how government operates and spends.

Finally, advocates of participatory budgeting ought to safeguard it against low expectations. It is the view of this author that PB need not be relegated to small-stakes projects and politics. PB offers a rare opportunity to think more creatively about what democracy can look like. Therefore, institutionalizing innovations in PB should not be simply limited to a new app or an additional tech component divorced from the overall process. Those invested in the future of participatory budgeting can work to ensure it does not fall prey to pressures that dilute its core objective: engaging citizens in governance and decisionmaking.

8

Civic Innovation in America

Participation does make better citizens. I believe it, but I can't prove it. And neither can anyone else. The kinds of subtle changes in character that come about, slowly, from active, powerful participation in democratic decisions cannot easily be measured with the blunt instruments of social science. Those who have actively participated in democratic governance, however, often feel that the experience has changed them. And those who observe the active participation of others often believe that they see its long run effects on the citizens' character.[1]

Jane Mansbridge spoke these words at a conference titled "Citizen Competence and the Design of Democratic Institutions," convened by the Committee on the Political Economy of the Good Society (PEGS), in February 1995 in Washington, D.C. In the intervening twenty years, we have yet to see dramatic participatory initiatives take hold in the United States. Since 1995 participatory budgeting (PB) has spread across the world to such diverse places as Ireland, Canada, India, Uganda, Brazil, and South Africa. The World Bank and the United Nations declared it a "best practice" and have devoted many millions of dollars toward its implementation.[2] In 2009 participatory budgeting arrived in America.

1. Jane Mansbridge, "Does Participation Make Better Citizens?" paper delivered at "Citizen Competence and the Design of Democratic Institutions," conference of the Committee on the Political Economy of the Good Society (PEGS), February 10–11, 1995.
2. Second United Nations Conference on Human Settlements in Istanbul in 1996 cited Porto Alegre's participatory budgeting as one of forty-two best practices in urban governance throughout the world.

Participatory budgeting represents one promising innovation within a broader field of attempts to add participatory elements to governance, including in zoning, housing, and other areas of concern in both civil society and the private sector.[3] In the past decade and a half, the United States has seen the rise of privatization as a tool to address public problems without the necessary emphasis on deliberation.[4] New urban "apps" proliferate, but diverse and substantive civic engagement is not always placed at a premium. As a result, robust participatory mechanisms that genuinely involve citizens in governance, politics, or service delivery have yet to become mainstream in the United States.

This has not entirely been for lack of trying. Attempts to increase participatory governance, especially in cities, have been numerous. These efforts include building participatory deliberation into energy use decisions in Texas and urban revitalization in downtown Minneapolis and at the Philadelphia waterfront.[5] Several of these efforts, however, lack the enforceability mechanisms of participatory budgeting.[6] Government invites citizens to give input and feedback or to take part in deliberate exercises, such as those put on by AmericaSpeaks.[7] In Oregon, citizens have been asked to weigh in on critical policy issues over a digital "kitchen table." This includes exploring opportunities for peer-to-peer micro lending to start new businesses in Oregon and civic crowdfunding for communal public projects.[8] Cities have engaged citizens in visioning exercises to set policy priorities for new mayors. While these types of engagements enable fruitful deliberation and foster civic engagement, they are not binding in the same way that PB is.

In this chapter, I discuss PB as one example within a varied civic tech and innovation ecosystem, bringing together projects that are not typically associated with one another. The goal of this chapter is to provide further insight into current civic experiments in the United States in order to shed light on potential future trends.

---

3. Two promising innovations in the United States include "Imagine Philadelphia" and "Strong Starts for Children" in New Mexico. The former involved citizens in designing the new city plan. See Participedia, "Imagine Philadelphia: Laying the Foundation (Philadelphia, Pennsylvania)," public wiki (http://participedia.net/cases/imagine-philadelphia-laying-foundation-philadelphia-pennsylvania). "Strong Starts for Children" involved dialogue circles in New Mexico, with a focus on improving education. See Participedia, "Strong Starts for Children (Albuquerque, New Mexico, USA)," public wiki (http://participedia.net/cases/strong-starts-children-albuquerque-new-mexico-usa).

4. See Crenson and Ginsberg (2004).

5. Lehr and others (2003); Fagotto and Fung (2006); Sokoloff, Steinberg, and Pyser (2005).

6. Citizen input translates into direct policy implementation. By contrast, citizens in other forms of engagement are usually in consultative or advisory roles.

7. This was one of the most evolved participatory processes. See AmericaSpeaks, "AmericaSpeaks: A Legacy of Critical Innovations in Deliberative Democracy and Citizen Engagement," online pamphlet, 2014 (https://dl.dropboxusercontent.com/u/6405436/AmericaSpeaks_Legacy.pdf).

8. See OregonsKitchenTable.org for an example of a groundbreaking approach to engaging citizens.

The Locality: A Global Twenty-First-Century Public Sphere

The civic innovations I have discussed are often local-level phenomena; however, they increasingly tie into broader international networks. As mentioned in chapter 1, the United Nations' Millennium Development Goals (MDGs) and the post-2015 Development Agenda of the United Nations Development Program (UNDP) have led to an ongoing effort to formulate sustainable development goals (SDGs).[9] This effort incorporates targets for inclusive governance and civic participation in decisionmaking.[10] The World Bank has issued a commitment to seeking and including "beneficiary feedback" in all their programs by 2018.[11] A demand exists to take lessons from local, especially urban, contexts and spread them globally.

Cities are increasingly emerging as local innovation hubs that function within a global context. Urban areas are using advances in digital technologies to be leaner and more agile as well as to perform "smarter" (more targeted, responsive, and efficient) governance.[12] For example, cities are releasing their government data to the public.[13] The availability of this open data, in turn, empowers a new set of public and private actors to help governments improve their performance. As Stephen Goldsmith and Susan Crawford reflect in their study of new uses of data in governance, "government's authority comes from its cooperation with a vibrant community, and the community's respect for that authority flows from government's responsiveness."[14]

Of course, civic innovation is not restricted to the local level. However, local levels of governance, including rural towns and exurbs as well as cities, offer polities at sizes that allow citizens to be more closely connected to the policies that have the most impact on them. Within the context of globalization, local politics is viewed as more susceptible to being shaped by local citizens than national politics.[15] Patrick Heller and Peter Evans note that local governments are increas-

9. United Nations Economic and Social Council, "Millennium Development Goals and Post-2015 Development Agenda" (http://www.un.org/en/ecosoc/about/mdg.shtml).

10. SDG, 16.7, calls on signatories to "ensure responsive, inclusive, participatory and representative decision-making at all levels." See United Nations, Sustainable Development Knowledge Platform, "Open Working Group Proposal for Sustainable Development Goals" (https://sustainabledevelopment.un.org/sdgsproposal).

11. David Bonbright and Fredrik Galtung, "Jim Kim's Bold Vision of Beneficiary Feedback in Development," Keystone Accountability (blog), January 20, 2015 (https://keystoneaccountability.wordpress.com/2015/01/20/jim-kims-bold-vision-of-beneficiary-feedback-in-development/).

12. Goldsmith and Crawford (2014).

13. Goldsmith and Crawford (2014).

14. Goldsmith and Crawford (2014, p. 62).

15. Keil (1998).

ingly functioning as focal points for public authority and socially transformative projects.[16] The practice of participatory budgeting, which has been implemented in more than 1,500 localities around the world, is particularly well suited for galvanizing both civil society and citizens at the local level.

Local innovations can generate global lessons and opportunities. Viewed in the context of globalization, the study of local politics seems more pressing than ever, while participation often emerges as a "redemptive" element for a community.[17] Jeffrey M. Berry, Kent E. Portney, and Ken Thompson posit that participatory democracy is redemptive for local politics insofar as

> participation nourishes the democratic spirit of individuals. . . . It builds community, which in turn nurtures shared values such as compassion, tolerance, and equality. . . . Participation transforms institutions so that they become more effective instruments of democracy.[18]

Experimentation occurring on the local level creates important models for an international community of practitioners and researchers across diverse localities, who can share best practices, impart lessons learned, and build stronger networks for collaboration. Much further research is needed. What works and why? How do we separate civic fads from meaningful contributions to the evolution of governance? Can engagement lead to stronger, more resilient communities?

Democratic Innovation beyond Participatory Budgeting

Can PB work within existing civil society to strengthen opportunities for citizen engagement, building more inclusive governance? Numerous experiments in strengthening governance, comprising civic, social, and democratic innovations, have been undertaken.[19]

Participatory budgeting is an important civic innovation because it opens up traditionally closed institutions of governance. Citizens do not merely consult; they are empowered with tangible decisionmaking power. Yet PB is not alone in

16. Heller and Evans (2010).

17. Jessica Trounstine, like Robert Dahl (Dahl 1967) before her, outlines the methodological strengths of studying local areas as well as the many opportunities they offer for witnessing ways that most Americans interact with their government (Trounstine 2008).

18. Berry, Portney, and Thomson (1993, p. 5).

19. For an expanded take on this subject, see my work with New America, in particular with their Open Technology Institute, focusing on civic innovation. Georgia Bullen and Laurenellen McCann have been indispensable intellectual collaborators in this work.

attempting to do so. A broader movement in support of innovations aims at reengaging citizens in governance. Citizens are working together to co-create, share, and develop public goods, deepening communities in ways that go beyond simply improving public service delivery. A vision of more inclusive governance involves institutions that open up spaces for civic participation as well as citizens and civil society who self-organize to solve social problems. Citizens can take responsibility for where they live.

These examples illustrate a broadened understanding of what constitutes the public sector. Its scope includes not only government, but also a variety of other actors across civil society, academia, and the private and social sectors (e.g., see table 8-1). Understanding this diverse set of actors places PB in a more widely available ecosystem. Some of the most dynamic innovations in governance involve collaborations between multiple stakeholders working together to build stronger civil society capacity in conjunction with governments. Primary examples include the Open Government Partnership, as discussed in chapter 7, as well as Smart Chicago, a collaborative effort between the city of Chicago, the Chicago Community Trust, and the John D. and Catherine T. MacArthur Foundation. It is a civic organization that fosters a network aiming to apply emerging technology to public problems, including city services, open data, and infrastructure for health, education, and technology.[20]

These initiatives engender a broad ecosystem for civic innovation, spread across several dimensions involving economic development, governance, and community-building. Box 8-1 shows a typology of civic tech and innovations.

Institutionalization at scale is not equally important across all the categories shown in box 8-1. Some experiments will be most effective if they are deeply embedded within a community and not institutionalized. Criteria for assessing impact should include whether a process effectively solves a public problem and whether it is inclusive and representative of diverse stakeholder needs. Opportunities for iterative learning are essential. Becoming comfortable with failure will help ensure a learning element is baked into innovation processes from the beginning.

Institutionalization is critical for participatory budgeting, however, because PB is a process of public decisionmaking. It works alongside existing government structures. It depends on government buy-in and support. Innovations focused on institutional decisionmaking should work to become embedded in those structures to persist and to demonstrate their staying power, legitimacy, and relevance.

---

20. Goldsmith and Crawford (2014, p. 39).

Table 8-1. *Multistakeholder Collaborations Engaged in Civic Innovation*

Type	Features
Individual	Individual people not tied directly to an organization structure E.g., First activity happens as a result of a single actor
Nongovernmental organizations (NGOs)	Includes civil society organizations, nonprofits, and foundations Can be domestic, international E.g., World Bank, the Participatory Budgeting Project
Community	Associations of people, often on the local level, that fall outside of the context of NGOs due to their structure, resources, or capacity E.g., Faith organizations and other place-based groups such as farmers markets, one-off hyperlocal groups, informal alliances (that is, "activists" generally), digital gatherings (listservs, forums), issue advocacy groups
Government	International, federal, state, county, other local E.g., Libraries, post offices, elected officials
Private sector	For-profit organization with private capital and the goal of generating profits for stakeholders E.g., Local business, start-ups, large multinational corporations (for example, McDonald's, Verizon)
Academia	Research-based institutions E.g., Universities, think tanks, research centers, and other research-based organizations
Philanthropy	Grant-making organizations and foundations, including charitable trusts E.g., private philanthropy, charitable givers, state-based foundations (primarily outside of the United States)

BOX 8-1
Civic Tech and Innovation Typology

Economy—Resources, Goods, Services

Economic services, goods, and resources are being divided, organized, and reorganized by a variety of different types of large and small communities. Innovations are changing the way people share, acquire, and effectively produce resources and goods. This is occurring along several tracks:

Collaborative Funding

Citizinvestor An online platform that crowdfunds public sector projects.[a]

Cash mobs Groups of people who assemble at a local business to make purchases.[b]

The Awesome Foundation Pools $1,000 grants from self-organized "micro-trustees" to give to "awesome" creative projects in technology and arts and for the social good.

Sharing Economy

Capital Bikeshare A public-private partnership that runs a bicycle-sharing system in Washington, D.C.

Popuphood A small-business incubator that revitalizes neighborhoods in Oakland, California.

Time-banked currency Alternative currency where the unit of exchange is person hours.[c]

Tool libraries Communities investing in shared tool collections.[d]

These innovations represent shifts in ways that communities conceive of and deploy their common economic resources. As with PB, many of these innovations do not include a required gadget or app; rather, the innovation consists of changing a process, bringing people together in a new way and ushering in a culture shift in how governance is conducted.[e] They involve public as well as private partners and require new thinking, new technology, and new collaborations in order to bring new services to the community.

Government—Institutions and Process

Government institutions are exploring ways to increase participation, transparency, and collaboration internally and externally. Elected officials are devolving decisionmaking opportunities back to the very citizens who elected them. Agency officials are donating their time, after hours, to work with their constituents. Changes are happening throughout all levels and branches of government, and they include governance institutions in the broadest sense.

Collaborative Decisionmaking

Participatory budgeting Empowers citizens to make binding recommendations on spending public money.

Citizen juries Groups of randomly selected, representative citizens who deliberate on an issue.[f]

Citizens' Initiative Reviews In Arizona, Colorado, and Oregon, these panels of randomly selected representative voters are called upon to fairly evaluate ballot measures.[g]

Process Improvement

Regulations.gov An online portal created by the U.S. government to make public regulatory review during notice and comment periods more transparent and accessible.[h]

City Hall to Go A refurbished truck in Boston that delivers city services directly to people.[i]
Citizens Connect A mobile app for citizens of Boston to report and track service delivery complaints, with a collaborative component.[j]

These innovations directly involve government actors, and they open up governance processes to new audiences via new technologies and new means of organization.

Communities—Local, Online and Off, and Context Specific
Communities are networks formed around shared interests, resources, locations, and needs. The currency of communities is communication—the creation and exchange of goods and knowledge. As locality reemerges as a sphere for civic life, community-based innovations increasingly tie place-based interventions—whether digital or physical—to the needs of individuals and collectives.

Knowledge Transfer
Makerspaces Workshops that provide space with industrial equipment for communal use.[k]
TEDx Independently organized events to spread innovative ideas, granted permission to use the branding of the TED organization.[l]

Co-creating
Parklets Small plots of land converted into parks in urban areas.[m]
OldWeather.org A crowdsourcing project that began by enrolling citizens to collectively transcribe old British ship logs to determine climate patterns.[n]
Parent Teacher Associations (PTAs) Local organizations of parents improving education.[o]

Community-based innovations frequently focus on how knowledge can be produced, distributed, and accessed more efficiently or creatively by people and groups with shared interests, practices, and needs.

---

[a] See Citizinvestor.com for more details.
[b] See Cash-mobs.com for more details.
[c] TimeBanks.org offers a central knowledge bank on such projects around the world.
[d] The tool library in the neighborhood of Atwood in Madison, Wisconsin, is one such example (http://sustainableatwood.org/tool-library/).
[e] Sirianni (2009) discusses culture change in government.
[f] Jefferson Center, "Citizen Juries" (http://jefferson-center.org/what-we-do/citizen-juries/).
[g] Healthy Democracy, "Citizens' Initiative Review: Background" (http://healthydemocracy.org/citizens-initiative-review/).
[h] See Regulations.gov for more details.
[i] City of Boston, "City Hall to Go" (www.cityofboston.gov/cityhalltogo/).
[j] City of Boston, "Citizens Connect" (www.cityofboston.gov/doit/apps/citizensconnect.asp).
[k] MakerSpace.com sponsors public events promoting do-it-yourself technology tinkering called Maker Faires and maintains a directory of shared workshops (http://spaces.makerspace.com/).
[l] TED, "TEDx Program" (www.ted.com/about/programs-initiatives/tedx-program).
[m] ParkletDC.org demonstrates how one group in Washington, D.C., is trying to bring microparks to the nation's capital.
[n] It has since expanded, involving collaboration between several national-level agencies in the United States and the United Kingdom to make historical weather data available for research, while continuing to enroll citizen participation in processing archival material.
[o] The National PTA (PTA.org) supports local parent teacher associations across the country.

Working toward institutionalization requires civil society engagement at every stage, from conception through implementation. However, not every democracy has a diverse or robust civil society. For example, many developing democracies suffer from weak and underdeveloped civil society sectors, with only a handful of thriving, independent organizations. Currently, civil society in the United States faces a different kind of challenge. In some sectors, it can be oversaturated or fragmented, with many groups fighting over limited resources. Funding models can discourage collaboration. In some cases, options and opportunities for peer organizations to share institutional knowledge or work together closely are lacking. I propose a networked model of civil society engagement—one that values collaboration, not competition, and pushes for more inclusive participation and governance *within* organizations themselves. This model includes the option of tying resource allocations to governance structures, suggesting ways that funding organizations can evaluate partnerships and collaborations.

Strategic choices by civil society, ranging from local community-based groups to the World Bank, can identify and foster conditions under which inclusive governance is more or less likely to grow. Strategic choices can build up communal resilience. For example, the small city of Mount Rainier, Maryland, has built up a strong civic community. Their tool library and bicycle co-op engage a large swath of this connected, perhaps self-selecting, suburban community. Anchor institutions are one ingredient of the area's success: the Community Forklift home improvement center in nearby Bladensburg, Maryland, lends tools the community can use, while Joe's Movement Emporium is a performing arts center that offers education on production and artist services for residents.[21]

Anchor institutions help foster face-to-face engagement and networks of trust that are more important than ever in a highly digitized world. However, many organizations face a climate of fewer available resources for mobilizing people and keeping them involved. One strategy for promoting long-term civic innovation and resilience could be to find and strengthen existing anchor institutions across many different local contexts.

I view examples like the above as important to working toward a vision of more participatory and engaged society. Building structured engagement opportunities can help create connective tissue to empower citizens in a variety of governance issue areas.

---

21. See CommunityForklift.org and JoesMovement.org.

Toward Inclusive Governance

> By giving people a direct voice in shaping regulations, we can make agencies more responsive and accountable, and give citizens a direct stake in policy-making, beyond just voting every four years.[22]

This book illustrates opportunities for citizens to be involved in public discretionary spending. More inclusive and collaborative governance involves taking existing institutions of government and redefining how citizens can take part in them. There is a wide range of opportunities for more participation in governance, beyond discretionary budgets.[23]

Regulations represent just one arena in which citizens could have more direct decisionmaking power. Regulations.gov is a federal government website with an easy-to-use interface that enables individuals to submit comments on proposed regulations. The website also enables users to search and view original regulatory documents and previously submitted comments. Regulations.gov also released an application program interface (API) that allows programmatic access to regulatory data.[24] Developers and programmers alike can use the API to create easily accessible tools for a variety of civic stakeholders.

Citizen engagement with governance can take a variety of forms. There are some basic underlying conditions:

—First, citizens need information in order to understand how decisions are made. Ideally, this will also involve creating or improving information systems that allow citizens to better monitor their government. It may include identifying and addressing current deficiencies in the information environment.

—Second, public institutions can provide two-way opportunities for citizens to engage. This can include citizens collaborating with other citizens to formulate solutions to public problems.

—Finally, engagement works best when it aims at more sustainable systems for greater transparency, accountability, and long-term engagement. This is why internal and external validation is critical. International partnerships between

22. K. Sabeel Rahman, "Is Participatory Rule-Making Possible?" *The Nation*, March 21, 2012 (www.thenation.com/article/166959/participatory-rule-making-possible).

23. K. Sabeel Rahman, "Beyond the Free Market," *Salon*, March 4, 2012 (http://www.salon.com /2012/03/04/beyond_the_free_market/); Smith (2005).

24. See Data.gov, "Regulations.gov API" (http://api.data.gov/docs/regulations/); and Andrew Pendleton, "Regulations.gov Continues to Improve, but Still Has Potential for Growth," Sunlight Foundation blog, April 9, 2013 (http://sunlightfoundation.com/blog/2013/04/09/regulations-gov-continues-to -improve-but-still-has-potential-for-growth/).

multiple stakeholders can hold local governments to account by providing another pressure point and an international context for civic engagement at the local level.

Ideally, information to inform policy choices would be accompanied by structured opportunities for civic participation. Without this, citizens could simply feel inundated by information and further disillusioned or disenfranchised.

Many reasons can be cited to engage citizens in governance and decisionmaking. In the introduction, I discussed a lack of transparency and accountability as primary concerns for contemporary governments. Decisions made through collaborative processes can improve effectiveness and legitimacy. Involving more voices in governance makes it easier for traditionally marginalized groups to work cooperatively with entrenched actors and can help government capitalize on diverse expertise diffused throughout society.[25]

The Potential of Information and Communications Technologies (ICTs)

Information and communications technologies (ICTs) provide a range of additional opportunities to engage citizens in decisionmaking.[26] These opportunities include, for example, more easily accessible data on where and how elected officials receive and allocate funds, which can lead to greater accountability.

In India, Mumbai Votes is an NGO that does just this. Volunteers and students play an integral part. Through crowdsourcing, Mumbai Votes provides information that allows constituents to hold elected officials accountable to their campaign promises. This information is viewed as more credible than that provided in some news outlets in which paid news is a widespread problem.[27] When embedded advertisements are placed as news in mainstream sources of journalism, this reduces the overall credibility of the system. Mumbai Votes empowers people to address this problem themselves and provides valuable information that can put necessary pressure on elected officials. The actual website that Mumbai Votes runs is less important than its ability to host this information and thereby hold governments to account. Mumbai Votes provides a viable alternative information source to traditional news.

Similarly, governments can take steps to support a more democratic information ecosystem. By choosing "open by default" as a governmental data standard— as stipulated by the Obama administration's Executive Order 13642, for

25. See Noveck (2009).
26. Although, as discussed elsewhere, the information conveyed is usually more important to the outcome than the specific technology that conveys it.
27. Fung, Gilman, and Shkabatur (2010).

example—governmental entities can ensure that open, machine-readable data are readily available to the public.[28] This, in turn, empowers outside parties, including NGOs and private companies as well as journalists and others, to use this data in a variety of ways.[29] Open data are a means to an end. On their own, they do not lead to a more engaged citizenry or improved governance. It is incumbent upon others—citizens and civil society groups, such as civic entrepreneurs and NGOs—to build applications for civic use. This should include easily accessible applications designed for use by citizens who are not technological elites.

Distributed ICTs can go beyond merely informing citizens to prompt and enable them to take a more active role in governance. One example is the "Text Talk Act" platform devised by Creating Community Solutions (CCS), a coalition of deliberative democracy organizations that have led a national dialogue on mental health. Text Talk Act, as its name implies, uses SMS messages to facilitate face-to-face conversations in small groups of three to five people.[30] Participants receive discussion and polling questions. Results from the live polling questions are collected and can be viewed in real time. Participants in CCS's Text Talk Act events were also invited to share the progress of their conversations via social media so as to further expand the reach of the event. To date, CCS has used Text Talk Act to engage more than 26,000 young people across the country in face-to-face dialogues on mental health issues, generating at least 13.58 million Text, Talk, Act impressions and 6,000 tweets on social media. Importantly, while technology was leveraged as a process improvement to facilitate in-person dialogue and deliberation, a key ingredient to the success of Text, Talk, Act was the creation of a robust network of promoters and supporters, including a variety of national partner organizations and a cadre of youth organizers.[31]

Another example is SeeClickFix.com—a site to help residents report, view, and discuss problems directly with their local governments by simply locating them on a map and submitting a report.[32] The site creates a permanent record of the issue, submitted to the relevant public officials. In addition, citizens can

---

28. Executive Order 13642 of May 9, 2013, Making Open and Machine Readable the New Default for Government Information, *Federal Register* 78 (93): 28111–13 (http://www.gpo.gov/fdsys/pkg/FR -2013-05-14/pdf/2013-11533.pdf).

29. See DJ Patil, "A Six Month Update on How We've Been Using Data, and How It Benefits All Americans," *Medium*, August 19, 2015 (https://medium.com/@WhiteHouse/a-six-month-update-on -how-we-ve-been-using-data-and-how-it-benefits-all-americans-b1221b5cbb0e).

30. See "Text, Talk, Act," Creating Community Solutions, 2015 (http://creatingcommunitysolutions .org/texttalkact).

31. See Matt Leighninger, "Text, Talk, Act," Deliberative-Democracy.net, November 18, 2013 (www .deliberative-democracy.net/index.php/projects-general/188-texttalkact) and www.creatingcommunity solutions.org. Thank you to Carolyn Lukensymer.

32. See Sifry (2014, pp. 177–94).

discuss the problem with others on the website and, together, they can lobby city officials to fix it. SeeClickFix also empowers citizens to take action within their communities.[33] There are "civic points" for engagement, which range from reporting an issue to starting a watch group, and even a "thank you" button sent directly to the public official who fixed the problem.[34]

It is important to remember that processes such as "SeeClickFix" work best when they are buttressing, not replacing, government. As a tech-policy practitioner once put it: "'See-Click-Fix' without government is only 'See-Click.'"[35] The approach taken by SeeClickFix.com ultimately requires government intervention.

Cities are taking a more open approach to small issues of hyperlocal governance by increasingly pairing existing 311 infrastructures for reporting nonemergency problems with technical solutions like those of SeeClickFix.com to create more participation and transparency. If they choose to use SeeClickFix.com rather than their own solution, cities can receive both an activity and a results score to track use of the system and complaint resolution.[36] This empowers people and governments to work together as collaborative problem solvers. A common feature of most open 311 systems is that citizens are empowered to supply new public data for improved governance, enhancing government transparency and accountability in service delivery.[37]

Technology alone cannot transform the public sector. Yet these democratic innovations are important because they show how carefully designed technology can work to engage citizens in more collaborative models of decisionmaking. The lessons drawn from PB and discussed throughout this book can help provide tangible knowledge for how to get citizens more deeply involved in governance. I have shown that the task of empowering citizens is neither straightforward nor easy; rather, it requires a nuanced understanding of incentives, people, and politics. Hopefully, these lessons can help buttress efforts to harness digital technology to bring about a variety of political reforms.

These lessons and observations regarding PB and ICTs stand in contrast to a wave of democratic technological utopianism that arose amid the broad adop-

---

33. See Micah Sifry, "Civic Tech and Engagement: How SeeClickFix Is Changing the Fabric of Local Reality," *TechPresident*, July 24, 2014 (http://techpresident.com/news/25206/civic-tech-and-engagement-how-seeclickfix-changing-fabric-local-reality).

34. SeeClickFix, "Click Thank You," November 28, 2013 (http://blog.seeclickfix.com/2013/11/28/click-thank-you).

35. Fung, Gilman, and Shkabatur (2013, p. 8).

36. Luke Fretwell, "Get the 311 with SeeClickFix," *Govfresh*, January 10, 2010 (www.govfresh.com/2010/01/get-the-311-with-seeclickfix/).

37. See Open311(http://www.open311.org/about/) and GeoReport v2, Open 311 (http://wiki.open311.org/GeoReport_v2/).

tion of the Internet. During this period, there was a normative aspiration that digital tools should transform civic engagement and help mitigate some of its traditional perceived messiness. The rationale was that as ICTs dramatically reduce transactional costs, communication and participation in governance would be easier. Many scholars and activists were hopeful that these technologies could create a transformed, more egalitarian public sphere.

For example, in 2008, Clay Shirky noted:

> Newly capable groups are assembling, and they are working without the managerial imperative and outside the previous strictures that bounded their effectiveness. These changes will transform the world everywhere groups of people come together to accomplish something, *which is to say everywhere.*[38]

The intervening years have made clear significant obstacles to achieving this vision. Technology has yet to dramatically democratize the public sphere as some scholars have suggested it would.[39] This book seeks to contribute to this ongoing discussion—particularly by looking at the interplay of technology, institutions, and people in the practice of democratic governance.

It is essential to put people—not a piece of software or hardware—and their specific communities and contexts at the center of improvements to democracy. Of course, online tools can buttress, support, and enhance existing opportunities to improve governance. ICTs have the ability to push democratic institutions to evolve. In many instances, building inclusive governance resilient to electoral transition may well require online tools. NGOs, foundations, and private companies can support the use of digital tools to strengthen civil society and deepen democracy, building capacity for civic engagement. Yet digital tools alone simply cannot replace face-to-face interactions, which are more important than ever. At the end of the day, inclusive governance requires understanding politics and institutions. Democratic innovations that leverage technology within existing political incentive structures are more likely to effect change.

Institutional Barriers

How and why democracy changes is complex. There is no quick answer—neither finding the right tool nor electing a political reformer ensures it. Many public

---

38. Shirky (2008, p. 3), italics added.
39. See Trippi (2004); Benkler (2006); and Shirky (2008).

institutions face the added challenge of launching and executing experimental civic innovations without knowing the consequences. Stakeholders worry that the results of change may be politically costly. Even when results are positive, there is a concern regarding limited resources. For example, if citizens actually participate in processes like PB, there could be a lack of institutional capacity to effectively manage and engage such participation.[40] A concern exists that civil servants with high work burdens will be unable to respond to citizens properly and directly and that engaging citizens without a capacity to respond could result in further disillusionment.[41]

The following factors contribute to a general lack of experimentation in public institutions:

—*Lack of capacity:* Public institutions lack resources and the capacity to engage.

—*Lack of political will:* Public institutions lack the political will to experiment.

—*Fear of failure:* They are especially vulnerable to criticism as it relates to experimentation—and potential failures include electoral costs.

—*Lack of agility:* Typically large, bureaucratic structures are not well designed to execute on the lean, agile approach.

—*Limited research:* Insufficient independent studies assess *what works* and *why*.

—*Communication gaps:* Robust research containing nuanced results on nascent experimentation and innovation, information that is difficult for large institutions to publicly convey.

Challenges in innovation and experimentation have as much to do with uncertainty in an emerging sector as with longstanding structural obstacles. A chicken-and-egg dilemma emerges when public institutions are asked to innovate in ways they never have before. To understand what works, trials and tests must be conducted so that institutions can learn and then adopt what works. Yet doing so requires many early adopters and resources. It also means that these institutions have to accept a greater potential for failure. Such an approach challenges basic underlying assumptions about the stability of public sector institutions. Budget constraints only add another dimension of complexity. As a result, the lean, agile, empirical method of innovation is the exception, not the norm, in this sector.

Despite the opportunities for emerging technologies and democratic innovations to organize, galvanize, and mobilize citizens, basic functions and complex

---

40. When working in government, I heard a steady refrain of such concerns from dedicated public servants who wanted to engage citizens.

41. See Sirianni (2009).

issues remain that require traditional, stable governance institutions. Public problems require public funds.[42] This is partially due to the nature of public problems, which demonstrate and address the following social concerns and dynamics:[43]

—*The collective action dilemma:* Also known as the free rider problem, this dilemma results in situations in which even the most civic-minded citizens will still underproduce public goods (e.g., ensuring a public park is clean).

—*Globally connected problems:* Many complex issues require stakeholders across nation-states and sectors to collaborate to effectively address them (e.g., climate change).

—*Market inefficiencies:* Large-scale economic issues that affect entire markets require advance planning and may not immediately turn a profit (e.g., public infrastructure).

—*Laws and regulations:* Solutions that hinge upon independent legal and policy structures require entities with the authority to govern and enforce rules (e.g., patents).

Conclusion

Public sector institutions are tasked with authority over large and important societal concerns. These characteristics of public sector dilemmas illustrate the importance of studying institutions as a primary unit of analysis within a broader discussion of civic innovation. The importance of public institutions means that the stakes of innovation are sometimes perceived as particularly high—they cannot afford to lose public trust, either through unreliable service delivery or through stagnation and disillusionment.

Further, while public institutions are anything but monolithic, many institutions face certain intrinsic obstacles to fulfilling the norms of civic politics, including:

—*Path dependency:* Inertia that makes them slow to innovate and change.
—*Electoral accountability:* Fear of elections that makes them risk averse.
—*Focus on efficiency not effectiveness:* A focus on outputs rather than outcomes.

At a time of budget deficits and austerity in many developed economies and slowing growth rates in many emerging economies, these hindrances become even

---

42. Even within multisector partnerships, there is typically some public investment.
43. See also Young and others (2013).

more pronounced. Governments continually look to reduce costs, which can reduce capacity. Engagement takes resources. Expanding meaningful and effective citizen participation will require continued devotion to the principles of *participation, deliberation,* and *institutionalization* that I have espoused in this book.

I have outlined some of the institutional challenges to robust civic innovation. Leadership turnover poses a further obstacle. It is difficult to focus on long-term civic engagement if innovations are at the mercy of changing leaders. Another wrinkle relates, in particular, to open data. Governments fear that opening up institutions to the scrutiny of the public will create information flows that are more intense than they can adequately handle. These factors contribute to suppressing civic experimentation and creating a climate that is insufficiently tolerant of lean, agile research.

It is worth recalling that institutions are not monolithic; rather, they have varied functions and properties. Nonetheless, the overarching principles outlined in this chapter can help practitioners to guide and to operate individual efforts.

9

Why Engage Citizens?

Throughout this book, I have identified (1) substantive participation, (2) deliberation, and (3) opportunities for institutionalization as critical dimensions for assessing PB's effectiveness and legitimacy. Components of this framework may be applicable to other civic experiments, depending on their nature and goals. Deliberation and participation are vital to deepening democracy. However, democratic innovations cannot meaningfully and enduringly enhance citizens' political efficacy on a large scale unless they can move beyond pilot periods and become institutionalized.

I have zeroed in on PB in the United States as one compelling example within an ecosystem of civic tech and innovation, a study that may offer lessons for other attempts to deepen democracy. This book has focused on the specific processes of deliberation and participation found within the practice of participatory budgeting in the United States, looking at the pilot year in New York, Chicago, and Boston. Because the book focuses on pilots, some characteristics may have already evolved in the natural life cycle of innovation. My framework privileges civic participation that is more substantive than transactional, prioritizing effective civic engagement over reducing transaction costs or simply maximizing the efficiency of service delivery. It values deep, sustained, and civically transformative participation.[1]

My theory requires that participation be measured not simply by metrics common to the digital world, such as "total page views" or "number of contacts," but rather in terms of the nature and quality of that participation, which must include genuine opportunities for deliberation and dialogue. Some scholars posit

---

1. See also Han (2014).

that deliberation stands in tension with participation because people are risk averse.[2] I assert that democratic processes can, in fact, create meaningful opportunities for both participation and deliberation. However, this requires careful planning and, above all, recognition of the importance of the values inherent within civic engagement.

Institutionalizing innovation is the other critical dimension of my framework. As outlined in chapter 7, this is especially important for innovations that increase engagement in governance decisionmaking. As these become embedded in political procedure, a snowball effect can emerge that promotes scale and broadens scope. Scalability can also lend political clout. Ad hoc processes will be less successful at creating sustainable channels for inclusive governance and maintaining the necessary political pressure for lasting change.

My hope is that these criteria will also prove useful to researchers and practitioners looking beyond participatory budgeting. Practitioners can use them to design participatory processes with intent. Researchers can look to them in order to move beyond only quantitative metrics toward more textured and nuanced indicators.

The framework illustrates varied opportunities for citizens to flex their civic muscles—the knowledge, experience, and motivation that arise from meaningful participation in governance—to contribute beyond simply voting in elections every other year. The goal is to identify and create opportunities for citizens to train themselves to seek deeper democratic involvement. I posit that citizens can strengthen their civic muscles through participation. PB's ability to provide numerous opportunities for citizens to participate enables a variety of channels for people to flex and develop their civic muscles.

Deepening Democracy

Why participate? Robust civic participation is a key indicator of democratic health. PB's civic rewards can deepen democracy; by providing channels for meaningful citizen engagement, PB promotes civic learning. Strengthening these civic muscles fosters a healthy democratic society, which, in turn, engenders trust in decisionmaking and grants more legitimacy to governance. PB serves as a civic training school for citizens, who, in turn, can strengthen the quality of governance in other venues as well.

Numerous scholars, from Robert Putnam to Michael J. Sandel, note the importance to civic virtue of being involved in associational relationships.[3] Nancy L. Rosenblum discusses the multifaceted ways in which such associations

---

2. Mutz (2008).
3. Putnam (2001); Sandel (1998).

benefit an individual's character.[4] PB connects people with one another at the local level and builds social capital for participants while also bridging their individual relationships via the larger project of civic engagement within a democracy.[5]

Participatory budgeting enables people to think more creatively—to think on a bigger scale than that of their day-to-day tasks. In the process of PB, citizens are suddenly engaging with each other and their elected officials in nontraditional roles. PB opens up spaces for civic creativity. The civic rewards of the process motivate a diverse swath of people, granted the opportunity that PB affords, to experience for themselves what it means to think expansively about how they might channel the resources of government to better their communities.

Civic engagement can generate many positive returns for both the larger society and the individual character. Mark E. Warren has an enthusiastic list of civic virtues associated with democracy, including attentiveness to the common good and concerns for justice; tolerance of the views of others; trustworthiness; willingness to participate, deliberate, and listen; respect for the rule of law; and respect for the rights of others, to name but a few.[6] While such civic benefits extend beyond the temporal limits of the PB process, there are also many material benefits to PB, including projects that more creatively address community needs than status quo budgeting efforts. Elected officials get to interact with a wider set of their constituents. PB places decisionmaking at the neighborhood level—engaging many who are not typically involved in civic life.

This book has shown that fulfilling the norms that PB aims to advance is a complex process. Some citizens ended up participating in the design of participatory institutions, despite the intent of initiators. While participation in the PBNYC pilot was generally meaningful for participants, some parts of the process, such as the vote, were more effective than others at achieving inclusive and diverse representation.

The budget delegate process was less diverse and inclusive. That setting, however, allowed for deliberative discourse, which exhibited trade-offs between two norms of deliberation—efficiency and inclusiveness. These two norms emerged out of a broader context: in the United States, PB tries to accommodate dual goals of improving short-term service delivery while also deepening the democratic process.

Participants in PB can help to determine the criteria for its success. PB is not beholden to a simple understanding of governmental efficiency as the sole criterion

4. Rosenblum (1998).
5. Putnam (2001).
6. Warren (2001, p. 73); see also Fung (2003a).

of civic achievement. I have argued that PB is impactful because its participants are motivated by how the process creates civic rewards. My research points to ways that participants' varying values and notions of success have the potential to be incorporated into process design, opportunities for engagement, and evaluation.

PB shows that ordinary citizens can be involved in decisionmaking. PB breaks down complex challenges into manageable projects that can be tackled neighborhood by neighborhood. As a result, it generates "new citizens"—members of the public who have not previously participated in elections or political discourse but who are able to exercise voice and power through this process.[7] PB participants are diverse not only in terms of traditional demographic indicators but also in terms of civic experience levels, as the process attracts and engages many beyond just the "usual suspects." The opportunity to exercise direct agency over the spending of government funds draws new actors into the political process in all of its facets, awakening dormant interests and energies and reinvigorating local democracy. New citizens pave the way for more inclusive engagement with local government.

Next Steps: Participatory Budgeting in the United States

PB may not be the most efficient way to deliver public services, but its rapid expansion suggests the importance of citizen involvement for effective governance.

The demand signal for PB and other civic innovations like it suggests that perhaps contemporary democracies have mistakenly devalued citizens' buy-in and input in decisionmaking. Democracy is not only about timely and reliable public service delivery or even about electing representatives. Engaging citizens directly as decisionmakers can lead to better policy. By tapping into the varying knowledge of individual people, and using that knowledge to formulate public projects decided upon via small-group deliberation, local policy can more accurately reflect the will of the people in common. This, in turn, can lead to better outcomes and help restore trust in governance.

Participatory budgeting can create more effective processes that make government more transparent, participatory, and collaborative. I have argued that PB produces significant civic rewards, including enhanced civic knowledge, strengthened relationships with elected officials, and greater community inclusion. Participatory processes have the potential to be more creative than the status quo urban bureaucratic process. Overall, PB is a viable and impactful model for citi-

---

7. Again, I use the term "citizen" to refer to people engaged in civic processes, including especially participants in PB. I am not referring to formal citizenship status.

zen engagement, one that leads to improved outputs and outcomes. It is an informative, democratic innovation for strengthening civic engagement within the United States that can be streamlined and adopted to scale.

As participatory budgeting expands to encompass different pots of monies, forms of influence, and stakeholders and participants, new challenges will inevitably arise. Bigger public budgets allocated through PB will mean greater attention will be paid to who participates. A tension exists between aiming for broad mobilization and focusing on populations of need, especially given the current constraints on funding the actual process itself. Champions of PB should anticipate further questions regarding how to measure and weigh who participates as well as how to prevent special interests from co-opting the process, if more money is decided through it. Supporters may need to find ways to mitigate political competition, which can occur in connection with it. The process should be safeguarded against co-option by special interests or its use as primarily a vehicle for electoral ambitions. Similarly, thus far, community representatives have not been elected in implementations of PB in the United States. Process expansion could include revisiting this question of elected representation.

There are challenges to sustained participation in the current model, including the high costs of engagement, frequent chances for frustration and disillusionment, and obstacles related to its scalability. Expansion of PB will necessitate change. The process could be more streamlined to make it less time and resource intensive. Through reforms and modifications to PB, barriers to entry can be lowered, exhaustion with the process can be minimized, and the potential for process co-option by determined political actors can be reduced.

Even if these necessary changes are made, formidable challenges will remain, especially in terms of providing sufficiently uniform process quality and scalable institutionalization. The high level of variance within the PBNYC pilot—presumably a self-contained process conducted across only four districts—demonstrates a potential obstacle to bringing PB to scale. Is variance a necessary by-product of PB? Bringing PB to its full potential in the United States will require navigating the tension between creative autonomy on the local level and practical institutionalization.

Empirical data on PB in the United States illustrate variance at all levels—from process governance to budget subcommittees. Even within districts there was variation in how individual facilitators and in-group dynamics have shaped discourse, decisionmaking, and mobilization. District demographics, political economies, and civil society capacity have shaped the experience of PB down to the subcommittee level.

Politics and political dynamics will continue to influence PB's adoption in different places. For example, the process in Chicago and New York started with small pots of discretionary funds already at the disposal of individual municipal officials. In other places, such as Buffalo, New York, PB is being driven by a collective legislative process: the Buffalo Common Council Members allocated $150,000 in the 2015–16 budget for PB.[8] The questions of which elected officials and mechanisms fund PB will continue to remain central to PB in the United States.

The policy recommendations in chapter 7 offer strategies for how to better pool process resources to enable continued growth. Currently, PB suffers from limited funds dedicated solely to process implementation. Increasing process funds could help streamline PB and make it less resource intensive. Yet the process will always require participant hours. Better communication between practitioners and improved process transparency, particularly regarding how and when specific projects are implemented, could help foster citizens' trust and build momentum.

To safeguard PB against criticisms of co-option, the process should continue to find more opportunities for engaging people. If PB is seen either as simply a mobilization effort of a specific organization or as an elaborate electoral project of a politician, the process will loose support and legitimacy. Yet numerous opportunities for process participation also create liabilities—as each one is subject to critique. For example, are people at neighborhood assemblies representatives of specific organizations? Does a budget delegate have an agenda tied to an outside group? How can the vote be protected from lobbyists and special interests? These kinds of questions will vary by context, but they are critical.

Over time, PB can increase the legitimacy and accountability of governance. If the process demonstrates that it enacts citizen input, it will begin to take root. This is why institutionalizing innovation is key. Advocates and practitioners of PB should work to communicate back to citizens how and where their money and time were spent. A centralized website would go a long way toward promoting process transparency. In addition, signs could illustrate which projects are funded as a result of PB—similar to standard funding signage often tied to infrastructure projects, such as that deployed in conjunction with federal "project[s] funded by the American Recovery and Reinvestment Act." This could include signage at sites where PB projects have been funded but are not yet complete. PB is a reinvestment in democracy. Greater visibility can help connect the PB process to larger stakes. In New York, Melissa Mark-Viverito, the speaker of the city council, called for PB to be applied to New York Tenant Participation Activity (TPA) funds as part of City Housing Authority (NYCHA)

8. Alex Haight, "Buffalo Common Council Approves Participatory Budgeting for the First Time," *Time Warner Cable News*, May 19, 2015 (www.twcnews.com/nys/buffalo/news/2015/05/19/buffalo -common-council-approves-participatory-budget-for-first-time.html).

grants. The coming years will make clear how these funds are ultimately allocated and whether this spurs other government agencies and offices to put funding into PB.

Only a few years into a PB experiment, the city of Vallejo, California, is already seeing pushback.[9] Opponents of PB have emerged, arguing that the process should be constricted in favor of other city priorities. In 2014 the city council of Vallejo pushed back on many of the individual projects proposed via PB. The process has also started strong and faded in other places, such as in Buenos Aires.[10] Marrying an implementation of PB in the context of a strong civil society with commitments to internal participatory governance can go a long way to ensure its continuing use.[11] Where civil society is healthy—with numerous independent and inclusive organizations that show a genuine commitment to engaging citizens—the process can enhance its resiliency in the face of electoral change.[12]

PB faces a challenge shared by many democratic innovations: it must be viewed as more than a shiny new toy or a tool for electoral gain. Throughout this book I have argued that ideology has played a less critical role in PB in the United States than it has in global counterparts. Ideological commitment from government officials alone will not suffice. Instead, I view PB as one example within a more broadly based effort toward promoting inclusive governance throughout a democratic society.

A Broader Project to Reinvent Democracy

The commanding beliefs of the American people—that everything is possible, that vast problems can be solved if broken up into pieces and answered one by one, and that ordinary men and women contain within themselves, individually and collectively, the constructive genius with which to craft such solutions—now find themselves without adequate political expression.[13]

Participatory budgeting has never just been about effective and legitimate decisionmaking, though that is a worthy, important goal integral to the process. If

9. Alana Semuels, "The City That Gave Its Residents $3 Million," *The Atlantic,* November 6, 2014 (http://www.theatlantic.com/business/archive/2014/11/the-city-that-gave-its-residents-3-million /382348/).
10. For more on the process in Buenos Aires, see Fung (2011, p. 867).
11. Fung (2011).
12. Fung (2011).
13. Unger (2009, p. 6).

efficiency is viewed as making a decision in the least amount of time, PB will not be a first choice. Rather, PB began in Brazil as a way to reimagine the relationship between citizens and the state. PB is about redistributing power to citizens. Part of this normative project works to recapture an ancient ideal of the power of civic engagement.

From the beginning of Western thought, Plato and Aristotle envisioned a polis that would enable man to perform a particularly human activity: speech.[14] This activity in the political sphere was important for a variety of reasons, including its effect on the human soul. In the ancient ideal of the polis, citizens were freed from their material constraints and could work to achieve something larger than their individual lives. This promise of politics has helped keep the allure of democracy alive, despite its evident shortcomings.

Concerns about the feasibility of this democratic ideal are as old as the ideal itself. Hannah Arendt notes in her 1958 work *The Human Condition*:

> Through many ages before us—but now not any more—men entered the public realm because they wanted something of their own or something they had in common with others to be more permanent than their earthly lives.[15]

Many scholars, activists, and critics have been concerned about the declining quality of democratic engagement. In a sense, these concerns reflect a decline in opportunities to pursue the type of civic rewards I have contended exist in participatory budgeting. Yet my terminology is far removed from the common language used in contemporary American politics, which is much more comfortable with discussions of good governance than discourses on power and civic engagement, let alone politics as a way to achieve a type of Athenian immortality. As a result, we are left with a political discourse that cannot capture the full range of why people participate.[16]

Throughout this book, I have argued that civic rewards drive people to both participate in and remain engaged in collaborative public efforts like participatory budgeting. It is these civic rewards that inspire people to believe that participatory budgeting is a viable process. Participation is difficult. It can be filled with frustrations and disappointments, and it can leave people exhausted and fatigued. My research has consistently affirmed that people remain involved nonetheless because of civic rewards. People make friends, form new networks, and enjoy being a part of something larger than their personal day-to-day concerns.

14. See Arendt's discussion of Aristotle and Plato (1998, p. 27).
15. Arendt (1998, p. 55).
16. Davies (2014) notes in his discussion of civic crowdfunding that the rhetoric of entrepreneurship and ownership is much more common than narratives of ties to community (p. 22).

Not everyone espouses this view. Many fears surround participation, including concerns that it will lead to suboptimal outcomes, and that ordinary citizens are not equipped to make policy decisions. Yet there is another often overlooked fear of citizen engagement: What if participation actually undermines representative democracy?

None of our founding fathers thought direct democratic deliberation by the people was a good idea. The core theorists of the American Republic include those—Alexander Hamilton and James Madison—who were more skeptical about the value of the people's involvement as well as those—Thomas Jefferson and Woodrow Wilson—who were less skeptical. Yet throughout its history direct deliberative democracy has been anathema to the traditional vision of the United States. James Madison's Federalist No. 10 famously warns against the dangers of direct democracy and of factions:

> It may be concluded that a pure democracy, by which I mean a society consisting of a small number of citizens, who assemble and administer the government in person, can admit no cure for the mischiefs of faction.[17]

In Hannah Arendt's depiction, Thomas Jefferson comes closest to championing an ideal of participatory democracy, but this ideal is neither as robust nor as binding as participatory budgeting.[18] In addition to the fear of factionalism espoused by the founding fathers, another political concept identified at the turn of the nineteenth century presents an obstacle to the normative value of participation. It is possible that citizens want the type of modern liberty outlined by Benjamin Constant, wherein they are freed from politics itself.[19] What if people do not *want* to participate in their democracy?[20]

In response to these challenges, I contend that the current political atmosphere does not give citizens the background knowledge needed to assess these value propositions. No functional system of supply and demand for civic engagement exists that would allow a fair assessment of citizens' desires for political activity. Citizens do not even know the scope of the existing realm of possibilities for engaging with politics. Participatory budgeting is one attempt to provide more opportunities for citizens to begin a discussion.

17. James Madison, "The Same Subject Continued: The Union as a Safeguard against Domestic Faction and Insurrection," *New York Packet,* November 23, 1787, known as *The Federalist,* no. 10 (http://thomas.loc.gov/home/histdox/fed_10.html).

18. The accuracy of Arendt's reading of Jefferson is subject to debate. Moreover, just as Arendt may assign more democratic inclinations to Jefferson than warranted, perhaps I do the same with Arendt.

19. Benjamin Constant, "The Liberty of the Ancients Compared with That of the Moderns," 1819 (2010) (www.earlymoderntexts.com/pdfs/constant1819.pdf).

20. As suggested by Hibbing and Theiss-Morse (2002).

Another counterargument may suggest that it does not go far enough. Participatory budgeting focuses the locus of power on budgets, perhaps too narrowly. If PB cannot scale beyond small discretionary funds in the United States, many will view it as a missed opportunity for innovations in participation to have an impact on political structures.

What if budgets are not a good locus of political involvement? What if civic efforts should aim instead to develop transformative leadership?[21] Participatory budgeting offers several entry points for engagement, including leadership development. Ideally, to restore citizens' faith in democratic governance, PB ought to be combined with a campaign for greater civic reform and with an expansion of citizens' political power beyond budgets.

Participatory budgeting is not enough, but it is one tool for deepening democracy in both developing and developed countries. I have outlined further opportunities for reengaging citizens, both in self-governance and in coproduction, arguing that PB fits within a broader toolkit to improve inclusive governance. It will be a missed opportunity if PB is not incorporated into a wider discussion of how to build and strengthen democratic institutions that reinvents the roles of "beneficiaries" and the state.

The Future

The secret message is that politics should become little so that individuals can become big.[22]

One of the greatest democratic contributions participatory budgeting can make is to create a new process for how citizens and institutions share information, interact, and make sustainable public decisions. Participatory budgeting reinvigorates a larger vision of democracy precisely by making the focal point of activity small.

Participatory budgeting, as per the discussion in this book, responds to the decline in citizen engagement in the United States. Among the culprits of that decline are the shortcomings of the hierarchical, bureaucratic model of government laid out by Max Weber. The realm of politics has become too "big" and complex for ordinary citizens to feel efficacious therein. The Weberian model lacks necessary mechanisms that would enable elected officials and citizens to respond to each other more directly and effectively.[23]

21. See Han (2014).
22. Unger (2005, p. 17).
23. Moynihan (2007).

Bureaucratic organizations have often alienated citizens and failed to serve as vehicles to form inclusive relationships with the people they serve.[24] Yet popular unease with a government seen as having grown too "big" has itself created new opportunities, spaces, and tools for citizen engagement and participation.[25] This frustration with bureaucratic growth has spurred the search for more participatory, democratic, and collective channels for citizens to communicate with their government. Localities and cities in particular are reemerging as critical engines to empower citizens and serve as laboratories for democratic experimentation.

Participatory budgeting also provides a way for citizens to be creative architects of public works, including in urban areas. This civic creativity enables a new understanding of civic participation. PB extends norms about participation, providing a framework for citizen involvement in politics that is applicable to the real world. Participatory budgeting is about more than a utopian experiment divorced from the rest of politics. Rather, it provides a blueprint for directly engaging citizens in the process of governance.

Some citizens may find they would prefer not to be so deeply involved in the process of governance. PB offers a variety of options for citizens in allowing them to determine when and if and how they want to engage. These choices—from one-time voting to spending nearly every week planning projects—offer numerous opportunities for different levels of participation. Some citizens may prefer to allow their neighbors to take on certain responsibilities, only weighing in at the end of the process. Currently, PB offers these self-selecting options. As the process continues to expand, a push for greater formal representation may emerge due to concerns about co-option by specific groups.

Participatory budgeting may need to reconcile another tension: Is the goal to create a new structure or to improve current structures? If PB were to accelerate pressures to make other budget processes fully transparent and accountable, perhaps its success would contribute to its extinction. For the near-term and medium-term future, this is not a realistic concern. Ultimately, creating more citizen input throughout public institutions will require building civil society capacity beyond only PB, ideally leveraging PB's organizing principles and expertise. Broadening capacities for greater civic engagement in governance requires interconnected systemic change. These are complex problems that need an "all hands on deck" approach, one that extends across actors, sectors, disciplines, and localities.

In addition, the future of participatory budgeting should be more than simply the domain of "toilets and trees." The process could move beyond small-stakes politics—helping, in turn, to ensure its longevity and safeguard it from being

24. Zajac and Bruhn (1999).
25. Peters (1996).

simply a self-serving mobilization exercise that supports elected officials. If PB constitutes a place of genuine political contestation, it will garner further legitimacy and deepen its offerings of civic rewards. Advocates of PB also need to ensure that the process does not "die on its own weight."

Early data show that the so-called millennial generation wants a results-oriented government. As millennials engage in civic life, their preferences will play a role in shaping political ecosystems. Although they tend to be critical of government—seeing it as insufficiently effective or representative—they still believe it has the potential to be a positive force in solving societal problems. For example, more than half of millennials are supportive of activist government—more than any other generation.[26] As a study by the Center for Information and Research on Civic Learning and Engagement (CIRCLE) succinctly sums up, millennials do not eschew politics altogether; rather, they do not see current politics as offering a viable option for achieving the outcomes they believe are important.[27] While millennials did turn out in substantial numbers to vote for Barack Obama for president in 2008, in general they vote and contact public officials at lower rates than their parents.[28]

Despite gravitating away from institutional forms of participation, this generation is finding other, more accessible avenues for contributing to their communities and engaging in the world.[29] While forms and levels of engagement vary among different socioeconomic segments of the cohort, millennials volunteer at a higher rate than other generations, frequently engage in consumer activism, and are spearheading civic uses of social media.[30] For example, 44 percent of millennials who use social networking sites use them to "like" or promote political material, 42 percent to post their own thoughts on issues, and 36 percent to encourage others to act.[31]

Obstacles to political engagement are not unique to millennials; in fact, they apply more broadly to the body politic. Doubts about the functioning of the country's democratic institutions are common throughout the populace. Gallup found in 2014 that 30 percent of Americans say they have "a great deal" or "quite a lot" of confidence in the Supreme Court, 29 percent in the presidency, and only 7 percent in Congress.[32] The perception that Washington is broken is a view shared by all generations.

26. Taylor and Keeter (2010).
27. Kiesa and others (2007).
28. Taylor and Keeter (2010).
29. Kawashima-Ginsberg (2011).
30. Taylor and Keeter (2010).
31. Rainie and others (2012).
32. Gallup (2014).

While policymakers seek to engage a generation that is particularly disaffected, but powerful and persuadable, they should focus on policies to improve the accessibility, representativeness, and functioning of democratic institutions for all generations. Currently, government has not done enough to harness or capture civic energy across generations. Well-designed democratic innovations could provide opportunities for robust civic rewards that transcend traditional demographic barriers.

Participatory budgeting can transform both individual citizens who partake in it as well as broader structures of representational democracy. Properly understood and supported, PB could revolutionize local democratic practice and transform current relationships between citizens and the state. But this requires grappling with tough questions: How much democracy is desirable? How best to work to achieve it? How to prevent digital divides that could further inequality? I argue that the norms of participation and deliberation are critical. ICTs cannot and should not replace human interaction. Properly deployed, however, they can enhance face-to-face engagements.

This book articulates a normative framework, guided by empirical questions. It is premised on the author's hope that participatory budgeting might lead to more accountable governance. Despite shortcomings, PB is an important step forward toward creating a revitalized political sphere. Getting it "right" will take practice and patience—and may ultimately prove less consequential than getting it going.

Today's civic innovations unfold against the backdrop of a troubling deficit of public faith in democracy. Democratic innovation can help restore that faith—but only if citizens suspend their cynicism long enough to give experiments in good governance the time, effort, and resources they need to demonstrate their potential. Democracy has never been monolithic in its practice. It should include trial and error. By being open to new structures, we can reinvest in the longstanding democratic norms that underpin our social contract: equality, justice, and fairness. Civic innovations that focus on participation and deliberation are uniquely effective in that endeavor. They unlock civic ingenuity and tap into the self-renewing power of democracy. They remind citizens that we are democracy.

Appendix: Methods

The research methods employed in this book aim to capture a nascent, dynamic, and evolving democratic innovation that is increasingly in evidence in the United States. My approach combines empirical results with a theoretical and normative framework. I conducted case study research on three pilots of PB in the United States (Chicago, New York City, and Boston), analyzing each so as to draw recommendations common to all three that are informed by experience in working closely with practitioners and as a policymaker. The work of building the body of quantitative and qualitative research that will support PB in the United States is just getting started. Rather than offering a complete history of PB or a comprehensive study of any one instance of PB, my goal has been to provide a rich and multifaceted analysis of an emerging civic process while also generating a theoretical understanding applicable beyond PB.

For the case studies, I employed a variety of methods, including formal interviews, field observations, site visits, process tracing, difference-in-difference analysis, and electronic sources. I have tried to be clear where my claims rest on personal observations based on my extensive firsthand experience of PB—and also about the extent to which I believe these observations can be generalized. My research has aimed to capture participatory activity throughout the ecosystem of stakeholders engaged in PB, including PB participants with little time for, or experience with, conducting formal interviews. I directly transcribed quotes, more or less verbatim, from firsthand encounters and conversations with relevant participants. Some passages are consolidated from extended interviews. All names have been omitted or changed to provide anonymity. Disparate demographic and personal characteristics of participants are highlighted in various chapters as they pertain to in-group dynamics.

For the first pilot year of Participatory Budgeting in NYC (PBNYC), I contributed to the research team led by the Community Development Project at the Urban Justice Center with the PBNYC Research Team. The chapters discussing PBNYC, chapter 4 in particular, draw heavily on their final report, as cited. This research employed a multimethod approach in the form of quantitative surveys of participants at neighborhood assemblies, budget delegate meetings, and voting sites. I conducted scores of structured and semi-structured interviews with individuals participating at varying levels of the process. Subjects were diverse in their levels of involvement in the various stages of the process as well as in terms of gender, race, and socioeconomic background. As the research progressed, subjects were also chosen to study the three main categories of my civic typology. That is, some interview subjects were selected as exemplars of the disparate types of citizens I lay out in chapter 4—namely "usual suspects," "active citizens," and "new citizens." I also conducted extensive conversations with policymakers, researchers, and leaders of foundations and community-based organizations.

During the PBNYC pilot, I took a process-tracing approach with a group of roughly thirty participants, employing participant observation throughout the various stages of the process. As analyzed in chapter 5, I used process tracing to do an in-depth analysis of attitudes and behavior of budget delegates on the thematic committees dedicated to parks and recreation found within each of the four districts of the New York City Council that implemented the PBNYC pilot.[1] I choose the parks and recreation committees for the variety of participants included on these committees as well as for the issues with which they dealt, which were well suited to PB.

To capture activity at the level of process governance in PBNYC, I attended meetings of the steering committee, which comprised members of the city council or their staff as well as leaders of civil society organizations (CSOs). I conducted in-depth interviews with council members, their staff, CSO staff, and other key leaders, activists, and scholars of civic engagement and democracy in New York City. I also conducted numerous semi-structured interviews over a period of a year and a half with active participants and leaders in the PB process in Chicago to better understand process governance there.

I conducted a difference-in-differences analysis, comparing capital projects in the four districts implementing the PBNYC pilot program before and after participatory budgeting. I employed a matched pair analysis: for each PBNYC district I chose a similar district that did not implement PB and compared capital funds projects implemented without PB with those projects emanating from

---

1. Parks are particularly fruitful for studying civic engagement experiments. Davies (2014) notes that parks are some of the most popular, and least controversial, uses of civic crowdfunding.

the PB process. To employ these research methods, I relied on a variety of communications to supplement in-person conversations, including phone conversations, e-mail correspondence, and Short Message Service (SMS) notifications relating to PBNYC.

As outlined in chapter 6, during Boston's Youth Lead the Change (YLC)—the first youth-oriented PB project—I served as part of a research team from the Harvard Kennedy School's Ash Center for Democratic Governance and Innovation. I helped with survey design, process implementation, and research analysis. I attended a variety of meetings throughout different stages of the process, including neighborhood assemblies, budget delegate or "change agent" meetings, and the vote. I conducted in-depth semi-structured interviews with different participants, including organizers, members of the YLC steering committee, government officials, assembly participants, and voters.

While my formal political science training informed the field research, my experience in policy and as a practitioner working closely with NGOs informed the policy recommendations. I have worked with the World Bank Institute to assess PB internationally, mainly in the Dominican Republic and the Democratic Republic of the Congo, specifically looking at the relationship of mobile technology to PB.

Serving as the open government and innovation adviser in the White House Office of Science and Technology Policy, I worked to incorporate participatory budgeting into the Second Open Government National Action Plan for the United States of America, prepared to comply with the open government commitments of the international Open Government Partnership. In this capacity, I worked closely with many community stakeholders to understand the political and policy challenges of bringing PB to scale across the United States. Additionally, I convened academics and practitioners to discuss metrics for public participation. These experiences shaped the lessons and recommendations I offer as well as my account of the broader civic innovation ecosystem that supports the growth of participatory budgeting.

References

Abers, Rebecca. 1998. "From Clientelism to Cooperation: Local Government, Participatory Policy, and Civic Organizing in Porto Alegre, Brazil." *Politics and Society* 26, no. 4, pp. 511–37. doi:10.1177/0032329298026004004.

———. 2000. *Inventing Local Democracy: Grassroots Politics in Brazil* (Boulder, Colo.: Lynne Rienner).

Ackerman, Bruce, and James S. Fishkin. 2005. *Deliberation Day* (Yale University Press).

Almond, Gabriel A., and Sidney Verba. 1965. *The Civic Culture: Political Attitudes and Democracy in Five Nations: An Analytic Study* (Boston: Little, Brown).

Arendt, Hannah. 1965. *On Revolution* (New York: Viking).

———. 1998. *The Human Condition*. 2nd ed. (University of Chicago Press).

———. 2005. *The Promise of Politics* (New York: Schocken).

Arian, Asher, Arthur S. Goldberg, John H. Mollenkopf, and Edward T. Rogowsky. 1991. *Changing New York City Politics* (New York: Routledge).

Arnstein, Sherry R. 1969. "A Ladder of Citizen Participation." *Journal of the American Institute of Planners* 35, no. 4, pp. 216–24. doi:10.1080/01944366908977225.

Arrow, Kenneth J. 1988. "Behavior under Uncertainty and Its Implications for Policy." In *Decision Making: Descriptive, Normative, and Prescriptive Interactions,* edited by David E. Bell, Howard Raiffa, and Amos Tversky (Cambridge University Press), pp. 497–507.

Avritzer, Leonardo. 2002. *Democracy and the Public Space in Latin America* (Princeton University Press).

———. 2006. "Modes of Democratic Deliberation: Participatory Budgeting in Brazil." In *Democratizing Democracy: Beyond the Liberal Democratic Canon,* edited by Boaventura de Sousa Santos (London: Verso), pp. 377–404.

———. 2009. *Participatory Institutions in Democratic Brazil* (Johns Hopkins University Press).

Bach, Laurent, and Mireille Matt. 2005. "From Economic Foundations to S&T Policy Tools: A Comparative Analysis of the Dominant Paradigms." In *Innovation Policy in a Knowledge-Based Economy: Theory and Practice,* edited by Patrick Llerena and Mireille Matt Berlin (Berlin: Springer), pp. 17–45.

Bachrach, Peter, and Morton S. Baratz. 1962. "Two Faces of Power." *American Political Science Review* 56, no. 4, pp. 947–52. doi:10.2307/1952796.

———. 1975. "Power and Its Two Faces Revisited: A Reply to Geoffrey Debnam." *American Political Science Review* 69, no. 3, pp. 900–04. doi:10.2307/1958398.

Baez, Nancy, and Andreas Hernandez. 2012. "Participatory Budgeting in the City: Challenging NYC's Development Paradigm from the Grassroots." *Interface* 4, no. 1, pp. 316–26.

Baierle, Sérgio Gregório. 1998. "The Explosion of Experience: The Emergence of a New Ethical-Political Principle in Popular Movements in Porto Alegre, Brazil." In *Cultures of Politics, Politics of Cultures: Re-Visioning Latin American Social Movements*, edited by Sonia E. Alvarez, Evelina Dagnino, and Arturo Escobar (Boulder, Colo.: Westview), pp. 118–38.

———. 2003. "The Porto Alegre Thermidor? Brazil's 'Participatory Budget' at the Crossroads." *Socialist Register* 39, pp. 304–28.

Baiocchi, Gianpaolo. 2001. "Participation, Activism, and Politics: The Porto Alegre Experiment and Deliberative Democratic Theory." *Politics and Society* 29, no. 1, pp. 43–72. doi:10.1177/0032329201029001003.

———. 2002. "Synergizing Civil Society: State-Civil Society Regimes and Democratic Decentralization in Porto Alegre, Brazil." *Political Power and Social Theory* 15, pp. 3–52.

———. 2003a. "Participation, Activism, and Politics: The Porto Alegre Experiment." In *Deepening Democracy: Institutional Innovations in Empowered Participatory Governance*, edited by Archon Fung and Erik Olin Wright (London: Verso), pp. 45–76.

———, ed. 2003b. *Radicals in Power: The Workers' Party (PT) and Experiments in Urban Democracy in Brazil* (London: Zed).

———. 2005. *Militants and Citizens: The Politics of Participatory Democracy in Porto Alegre* (Stanford University Press).

Baiocchi, Gianpaolo, and Ernesto Ganuza. 2014. "Participatory Budgeting as If Emancipation Mattered." *Politics and Society* 42, no. 1, pp. 29–50. doi:10.1177/0032329213512978.

Baiocchi, Gianpaolo, Patrick Heller, and Marcelo K. Silva. 2011. *Bootstrapping Democracy: Transforming Local Governance and Civil Society in Brazil* (Stanford University Press).

Bang, Henrik P. 2009. " 'Yes We Can': Identity Politics and Project Politics for a Late-Modern World." *Urban Research and Practice* 2, no. 2, pp. 117–37. doi:10.1080/17535060902979022.

Barber, Benjamin R. 1984. *Strong Democracy: Participatory Politics for a New Age* (University of California Press).

Bardin, Rachel, Marvin Francois, Christine Fulton, Jeremy Levkoff, Katelyn Mikuliak, and Melissa Stevenson. 2012. "Who Votes? Voter Turnout in New York City: Who Does Not Vote and What Can Be Done?" Report for the New York City Campaign Finance Board and the Robert F. Wagner School of Public Service, New York University, June (www.nyccfb.info/PDF/issue_reports/WhoVotes.pdf).

Barnett, Aleise, David Dembo, and Stefaan G. Verhulst. 2013. "Are We There Yet? And How Will We Know? The Promise and Challenge of Evaluating Innovations in How We Govern." GovLab working paper, version 1 (http://thegovlab.org/observatory/toward-metrics/).

Benkler, Yochai. 2006. *The Wealth of Networks: How Social Production Transforms Markets and Freedom* (Yale University Press).

Berry, Jeffery M., Kent E. Portney, Robin Liss, Jessica Simoncelli, and Lisa Berger. 2006. "Power and Interest Groups in City Politics." Report for the Rappaport Institute for Greater Boston, Kennedy School of Government, Harvard University (http://citeseerx.ist.psu.edu/viewdoc/download?doi=10.1.1.133.7133&rep=rep1&type=pdf).

Berry, Jeffrey M., Kent E. Portney, and Ken Thompson. 1993. *The Rebirth of Urban Democracy* (Brookings).

Bertot, John Carlo, Patrice McDermott, and Ted Smith. 2012. "Measurement of Open Government: Metrics and Process." *Hawaii International Conference on System Sciences (HICSS)* 45, pp. 2491–99. doi:10.1109/HICSS.2012.658.

Besharov, Douglas J., Alexey Barabashev, Karen Baehler, and Jacob Alex Klerman. 2012. "Notes on the Appam-Moscow Conference—Improving the Quality of Public Services: A Multinational Conference on Public Management." *Journal of Policy Analysis and Management* 32, no. 1, pp. 204–10. doi:10.1002/pam.21672.

Best, Nina, Sarah Brabender, Alexander Koop, Peter Spink, and Marco Teixeira. 2011. "Recife Brazil: Participatory Budgeting—Case Study." Report for *Vitalizing Democracy through Participation* (Reinhard Mohn Prize 2011), Bertelsmann Stiftung (www.vitalizing-democracy.org/site/downloads/1324_303_Case_Study_Recife.pdf).

Bishku-Aykul, Jeffrey. "Low Turnout Blamed for Participatory Budgeting Ending," *Hyde Park Herald,* Jan. 15, 2014 (http://hpherald.com/2014/01/15/low-turnout-blamed-for-participatory-budgeting-ending/).

Bobbio, Norberto. 1997. *Left and Right: The Significance of a Political Distinction*, translated by Allan Cameron (University of Chicago Press).

Boulding, Carew, and Brian Wampler. 2010. "Voice, Votes and Resources: Evaluating the Effect of Participatory Democracy on Well-Being." *World Development* 38, no. 1, pp. 125–35. doi:10.1016/j.worlddev.2009.05.002.

Bryan, Frank M. 2003. *Real Democracy: The New England Town Meeting and How It Works* (University of Chicago Press).

Cabannes, Yves. 2004. "Participatory Budgeting: A Significant Contribution to Participatory Democracy." *Environment and Urbanization* 16, no. 1, pp. 27–46. doi:10.1177/095624780401600104.

Cabannes, Yves, and Sergio Baierle. 2006. "Municipal Finance and Participatory Budgeting: Base Document." Launching Seminar of URBAL Network, no. 9. Sponsored by the Municipal Government of Porto Alegre (https://baierle.files.wordpress.com/2006/07/dbingles.pdf).

Caddy, Joanne, Tiago Peixoto, and Mary McNeil. 2007. "Beyond Public Scrutiny: Stocktaking of Social Accountability in OECD Countries." Paper prepared for the International Bank for Reconstruction and Development and the World Bank, Washington, D.C. (www.sasanet.org/documents/Curriculum/Strategic%20Communication/J%20Caddy.pdf).

CCNY (Council of the City of New York). 2009. City Council Fiscal Year 2010 Adopted Expense Budget: Adjustments Summary/Schedule C (http://council.nyc.gov/downloads/pdf/fy_2010_sched_c_final.pdf).

CDP and PBNYC (Community Development Project at the Urban Justice Center and the Participatory Budgeting in New York City Research Team). 2012. *A People's Budget: A Research and Evaluation Report on Participatory Budgeting in New York City* (New York: Urban Justice Center) (https://cdp.urbanjustice.org/sites/default/files/pbreport.pdf).

———. 2014. "Executive Summary." In *A People's Budget: A Research and Evaluation Report on Participatory Budgeting in New York City—Cycle 3* (New York: Urban Justice Center) (https://cdp.urbanjustice.org/sites/default/files/CDP.WEB.doc_Report_PBNYC-cycle3-ES_20141030.pdf).

Chambers, Simone. 2005. "Measuring Publicity's Effect: Reconciling Empirical Research and Normative Theory." *Acta Politica* 40, pp. 255–66. doi:10.1057/palgrave.ap.5500104.

Cohen, G. A. 2011. *On the Currency of Egalitarian Justice, and Other Essays in Political Philosophy*, edited by Michael Otsuka (Princeton University Press).

Cohen, Joshua. 1989. "Deliberation and Democratic Legitimacy." In *The Good Polity: Normative Analysis of the State*, edited by Alan Hamlin and Philip Pettit (Oxford: Blackwell), pp. 17–34.

———. 1997. "Procedure and Substance in Deliberative Democracy." In *Deliberative Democracy: Essays on Reason and Politics*, edited by James Bohman and William Rehg (MIT Press), pp. 407–37.

Cohen, Joshua, and Joel Rogers. 1995. "Secondary Associations and Democratic Governance." In *Associations and Democracy*, edited by Erik Olin Wright (New York: Verso), pp. 9–98.

Commonwealth Foundation. 1999. *Citizens and Governance: Civil Society in the New Millennium* (London: Commonwealth Foundation).

Crenson, Matthew A., and Benjamin Ginsberg. 2004. *Downsizing Democracy: How America Sidelined Its Citizens and Privatized Its Public* (Johns Hopkins University Press).

Crosby, Ned, Janet M. Kelly, and Paul Schaefer. 1986. "Citizens Panels: A New Approach to Citizen Participation." *Public Administration Review* 46, no. 2, pp. 170–78. doi:10.2307/976169.

Crozier, Michel, Samuel P. Huntington, and Joji Watanuki. 1975. *The Crisis of Democracy: Report on the Governability of Democracies to the Trilateral Commission* (New York University Press).

Dahl, Robert A. 1961. *Who Governs? Democracy and Power in an American City* (Yale University Press).

———. 1967. "The City in the Future of Democracy." *American Political Science Review* 61, no. 4, pp. 953–70. doi:10.2307/1953398.

———. 1989. *Democracy and Its Critics* (Yale University Press).

Davidson, Jeffrey L. 1979. *Political Partnerships: Neighborhood Residents and Their Council Members* (Beverly Hills, Calif.: SAGE).

Davies, Rodrigo. 2014. "Civic Crowdfunding: Participatory Communities, Entrepreneurs, and the Political Economy of Place." Master's thesis, MIT. doi:10.2139/ssrn.2434615.

Dias, Nelson, ed. 2014. *Hope for Democracy—25 Years of Participatory Budgeting World Wide* (São Bras de Alportel, Portugal: In Loco) (https://democracyspotdotnet.files.wordpress.com /2014/06/op25anos-en-20maio20141.pdf).

Dietz, Thomas, and Paul C. Stern, eds. 2008. *Public Participation in Environmental Assessment and Decision Making* (Washington, D.C.: National Academies Press) (www.nap.edu /catalog/12434/).

Downs, Anthony. 1965. *An Economic Theory of Democracy* (New York: Harper & Row).

Dryzek, John S. 2000. *Deliberative Democracy and Beyond: Liberals, Critics, Contestations* (Oxford University Press).

———. 2007. "Theory, Evidence and the Tasks of Deliberation." In *Deliberation, Participation, and Democracy: Can the People Govern?* edited by Shawn W. Rosenberg (New York: Palgrave Macmillan), pp. 237–50.

Dutra, Olívio. 2002. "El Presupuesto Participativo y La Cuestión del Socialismo." Cited in Anwar Shah, ed. 2007. *Participatory Budgeting* (Washington, D.C.: World Bank).

Eaves, David. 2010. "After the Collapse: Open Government and the Future of Civil Service." In *Open Government: Collaboration, Transparency, and Participation in Practice*, edited by Daniel Lathrop and Laurel Ruma (Sebastopol, Calif.: O'Reilly), pp. 139–51.

Edstrom, Judith. 2002. "Indonesia's Kecamatan Development Project: Is It Replicable? Design Considerations in Community Driven Development." *Social Development Papers* (Environmentally and Socially Sustainable Development Network / World Bank), no. 39 (www-wds.worldbank.org/servlet/WDSContentServer/WDSP/IB/2005/02/22/000009486_20050222171656/Rendered/PDF/316150SDP13901public1.pdf).

Edwards, Bob, and John D. McCarthy. 2004. "Resources and Social Movement Mobilization." In *The Blackwell Companion to Social Movements*, edited by David A. Snow, Sarah A. Soule, and Hanspeter Kriesi (Oxford: Blackwell), pp. 116–52.

Elster, Jon. 1998. "Deliberation and Constitution Making." In *Deliberative Democracy*, edited by Jon Elster (Cambridge University Press), pp. 97–122. doi:10.1017/CBO9781139175005.

Evans, Angela M., and Adriana Campos. 2013. "Open Government Initiatives: Challenges of Citizen Participation." *Journal of Policy Analysis and Management* 32, no. 1, pp. 172–85. doi:10.1002/pam.21651.

Evans, Peter. 1996. "Government Action, Social Capital, and Development: Reviewing the Evidence on Synergy." *World Development* 24, no. 6, pp. 1119–32. doi:10.1016/0305-750X(96)00021-6.

Fagotto, Elena, and Archon Fung. 2006. "Empowered Participation in Urban Governance: The Minneapolis Neighborhood Revitalization Program." *International Journal of Urban and Regional Research* 30, no. 3, pp. 638–55. doi:10.1111/j.1468-2427.2006.00685.x.

Fainstein, Susan S. 2009. "Spatial Justice and Planning," translated by Philippe Gervais-Lambony. *Justice Spatiale*, no. 1 (www.jssj.org/wp-content/uploads/2012/12/JSSJ1-5en1.pdf).

Fauss, Rachael. 2012. "Creating a More Equitable and Objective Discretionary Funding Process in New York City." Report for Citizens Union of the City of New York (www.citizensunion.org/www/cu/site/hosting/Reports/CU_Report_NYC_Discretionary_FundingFY2009-2012_May2012.pdf).

Fedozzi, Luciano Joel, and Kátia Cacilda Pereira Lima. 2014. "Participatory Budgets in Brazil." In *Hope for Democracy: Twenty-Five Years of Participatory Budgeting*, edited by Nelson Dias (São Brás de Alportel, Portugal: In Loco), pp. 153–63 (http://www.buergerhaushalt.org/sites/default/files/downloads/Studie_Hope_for_democracy_-_25_years_of_participatory_budgeting_worldwide.pdf).

Ferreira, Dimas Enéas Soares. 2012. "Inclusão, participação, associativismo e qualidade da deliberação pública no Orçamento Participativo Digital de Belo Horizonte." Paper presented at the 34th annual meeting of the Associação Nacional de Pós-Graduação e Pesquisa em Ciências Sociais (ANPOCS) (www.anpocs.org/portal/index.php?option=com_docman&task=doc_view&gid=1322&Itemid=350).

Fiorina, Morris P. 1975. "Formal Models in Political Science." *American Journal of Political Science* 19, no. 1, pp. 133–59. doi:10.2307/2110698.

Fisher, Dana, Erika Svendsen, and James Connolly. 2015. *Urban Environmental Stewardship and Civic Engagement: How Planting Trees Strengthens the Roots of Democracy* (New York: Routledge).

Fishkin, James S. 1993. *Democracy and Deliberation: New Directions for Democratic Reform* (Yale University Press).

Fishkin, James, and Cynthia Farrar. 2005. "Deliberative Polling: From Experiment to Community Resource." In *The Deliberative Democracy Handbook: Strategies for Effective Civic Engagement in the Twenty-First Century*, edited by Peter Levine and John Gastil (San Francisco: Jossey-Bass), pp. 68–79.

Fölscher, Alta, ed. 2002. *Budget Transparency and Participation: Five African Case Studies*. (Cape Town: IDASA).

———. 2007a. "Participatory Budgeting in Asia." In *Participatory Budgeting*, edited by Anwar Shah (Washington, D.C.: World Bank), pp. 157–89.

———. 2007b. "Appendix: A Primer on Effective Participation." In *Participatory Budgeting*, edited by Anwar Shah (Washington, D.C.: World Bank), pp. 243–55.

———. 2007c. "Participatory Budgeting in Central and Eastern Europe." In *Participatory Budgeting*, edited by Anwar Shah (Washington, D.C.: World Bank), pp. 127–55.

Fölscher, Alta, Warren Krafchik, and Isaac Shapiro. 2000. "Transparency and Participation in the Budgeting Process." Paper presented at the third conference of the International Budget Project, Mumbai, November 4–9.

Ford, Alberto. 2009. "¿Para qué sirve una política participativa? Un balance del Presupuesto Participativo en Rosario, 2002–2008." Paper presented at IX Congreso Nacional de Ciencia Política, Ciudad de Santa Fe, Argentina, August 19–22 (www.academia.edu/5298447/).

Foroughi, Behrang, and Erica McCollum. 2013. "Learning Participatory Citizenship: Exploring the Informal Learning of Tenant Volunteers at Toronto Community Housing Corporation (TCHC)." In *Volunteer Work, Informal Learning and Social Action*, edited by Fiona Duguid, Karsten Mündel, and Daniel Schugurensky (Rotterdam: Sense), pp. 141–58.

Fox, Charles J., and Hugh T. Miller. 1994. *Postmodern Public Administration: Toward Discourse* (Thousand Oaks, Calif.: SAGE).

Fung, Archon. 2003a. "Associations and Democracy: Between Theories, Hopes, and Realities." *Annual Review of Sociology* 29, pp. 515–39. doi:10.1146/annurev.soc.29.010202.100134.

———. 2003b. "Deliberative Democracy and International Labor Standards." *Governance* 16, no. 1, pp. 51–71. doi:10.1111/1468-0491.t01-1-00204.

———. 2003c. "Recipes for Public Spheres: Eight Institutional Design Choices and Their Consequences." *Journal of Political Philosophy* 11, no. 3, pp. 338–67. doi:10.1111/1467-9760.00181.

———. 2004. *Empowered Participation: Reinventing Urban Democracy* (Princeton University Press).

———. 2011. "Reinventing Democracy in Latin America." *Perspectives on Politics* 9, no. 4, pp. 857–71.

Fung, Archon, Hollie Russon Gilman, and Jennifer Shkabatur. 2010. "Impact Case Studies from Middle Income and Developing Countries: New Technologies." Report for the Transparency and Accountability Initiative of the Open Society Foundation (www.transparency-initiative.org/wp-content/uploads/2011/05/impact_case_studies_final1.pdf).

———. 2013. "Six Models of Internet+Politics." *International Studies Review* 15, pp. 30–47.

Fung, Archon, and David Weil. 2010. "Open Government, Open Society." In *Open Government: Collaboration, Transparency, and Participation in Practice*, edited by Daniel Lathrop and Laurel Ruma (Sebastopol, Calif.: O'Reilly), pp. 105–14.

Fung, Archon, and Erik Olin Wright. 2001. "Deepening Democracy: Innovations in Empowered Participatory Governance," *Politics & Society* 29, pp. 5–41. doi:10.1177/0032329201029001002.

Gallup. 2014. "Trust in Government" (www.gallup.com/poll/5392/trust-government.aspx).

Ganuza, Ernesto, and Gianpaolo Baiocchi. 2012. "The Power of Ambiguity: How Participatory Budgeting Travels the Globe." *Journal of Public Deliberation* 8, no. 2, article 8 (http://www.publicdeliberation.net/jpd/vol8/iss2/art8).

Gastil, John. 2000. *By Popular Demand: Revitalizing Representative Democracy through Deliberative Elections* (University of California Press) (http://ark.cdlib.org/ark:/13030/kt596nc7dp/).

Gastil, John, and Peter Levine, eds. 2005. *The Deliberative Democracy Handbook: Strategies for Effective Civic Engagement in the Twenty-First Century* (San Francisco: Jossey-Bass).

Gaventa, John. 1980. *Power and Powerlessness: Quiescence and Rebellion in an Appalachian Valley* (University of Illinois Press).

———. 2007. "Participation and Citizenship: Exploring Power for Change." Public meeting in conjunction with the "Development Horizons: Future Directions for Research and Policy" series, January 22, London, organized by the Institute for Development Studies, the International Institute for Environment and Development, and the Overseas Development Institute (www.odi.org/events/139-participation-citizenship-exploring-power-change).

Genro, Tarso Ferndinando, and Ubiratan Jorge Iorio de Souza. 1997. *Orçamento participativo: A experiência de Porto Alegre* (Porto Alegre, Brazil: Fundação Perseu Abramo).

Gilman, Hollie Russon. 2012. "The Participatory Turn: Participatory Budgeting Comes to America." PhD diss., Harvard University (http://nrs.harvard.edu/urn-3:HUL.InstRepos: 10947513).

Goldfrank, Benjamin. 2001. "Deepening Democracy through Citizen Participation? A Comparative Analysis of Three Cities." Paper presented at the annual meeting of the American Political Science Association, San Francisco, September.

———. 2002. "Urban Experiments in Citizen Participation: Deepening Democracy in Latin America." PhD diss., University of California at Berkeley.

———. 2006. "Lessons from Latin American Experience in Participatory Budgeting." Paper presented at the Latin American Studies Association Meeting, San Juan, Puerto Rico, March (www.internationalbudget.org/themes/PB/LatinAmerica.pdf).

———. 2007a. "Lessons from Latin America's Experience in Participatory Budgeting." In *Participatory Budgeting*, edited by Anwar Shah (Washington, D.C.: World Bank), pp. 91–121.

———. 2007b. "The Politics of Deepening Local Democracy: Decentralization, Party Institutionalization, and Participation." *Comparative Politics* 39, no. 2: pp. 147–68. doi:10.2307/20434031.

———. 2011. *Deepening Local Democracy in Latin America: Participation, Decentralization, and the Left* (Pennsylvania State University Press).

———. 2012. "The World Bank and the Globalization of Participatory Budgeting." *Journal of Public Deliberation* 8, no. 2, article 7 (http://www.publicdeliberation.net/jpd/vol8/iss2/art7).

Goldfrank, Benjamin, and Aaron Schneider. 2006. "Competitive Institution Building: The PT and Participatory Budgeting in Rio Grande do Sul." *Latin American Politics and Society* 48, no. 3, pp. 1–31. doi:10.1111/j.1548-2456.2006.tb00354.x.

Goldsmith, Stephen, and Susan Crawford. 2014. *The Responsive City: Engaging Communities through Data-Smart Governance* (San Francisco: Jossey-Bass).

Gonçalves, Sónia. 2014. "The Effects of Participatory Budgeting on Municipal Expenditures and Infant Mortality in Brazil." *World Development* 53, pp. 94–110. doi:10.1016/j.worlddev.2013.01.009.

Goodin, Robert E., and John S. Dryzek. 2006. "Deliberative Impacts: The Macro-political Uptake of Mini-Publics." *Politics and Society* 34, no. 2, pp. 219–44. doi:10.1177/003232 9206288152.

Gordon, Victoria. 2014. "Participatory Budgeting: Ten Actions to Engage Citizens via Social Media." Report for the IBM Center for the Business of Government (www

.businessofgovernment.org/report/participatory-budgeting-ten-actions-engage-citizens -social-media).

Goren, Paul, Christopher M. Federico, and Miki Caul Kittilson. 2009. "Source Cues, Partisan Identities, and Political Value Expression." *American Journal of Political Science* 53, no. 4, pp. 805–20. doi:10.1111/j.1540-5907.2009.00402.x.

Gradel, Thomas J., Dick Simpson, Andris Zimelis, Kirsten Byers, and Chris Olson. 2009. "Curing Corruption in Illinois: Anti-corruption Report Number 1." Department of Political Science at the University of Illinois at Chicago (http://pols.uic.edu/docs/default -source/chicago_politics/anti-corruption_reports/anti-corruptionreport.pdf).

Gramberger, Marc. 2001. *Citizens as Partners: OECD Handbook on Information, Consultation, and Public Participation in Policy-Making* (Paris: OECD Publications Service) (http:// internationalbudget.org/wp-content/uploads/Citizens-as-Partners-OECD-Handbook .pdf).

Green, Donald, Bradley Palmquist, and Eric Schickler. 2002. *Partisan Hearts and Minds: Political Parties and the Social Identities of Voters* (Yale University Press).

Grillos, Tara. 2014. "Youth Lead the Change: The City of Boston's Youth-Focused Participatory Budgeting Process." Pilot year evaluation report for Youth Lead the Change (YLC), a project of the Leadership Institute at Harvard College (LIHC) and the City of Boston (http://scholar.harvard.edu/files/grillos/files/pb_boston_year_1_eval_0.pdf).

Guo, Hai (David), and Milena I. Neshkova. 2013. "Citizen Input in the Budget Process: When Does It Matter Most?" *American Review of Public Administration* 43, no. 3, pp. 331–46.

Gutmann, Amy, and Dennis Thompson. 1998. *Democracy and Disagreement* (Belknap Press of Harvard University Press).

———. 2004. *Why Deliberative Democracy?* (Princeton University Press).

———. 2012. *The Spirit of Compromise: Why Governing Demands It and Campaigning Undermines It* (Princeton University Press).

Habermas, Jürgen. 1975. *Legitimation Crisis*. Translated by Thomas McCarthy (Boston: Beacon).

———. 1991. *The Structural Transformation of the Public Sphere: An Inquiry into a Category of Bourgeois Society*. Translated by Thomas Burger with the assistance of Frederik Lawrence (MIT Press).

———. 1996a. *Between Facts and Norms: Contributions to a Discourse Theory of Law and Democracy*. Translated by William Rehg (MIT Press).

———. 1996b. "Three Normative Models of Democracy." In *Democracy and Difference: Contesting the Boundaries of the Political*, edited by Seyla Benhabib (Princeton University Press), pp. 21–30.

Hacker, Jacob S., and Paul Pierson. 2011. *Winner-Take-All Politics: How Washington Made the Rich Richer—And Turned Its Back on the Middle Class* (New York: Simon & Schuster).

Hailey, John. 2001. "Beyond the Formulaic: Process and Practice in South Asian NGOs." *In Participation: The New Tyranny?*, edited by Bill Cooke and Uma Kothari (New York: Zed Books), 88–101.

Han, Hahrie. 2014. *How Organizations Develop Activists: Civic Associations and Leadership in the 21st Century* (Oxford University Press).

Hansen, Mogens Herman. 1983. *The Athenian Ecclesia: A Collection of Articles, 1976–83* (Viborg, Denmark: Museum Tusculanum Press).

Hayward, Clarissa Rile. 2000. *De-Facing Power* (Cambridge University Press).

Heinrich, Carolyn J., and Yeri Lopez. 2009. "Does Community Participation Produce Dividends in Social Investment Fund Projects?" *World Development* 37, no. 9, pp. 1554–68. doi:10.1016/j.worlddev.2009.01.009.

Helbig, Natalie, Anthony M. Cresswell, G. Brian Burke, and Luis Luna-Reyes. 2012. "The Dynamics of Opening Government Data: A White Paper." Report for the Center for Technology in Government, State University of New York at Albany (www.ctg.albany.edu/publications/reports/opendata/opendata.pdf).

Heller, Patrick. 2001. "Moving the State: The Politics of Democratic Decentralization in Kerala, South Africa, and Porto Alegre." *Politics and Society* 29, no. 1, pp. 131–63. doi:10.1177/0032329201029001006.

Heller, Patrick, and Peter Evans. 2010. "Taking Tilly South: Durable Inequalities, Democratic Contestation and Citizenship in the Southern Metropolis." *Theory and Society* 39, pp. 433–50. doi:10.1007/s11186-010-9115-3.

Hellström, Tomas. 1997. "Boundedness and Legitimacy in Public Planning." *Knowledge, Technology, and Policy* 9, no. 4, pp. 27–42. doi:10.1007/BF02912435.

Hibbing, John R., and Elizabeth Theiss-Morse. 2002. *Stealth Democracy: Americans' Beliefs about How Government Should Work* (Cambridge University Press).

Hippel, Eric von. 2005. *Democratizing Innovation* (MIT Press) (http://web.mit.edu/evhippel/www/democl.htm).

Howard, Philip N. 2010. *The Digital Origins of Dictatorship and Democracy: Information Technology and Political Islam* (Oxford University Press).

Howard, Philip N., and Muzammil M. Hussain. 2011. "The Upheavals in Egypt and Tunisia: The Role of Digital Media." *Journal of Democracy* 22, no. 3, pp. 35–48. doi:10.1353/jod.2011.0041.

Howe, Jeff. 2008. *Crowdsourcing: Why the Power of the Crowd Is Driving the Future of Business* (New York: Crown Business).

Jackson, John L., Jr. 2001. *Harlemworld: Doing Race and Class in Contemporary Black America* (University of Chicago Press).

Kahn, Jonathan. 1997. *Budgeting Democracy: State Building and Citizenship in America, 1890–1928* (Cornell University Press).

Kaku, Michio. 2011. *Physics of the Future: How Science Will Shape Human Destiny and Our Daily Lives by the Year 2100* (New York: Doubleday).

Karpf, David. 2012. *The MoveOn Effect: The Unexpected Transformation of American Political Advocacy* (Oxford University Press).

Kawashima-Ginsberg, Kei. 2011. *Understanding a Diverse Generation: Youth Civic Engagement in the United States*. Report for the Center for Information and Research on Civic Learning and Engagement, at the Jonathan M. Tisch College of Citizenship and Public Service, Tufts University (http://www.civicyouth.org/wp-content/uploads/2011/11/CIRCLE_cluster_report2010.pdf).

Keck, Margaret E., and Kathryn Sikkink. 2002. "Transnational Advocacy Networks in International and Regional Politics." *International Social Science Journal* 51, no. 159, pp. 89–101.

Keil, Roger. 1998. *Los Angeles: Globalization, Urbanization, and Social Struggles* (New York: Academy Press).

Khondker, Habibul Haque. 2011. "Role of the New Media in the Arab Spring." *Globalizations* 8, no. 5, pp. 675–79. doi:10.1080/14747731.2011.621287.

Kiesa, Abby, Alexander P. Orlowski, Peter Levine, Deborah Both, Emily Hoban, Kirby Mark, Hugo Lopez, and Karlo Barrios Marcelo. 2007. "Millennials Talk Politics: A Study of College Student Political Engagement." Report for the Center for Information and Research on Civic Learning and Engagement (CIRCLE) and the Charles F. Kettering Foundation (www.civicyouth.org/PopUps/CSTP.pdf).

King, Cheryl Simrell, and Camilla M. Stivers. 1998. *Government Is Us: Public Administration in an Anti-government Era* (Thousand Oaks, Calif.: SAGE).

Knight Foundation. 2012. "Digital Citizenship: Exploring the Field of Tech for Engagement." Report for the Knight Foundation (www.knightfoundation.org/media/uploads/media_pdfs /Digital-Citizenship-tech4engage-summit-report.pdf).

Krause, Alanna. 2014. "Collaborative Funding: Dissolve Authority, Empower Everyone, and Crowdsource a Smarter, Transparent Budget." *Management Innovation eXchange,* March 30. (www.managementexchange.com/story/collaborative-funding-dissolve-authority -empower-everyone-and-crowdsource-smarter-transparent).

Kweit, Mary Grisez, and Robert Kweit. 1981. *Implementing Citizen Participation in a Bureaucratic Society: A Contingency Approach* (New York: Praeger).

Lathrop, Daniel, and Laurel Ruma, eds. 2010. *Open Government: Transparency, Collaboration, and Participation in Practice* (Sebastopol, Calif.: O'Reilly).

Lehr, R. L., W. Guild, D. L. Thomas, and B. G. Swezey. 2003. "Listening to Customers: How Deliberative Polling Helped Build 1,000 MW of New Renewable Energy Projects in Texas." Report for the National Renewable Energy Laboratory (http://apps3.eere.energy .gov/greenpower/resources/pdfs/33177.pdf).

Leighninger, Matt. 2011. "Using Online Tools to Engage—and Be Engaged by—the Public." Report for the IBM Center for the Business of Government (www.businessofgovernment .org/report/using-online-tools-engage-public).

Lerner, Josh. 2014. *Everyone Counts: Could "Participatory Budgeting" Change Democracy?* (New York: Cornell Selects).

Lerner, Josh, and Daniel Schugurensky. 2007. "Who Learns What in Participatory Democracy? Participatory Budgeting in Rosario, Argentina." In *Democratic Practices as Learning Opportunities,* edited by Ruud van der Veen, Danny Wildemeersch, Janet Youngblood, and Victoria Marsick (Rotterdam: Sense), pp. 85–100.

Lerner, Josh, and Donata Secondo. 2012. "By the People, for the People: Participatory Budgeting from the Bottom Up in North America." *Journal of Public Deliberation* 8, no. 2, article 2 (www.publicdeliberation.net/jpd/vol8/iss2/art2).

Lesbaupin, Ivo. 2000. *Poder Local X Exclusão Social: A experiência das prefeituras democráticas no Brasil* (Petrópolis, Brazil: Editora Vozes).

Lessig, Lawrence. 2011. *Republic, Lost: How Money Corrupts Congress—And a Plan to Stop It* (New York: Twelve) (http://lesterland.lessig.org/pdf/republic-lost.pdf).

Lloyd-Jones, David. 1981. "The Art of Enoch Powell: The Rhetorical Structure of a Speech on Immigration." In *Politically Speaking: Cross-Cultural Studies of Rhetoric,* edited by Robert Paine (Philadelphia: Institute for the Study of Human Issues), pp. 87–111.

Lukes, Steven. 2005. *Power: A Radical View.* 2nd ed. (London: Palgrave Macmillan).

Lynn, Laurence E., Jr. 2002. "Democracy's 'Unforgivable Sin.'" *Administration and Society* 34, no. 4, pp. 447–54. doi:10.1177/0095399702034004005.

Mansbridge, Jane J. 1983. *Beyond Adversary Democracy* (University of Chicago Press).

———. 1986. *Why We Lost the ERA* (University of Chicago Press).

———. 1995. "Does Participation Make Better Citizens?" *The Good Society* 5, no. 2, p. 1.

————. 1996. "Using Power/Fighting Power: The Polity." In *Democracy and Difference: Contesting the Boundaries of the Political*, edited by Seyla Benhabib (Princeton University Press), pp. 46–66.

Marquetti, Adalmir. 2002. "Democracia, equidade e effciencia: O, Caso do orçamento participativo em Porto Alegre." In *A inovação democrática no Brasil: o, Orçamento participativo*, edited by Leonardo Avritzer and Zander Navarro (São Paulo: Cortez Editora), pp. 129–56.

Marquetti, Adalmir, Carlos E. Schonerwald da Silva, and Al Campbell. 2012. "Participatory Economic Democracy in Action: Participatory Budgeting in Porto Alegre, 1989–2004." *Review of Radical Political Economics* 44, no. 1, pp. 62–81. doi:10.1177/0486613411418055.

Martin, Christine, Jessica Heinzelman, and Patrick Meier. 2010. "Assessment of the Ushahidi for the Carter Center's Peace Programs." Report on file with the authors.

McGee, Rosemary, with Nyangabyaki Bazaara, Jonathan Gaventa, Rose Nierras, Manoj Rai, Joel Rocamora, Nelson Saule Jr., Emma Williams, and Sergio Zermeño. 2003. "Legal Frameworks for Citizen Participation: Synthesis Report." Report for the Learning Initiative on Citizen Participation and Local Governance (LogoLink) (http://siteresources.world bank.org/INTPCENG/Resources/SynthesisRep-Web.pdf).

McNulty, Stephanie. 2012. "An Unlikely Success: Peru's Top-Down Participatory Budgeting Experience." *Journal of Public Deliberation* 8, no. 2, article 4 (www.publicdeliberation.net /jpd/vol8/iss2/art4).

Mendelberg, Tali. 2002. "The Deliberative Citizen: Theory and Evidence." In *Political Decision-Making, Deliberation, and Participation: Research in Micropolitics*, vol. 6, edited by Michael X. Delli Carpini and Robert Y. Shapiro (Greenwich, Conn.: JAI Press), pp. 151–93.

Miller, James. 1987. *Democracy Is in the Streets: From Port Huron to the Siege of Chicago* (New York: Simon & Schuster).

Mollenkopf, John H. 1992. *A Phoenix in the Ashes: The Rise and Fall of the Koch Coalition in New York City Politics* (Princeton University Press).

Morozov, Evgeny. 2011. *The Net Delusion: The Dark Side of Internet Freedom* (New York: PublicAffairs).

Mossberger, Karen, and Benedict Jimenez, with Carly Wobig, Martha Whipple, Lauren Bowman, and Brandon Chantavy. 2009. "Can E-Government Promote Civic Engagement? A Study of Local Government Websites in Illinois and the U.S." Report for the Institute for Policy and Civic Engagement, College of Urban Planning and Public Affairs, University of Illinois at Chicago (www.uic.edu/cuppa/ipce/interior/egovtfinalreport2009.pdf).

Mouffe, Chantal. 2000. "Deliberative Democracy or Agonistic Pluralism?" *Political Science Series Reihe Politikwissenschaft* 72 (www.ihs.ac.at/publications/pol/pw_72.pdf).

Moynihan, Donald P. 2003. "Normative and Instrumental Perspectives on Public Participation: Citizen Summits in Washington, D.C." *American Review of Public Administration* 33, no. 2, pp. 164–88.

————. 2007. "Citizen Participation in Budgeting: Prospects for Developing Countries." In *Participatory Budgeting*, edited by Anwar Shah (Washington, D.C.: World Bank), pp. 55–83.

Mutz, Diana C. 2008. "Is Deliberative Democracy a Falsifiable Theory?" *Annual Review of Political Science* 11, pp. 521–38. doi:10.1146/annurev.polisci.11.081306.070308.

NCoC (National Conference on Citizenship), CIRCLE (the Center for Information and Research on Civic Learning and Engagement), Mobilize.org, and the Institute of Politics,

Harvard University. 2013. *Millennials Civic Health Index* (Washington, D.C.: National Conference on Citizenship).

Neblo, Michael A., Kevin M. Esterling, Ryan P. Kennedy, David M. J. Lazer, and Anand E. Sokhey. 2010. "Who Wants to Deliberate—and Why?" *American Political Science Review* 104, no. 3, pp. 566–83. doi:10.1017/S0003055410000298.

Netherland, Wynn, and Chris McCroskey. 2010. "Case Study: Tweet Congress." In *Open Government: Collaboration, Transparency, and Participation in Practice,* edited by Daniel Lathrop and Laurel Ruma (Sebastopol, Calif.: O'Reilly), pp. 177–82.

Noble, David F. 2011. *Forces of Production: A Social History of Industrial Automation* (New Brunswick, N.J.: Transaction).

Norrander, Barbara. 1993. "Nomination Choices: Caucus and Primary Outcomes, 1976–1988." *American Journal of Political Science* 37, no. 2, pp. 343–64.

Noveck, Beth Simone. 2009. *Wiki Government: How Technology Can Make Government Better, Democracy Stronger, and Citizens More Powerful* (Brookings).

Novkirishka-Stoyanova, Malina. 2001. "Legislative Framework Supporting Citizen Participation in Local Government in Bulgaria." Local Government Initiative, Research Triangle Institute, Sofia, Bulgaria.

Nylen, William R. 2002. "Testing the Empowerment Thesis: The Participatory Budget in Belo Horizonte and Betim, Brazil." *Comparative Politics* 34, no. 2, pp. 127–45. doi:10.2307 /4146934.

———. 2003a. "An Enduring Legacy? Popular Participation in the Aftermath of the Participatory Budgets of João Monlevade and Betim." In *Radicals in Power: The Workers' Party (PT) and Experiments in Urban Democracy in Brazil,* edited by Gianpaolo Baiocchi (London: Zed), pp. 91–112.

———. 2003b. *Participatory Democracy versus Elitist Democracy: Lessons from Brazil* (Basingstoke, U.K.: Palgrave Macmillan).

Obama White House (Unsigned official document prepared by the Obama administration and issued via WhiteHouse.gov). 2013. "The Open Government Partnership: Second Open Government National Action Plan for the United States of America." December 5 (www .whitehouse.gov/sites/default/files/docs/us_national_action_plan_6p.pdf).

Office of the Mayor. 2015. "Mayor, Licata Announce Participatory Budgeting Project," Seattle .gov, July 7, 2015 (http://murray.seattle.gov/mayor-licata-announce-participatory-budgeting -project/#sthash.uI4XCkRs.dpbs).

Olivo, Christiane. 1998. "The Practical Problems of Bridging Civil Society and the State: A Study of Round Tables in Eastern Germany." *Polity* 31, no. 2, pp. 244–68. doi:10.2307 /3235228.

Olken, Ben. 2010. "Direct Democracy and Local Public Goods: Evidence from a Field Experiment in Indonesia." *American Political Science Review* 104, no. 2, pp. 243–67. doi:10.1017/S0003055410000079.

O'Reilly, Tim. 2010. "Government as a Platform." In *Open Government: Collaboration, Transparency, and Participation in Practice,* edited by Daniel Lathrop and Laurel Ruma (Sebastopol, Calif.: O'Reilly), pp. 11–40.

Ortega Hegg, Manuel. 2001. *Cultura política, gobierno local, y descentralización: Nicaragua* (San Salvador: FLACSO El Salvador).

———. 2003. "La conversion de un 'canal formal' en un 'espacio real' de participación social." In *Participación ciudadana y desarrollo local en Centroamérica,* edited by Nuria Cunill

Grau, Ricardo Córdova Macías, and Leslie Quiñónez Basagoitia (San Salvador, El Salvador: FundaUngo).

Participatory Budgeting Unit. 2011. "Now Is the Time to Trust Citizens on Budgets." *Participatory Budgeting Unit* (www.participatorybudgeting.org.uk/news-and-events/news/now-is-the-time-to-trust-citizens-on-budgets).

Pateman, Carole. 1976. *Participation and Democratic Theory* (Cambridge University Press).

———. 1988. *The Sexual Contract* (Stanford University Press).

———. 1989. "The Patriarchal Welfare State." In *The Disorder of Women: Democracy, Feminism, and Political Theory* (Stanford University Press), pp. 179–209.

———. 2012. "APSA Presidential Address: Participatory Democracy Revisited." *Perspectives on Politics* 10, no. 1, pp. 7–19. doi:10.1017/S1537592711004877.

PBNYC (Participatory Budgeting in New York City). 2012. *Participatory Budgeting in New York City: 2012–2013 Rulebook* (New York: Participatory Budgeting in New York City) (www.participatorybudgeting.org/wp-content/uploads/2012/07/Rulebook.pdf).

———. 2013. *Participatory Budgeting in New York City: 2013–2014 Rule Book* (New York: Participatory Budgeting in New York City) (www.participatorybudgeting.org/wp-content/uploads/2012/07/PBNYC-2013-2014-Rulebook-easy-print-version.pdf).

Peck, Jamie, and Nikolas Theodore. 2015. *Fast Policy: Experimental Statecraft at the Thresholds of Neoliberalism* (University of Minnesota Press).

Pederson, J., with D. Kocsis, A. Tripathi, A. Tarrell, A. Weerakoon, N. Tahmasbi, Jie Xiong, Wei Deng, Onook Oh, and G.-J. De Vreede. 2013. "Conceptual Foundations of Crowdsourcing: A Review of IS Research." *Hawaii International Conference on System Sciences (HICSS)* 46, pp. 579–88. doi:10.1109/HICSS.2013.143.

Peixoto, Tiago. 2008. "e-Participatory Budgeting: e-Democracy from Theory to Success?" Paper for *e-Working Papers*, E-Democracy Centre, Universität Zürich. doi:10.2139/ssrn.1273554.

———. 2009. "Beyond Theory: e-Participatory Budgeting and Its Promises for eParticipation." *European Journal of ePractice*, no. 7 (March).

Peters, B. Guy. 1996. *The Future of Governing: Four Emerging Models* (University Press of Kansas).

Pettit, Philip. 2001. "Deliberative Democracy and the Discursive Dilemma." *Philosophical Issues* 11, no. 1, pp. 268–99. doi:10.1111/j.1758-2237.2001.tb00047.x.

Posner, Richard A. 2003. *Law, Pragmatism, and Democracy* (Harvard University Press).

Putnam, Robert D. 2001. *Bowling Alone: The Collapse and Revival of American Community* (New York: Touchstone).

Putnam, Robert D., with Robert Leonardi and Raffaella Y. Nanetti. 1994. *Making Democracy Work: Civic Traditions in Modern Italy* (Princeton University Press).

Puttick, Ruth, Peter Baeck, and Philip Colligan. 2014. "The Teams and Funds Making Innovation Happen in Governments Around the World." Report for i-teams, Nesta, and Bloomberg Philanthropies (www.theiteams.org/resources/read-i-teams-report-0).

Rae, Douglas W. 2005. *City: Urbanism and Its End* (Yale University Press).

Rahman, Atiur, Mahfuz Kabir, and Abdur Razzaque. 2004. "Civic Participation in Subnational Budgeting in Bangladesh." Paper for the World Bank Institute, Washington, D.C. (www.shamunnaybd.org/us/hplinked_contet/Reports/CIVIC%20PARTICIPATION%20IN%20Bangladesh.pdf).

Rahman, K. Sabeel. 2011. "Conceptualizing the Economic Role of the State: Laissez-Faire, Technocracy, and the Democratic Alternative." *Polity* 43, pp. 264–86. doi:10.1057/pol.2010.29.

Rainie, Lee, Aaron Smith, Kay Lehman Schlozman, Henry Brady, and Sidney Verba. 2012. "Social Media and Political Engagement." Report for the Pew Research Center (http://www .pewinternet.org/files/old-media/Files/Reports/2012/PIP_SocialMediaAndPoliticalEnga gement_PDF.pdf).

Rawls, John. 1999. *A Theory of Justice* (Belknap Press of Harvard University Press).

Raymond, Eric S. 2001. *The Cathedral and the Bazaar: Musings on Linux and Open Source by an Accidental Revolutionary* (Sebastopol, Calif.: O'Reilly).

Reagle, Joseph Michael, Jr. 2010. *Good Faith Collaboration: The Culture of Wikipedia* (MIT Press).

Reich, Brian. 2010. "Citizens' View of Open Government." In *Open Government: Collabora- tion, Transparency, and Participation in Practice*, edited by Daniel Lathrop and Laurel Ruma (Sebastopol, Calif.: O'Reilly), pp. 131–38.

Rheingold, Howard. 2002. *Smart Mobs: The Next Social Revolution* (Cambridge, Mass.: Basic Books).

Richardson, Henry S. 2002. *Democratic Autonomy: Public Reasoning about the Ends of Policy* (Oxford University Press).

Robinson, M. 2004. "Resources, Citizen Engagement, and Democratic Local Gover- nance." Paper prepared for a project-planning workshop organized by Resources, Citizen Engagement, and Democratic Local Governance (ReCitE), Thiruvananthapuram, Ker- ala, India, January 4–16.

Rose-Ackerman, Susan, and Thomas Perroud. 2013. "Policymaking and Public Law in France: Public Participation, Agency Independence, and Impact Assessment." *Columbia Journal of European Law* 19, no. 2, pp. 223–309 (http://ssrn.com/abstract=2217716).

Rosenblum, Nancy L. 1998. *Membership and Morals: The Personal Use of Pluralism in Amer- ica* (Princeton University Press).

Rosenstone, Steven J., and John Mark Hansen. 1993. *Mobilization, Participation, and De- mocracy in America* (New York: MacMillan).

Sampaio, Rafael Cardoso, and Tiago Peixoto. 2014. "Electronic Participatory Budgeting: False Dilemmas and True Complexities." In *Hope for Democracy: Twenty-Five Years of Participa- tory Budgeting*, edited by Nelson Dias (São Brás de Alportel, Portugal: In Loco), pp. 413– 25 (www.buergerhaushalt.org/sites/default/files/downloads/Studie_Hope_for_democracy _-_25_years_of_participatory_budgeting_worldwide.pdf).

Sandel, Michael J. 1998. *Democracy's Discontent: America in Search of a Public Philosophy* (Har- vard University Press).

Sanders, Lynn M. 1997. "Against Deliberation." *Political Theory* 25, no. 3, pp. 347–76. doi: 10.1177/0090591797025003002.

Sangsari, Marcel. 2013. "The European Citizens' Initiative: An Early Assessment of the Eu- ropean Union's New Participatory Democracy Instrument." Paper for Canada-Europe Transatlantic Dialogue (CETD), Carleton University (http://labs.carleton.ca/canadaeurope /wp-content/uploads/sites/9/CETD_Sangsari_ECI_Policy-Paper.pdf).

Sanjek, Roger. 1998. *The Future of Us All: Race and Neighborhood Politics in New York City* (Cornell University Press).

Santos, Boaventura de Sousa. 1998. "Participatory Budgeting in Porto Alegre: Toward a Re- distributive Democracy." *Politics and Society* 26, no. 4, pp. 461–510. doi:10.1177/0032329 298026004003.

———. 2005. "Participatory Budgeting in Porto Alegre: Toward a Redistributive Democ- racy." In *Democratizing Democracy: Beyond the Liberal Democratic Canon*, edited by Boaventura de Sousa Santos (New York: Verso), pp. 307–76 (www.boaventuradesousasantos.pt /media/Chapter%2011.pdf).

Sayre, Wallace Stanley, and Herbert Kaufman. 1960. *Governing New York City: Politics in the Metropolis* (New York: Russell Sage Foundation).

Schaper, Nick. 2010. "Entrepreneurial Insurgency: Republicans Connect with the American People." In *Open Government: Collaboration, Transparency, and Participation in Practice,* edited by Daniel Lathrop and Laurel Ruma (Sebastopol, Calif.: O'Reilly), pp. 183–92.

Schlozman, Kay Lehman, Sidney Verba, and Henry E. Brady. 2012. *The Unheavenly Chorus: Unequal Political Voice and the Broken Promise of American Democracy* (Princeton University Press).

Schudson, Michael. 2010. *The Good Citizen: A History of American Civic Life* (New York: Free Press).

Schugurensky, Daniel. 2006. "'This Is Our School of Citizenship': Informal Learning in Local Democracy." In *Learning in Places: The Informal Education Reader,* edited by Zvi Bekerman, Nicholas C. Burbules, and Diana Silberman-Keller (New York: Peter Lang), pp. 163–82.

———. 2013. "On Participatory Governance: A Memo to Colleagues." Paper presented at "Participatory Governance in the 21st Century" (seminar), American Society of International Law, Washington D.C., December 13.

Schumpeter, Joseph A. 1942. *Capitalism, Socialism, and Democracy* (New York: Harper & Brothers).

———. 2006. *Capitalism, Socialism, and Democracy.* 6th rev. ed. (New York: Routledge).

Scruggs, Greg. 2014. "Participatory Budgeting's Birthplace Uses the Mechanism to Build Resilience." *Next City,* July 3 (https://nextcity.org/daily/entry/participatory-budget ings-birthplace-uses-the-mechanism-to-build-resilience).

Secondo, Donata, and Pamela Jennings. 2014. "Building Sustainable Empowerment: Participatory Budgeting in North America." In *Hope for Democracy: Twenty-Five Years of Participatory Budgeting,* edited by Nelson Dias (São Brás de Alportel, Portugal: In Loco), pp. 241–53.

Seltzer, Ethan, and Dillon Mahmoudi. 2013. "Citizen Participation, Open Innovation, and Crowdsourcing: Challenges and Opportunities for Planning." *Journal of Planning Literature* 28, no. 1, pp. 3–18. doi:10.1177/0885412212469112.

Shah, Anwar, ed. 2007. *Participatory Budgeting* (Washington, D.C.: World Bank).

Shall, Adrienne. 2007. "Sub-Saharan Africa's Experience with Participatory Budgeting." In *Participatory Budgeting,* edited by Anwar Shah (Washington, D.C.: World Bank), pp. 191–222.

Shane, Peter M., ed. 2004. *Democracy Online: The Prospects for Political Renewal through the Internet* (New York: Routledge).

Shapiro, Edward S. 2006. *Crown Heights: Blacks, Jews, and the 1991 Brooklyn Riot* (Brandeis University Press).

Shirky, Clay. 2008. *Here Comes Everybody: The Power of Organizing without Organizations* (New York: Penguin).

Shkabatur, Jennifer. 2011. "Cities @ Crossroads: Digital Technology and Local Democracy in America." *Brooklyn Law Review* 76, no. 4, pp. 1413–85 (http://ssrn.com/abstract =1781484).

Sifry, Micah L. 2011. *Wikileaks and the Age of Transparency* (Berkeley, Calif.: Counterpoint).

———. 2014. *The Big Disconnect: Why the Internet Hasn't Transformed Politics (Yet)* (New York: O/R Books).

Singh, J. P. 2013. "Information Technologies, Meta-power, and Transformations in Global Politics." *International Studies Review* 15, no. 1, pp. 5–29. doi:10.1111/misr.12025.

Sintomer, Yves, Carsten Herzberg, Giovanni Allegretti, and Anja Röcke. 2010. "Learning from the South: Participatory Budgeting Worldwide—an Invitation to Global Cooperation." Special issue. *Dialog Global,* no. 25 (www.service-eine-welt.de/images/text_material -2152.img).

Sintomer, Yves, Carsten Herzberg, and Anja Röcke. 2014. "Transnational Models of Citizen Participation: The Case of Participatory Budgeting." In *Hope for Democracy—25 Years of Participatory Budgeting World Wide* (São Bras de Alportel, Portugal: In Loco), pp. 28–44. (www.buergerhaushalt.org/sites/default/files/downloads/Studie_Hope_for_democracy _-_25_years_of_participatory_budgeting_worldwide.pdf).

Sirianni, Carmen. 2009. *Investing in Democracy: Engaging Citizens in Collaborative Governance* (Brookings).

Sirianni, Carmen, and Lewis Friedland. 2001. *Civic Innovation in America: Community Empowerment, Public Policy, and the Movement for Civic Renewal* (University of California Press).

Smith, Graham. 2005. *Beyond the Ballot: 57 Democratic Innovations from Around the World* (London: Power Inquiry).

———. 2009. *Democratic Innovations: Designing Institutions for Citizen Participation* (Cambridge University Press).

Sokoloff, Harris, Harris M. Steinberg, and Steven N. Pyser. 2005. "Deliberative City Planning on the Philadelphia Waterfront." In *The Deliberative Democracy Handbook: Strategies for Effective Civic Engagement in the Twenty-First Century,* edited by Peter Levine and John Gastil (San Francisco: Jossey-Bass), pp. 185–96.

Souza, Celina. 2001. "Participatory Budgeting in Brazilian Cities: Limits and Possibilities in Building Democratic Institutions." *Environment & Urbanization* 13, no. 1, pp. 159–84 (www.ucl.ac.uk/dpu-projects/drivers_urb_change/urb_governance/pdf_part_budg /IIED_Souza_Budgeting_Brazil.pdf).

Spada, Paolo. 2010. "The Political and Economic Effects of Participatory Budgeting." Paper presented at the annual conference of the Latin American Studies Association, Rio de Janeiro.

———. 2013. "The Role of Redundancy and Diversification in Multi-channel Democratic Innovations." Paper presented at the annual meeting of the American Political Science Association (http://ssrn.com/abstract=2300683).

Spada, Paolo, and Giovanni Allegretti. 2014. "The Role of Redundancy and Diversification in Multi-channel Democratic Innovations." In *Lýðræðistilraunir: Ísland í hruni og endurreisn* [Experiments in Democracy: Iceland in Crisis and Recovery], edited by Jón Ólafsson (Reykjavík: Haskolautgafan, University of Iceland Press, Bifröst University).

Spada, Paolo, Jonathan Mellon, Tiago Peixoto, and Fredrik Matias Sjoberg. 2015. "Effects of the Internet on Participation: Study of a Public Policy Referendum in Brazil." Policy research working paper, no. WPS 7204 (Washington, D.C.: World Bank Group) (http:// documents.worldbank.org/curated/en/2015/02/24060569/effects-internet-participation -study-public-policy-referendum-brazil).

Stokes, Susan C. 1998. "Pathologies of Deliberation." In *Deliberative Democracy,* edited by Jon Elster (Cambridge University Press), pp. 123–39. doi:10.1017/CBO9781139175005.

Summers, Nicole. 2011. "Chicago's Participatory Budgeting Experiment." *Shareable,* April 6 (www.shareable.net/blog/chicagos-participatory-budgeting-experiment).

Sunstein, Cass R. 2009. *Republic.Com 2.0* (Princeton University Press).

Svara, James H. 1990. *Official Leadership in the City: Patterns of Conflict and Cooperation* (Oxford University Press).

Taylor, Paul, and Scott Keeter, eds. 2010. *Millennials: Confident, Connected, Open to Change.* Report for the Pew Research Center (www.pewsocialtrends.org/files/2010/10/millennials -confident-connected-open-to-change.pdf).

Thompson, Dennis F. 2008. "Deliberative Democratic Theory and Empirical Political Science." *Annual Review of Political Science* 11, pp. 497–520. doi:10.1146/annurev.polisci .11.081306.070555.

Touchton, Michael, and Brian Wampler. 2014. "Improving Social Well-Being through New Democratic Institutions." *Comparative Political Studies* 47, no. 10, pp. 1442–69. doi: 10.1177/0010414013512601.

Trippi, Joe. 2004. *The Revolution Will Not Be Televised: Democracy, the Internet, and the Overthrow of Everything* (New York: Regan).

Trounstine, Jessica. 2008. *Political Monopolies in American Cities: The Rise and Fall of Bosses and Reformers* (University of Chicago Press).

Tufekci, Zeynep, and Christopher Wilson. 2012. "Social Media and the Decision to Participate in Political Protest: Observations from Tahrir Square." *Journal of Communication* 62, no. 2, pp. 363–79. doi:10.1111/j.1460-2466.2012.01629.x.

Tyler, Tom R. 2006. *Why People Obey the Law*, 2nd ed. (Princeton University Press).

Unger, Roberto Mangabeira. 1998. *Democracy Realized: The Progressive Alternative* (London: Verso).

———. 2004. *False Necessity: Anti-Necessitarian Social Theory in the Service of Radical Democracy*, Rev. ed. (London: Verso).

———. 2005. *What Should the Left Propose?* (London: Verso).

———. 2009. *The Left Alternative*, 2nd ed. (London: Verso).

URI (Urban Research Institute, Tirana). 2004. "Participatory Budgeting Initiative in Albania." Project summary report for the Urban Research Institute (Tirana, Albania) and the Citizens Participation in Local Governance Project, sponsored by the World Bank and the Government of the Netherlands (http://www.ceecn.net/ceecn.net/old_site/downloads /PBP+Project+Note.pdf).

Valenzuela, Sebastián, Arturo Arriagada, and Andrés Scherman. 2012. "The Social Media Basis of Youth Protest Behavior: The Case of Chile." *Journal of Communication* 62, no. 2, pp. 299–314. doi:10.1111/j.1460-2466.2012.01635.x.

Waldron, Jeremy. 2012. "Political Political Theory: An Oxford Inaugural Lecture." New York University School of Law, Public Law Research Paper no. 12–26. doi:10.2139/ssrn.2060344.

Walzer, Michael. 1999. "Deliberation, and What Else?" In *Deliberative Politics: Essays on Democracy and Disagreement*, edited by Stephen Macedo (Oxford University Press), pp. 58–69.

Wampler, Brian. 2002. "Orçamento participativo: Uma explicação para as amplas variações nos resultados." In *A inovação democrática no Brasil: o, Orçamento participativo*, edited by Leonardo Avritzer and Zander Navarro (São Paulo: Cortez Editora).

———. 2004a. "Expanding Accountability through Participatory Institutions: Mayors, Citizens, and Budgeting in Three Brazilian Municipalities." *Latin American Politics and Society* 46, no. 2, pp. 73–99. doi:10.1111/j.1548-2456.2004.tb00276.x.

———. 2004b. "The Diffusion of Participatory Budgeting across Brazil." Paper presented at the annual meeting of the Latin America Studies Association, Las Vegas.

————. 2007a. "Can Participatory Institutions Promote Pluralism? Mobilizing Low-Income Citizens in Brazil." *Studies in Comparative International Development (SCID)* 41, no. 4, pp. 57–78. doi:10.1007/BF02800471.

————. 2007b. "A Guide to Participatory Budgeting." In *Participatory Budgeting*, edited by Anwar Shah (Washington, D.C.: World Bank), pp. 21–53 (http://works.bepress.com/brian_wampler/3).

————. 2007c. *Participatory Budgeting in Brazil: Contestation, Cooperation, and Accountability* (Pennsylvania State University Press).

————. 2012a. "Participatory Budgeting: Core Principles and Key Impacts." *Journal of Public Deliberation* 8, no. 2, article 12 (http://www.publicdeliberation.net/cgi/viewcontent.cgi?article=1236&context=jpd).

————. 2012b. "Participation, Representation, and Social Justice: Using Participatory Governance to Transform Representative Democracy." *Polity* 44, pp. 666–82. doi:10.1057/pol.2012.21.

Wampler, Brian, and Leonardo Avritzer. 2004. "Participatory Publics: Civil Society and New Institutions in Democratic Brazil." *Comparative Politics* 36, no. 3, pp. 291–312. doi:10.2307/4150132.

————. 2005. "The Spread of Participatory Budgeting in Brazil: From Radical Democracy to Participatory Good Government." *Journal of Latin American Urban Studies* 7, pp. 37–52 (http://depts.washington.edu/jlaus/JLAUS7.pdf).

Wampler, Brian, and Rafael Cardozo Sampaio. 2010. "Belo Horizonte, Brazil: Co-governance—Case Study." Report for *Vitalizing Democracy through Participation* (Reinhard Mohn Prize 2011 [finalist]), Bertelsmann Stiftung (www.vitalizing-democracy.org/site/downloads/241_304_Case_Study_Belo_Horizonte.pdf).

Warren, Mark E. 1996. "What Should We Expect from More Democracy? Radically Democratic Responses to Politics." *Political Theory* 24, no. 2, pp. 241–70. doi:10.1177/0090591796024002004.

————. 2001. *Democracy and Association* (Princeton University Press).

Warren, Mark E., and Hilary Pearse. 2008. "Introduction: Democratic Renewal and Deliberative Democracy." In *Designing Deliberative Democracy: The British Columbia Citizens' Assembly*, edited by Mark E. Warren and Hilary Pearse (Cambridge University Press), pp. 1–19. doi:10.1017/CBO9780511491177.

Weber, Max. (1919) 2004. "Politics as a Vocation." In *The Vocation Lectures* (Indianapolis: Hackett).

Weber, Steven. 2004. *The Success of Open Source* (Harvard University Press).

Weeks, Edwards C. 2000. "The Practice of Deliberative Democracy: Results from Four Large-Scale Trials." *Public Administration Review* 60, no. 4, pp. 360–72. doi:10.1111/0033-3352.00098.

Weinstock, Daniel, and David Kahane. 2010. "Introduction." In *Deliberative Democracy in Practice*, edited by David Kahane, Daniel Weinstock, Dominique Leydet, and Melissa Williams (University of British Columbia Press), pp. 1–18 (www.ubcpress.ca/books/pdf/chapters/2009/DeliberativeDemocracyInPractice.pdf).

Windhoff-Héritier, Adrienne. 1992. *City of the Poor, City of the Rich: Politics and Policy in New York City* (Berlin: Walter de Gruyter).

World Bank. 1996. *The World Bank Participation Sourcebook* (Washington, D.C.: World Bank). doi:10.1596/0-8213-3558-8.

————. 2008. *Brazil: Toward a More Inclusive and Effective Participatory Budget in Porto Alegre.* Vol 1. *Main Report* (Washington, D.C.: World Bank) (https://openknowledge.worldbank.org/handle/10986/8042).

Wright, Erik Olin. 2010. *Envisioning Real Utopias* (London: Verso).

Wu, Tim. 2010. *The Master Switch: The Rise and Fall of Information Empires* (New York: Knopf).

YLC (Youth Lead the Change). 2014. *Youth Lead the Change—Participatory Budgeting Boston: Rulebook 201* (www.participatorybudgeting.org/wp-content/uploads/2014/03/YPB-Rulebook.pdf).

Young, Andrew, Hollie Russon Gilman, Sabeel Rahman, Christina Rogawski, Shruti Sannon, and Stefaan G. Verhulst, with Joel Gurin. 2013. "Toward Reimagining Governance: Mapping the Pathway toward More Effective and Engaged Governance." Paper prepared for GovLab, New York University, April 18 (http://thegovlab.org/wp-content/uploads/2013/06/GovLabMapDocument.pdf).

Young, Iris Marion. 2000. *Inclusion and Democracy* (Oxford University Press).

Zajac, Gary, and John G. Bruhn. 1999. "The Moral Context of Participation in Planned Organizational Change and Learning." *Administration and Society* 30, no. 6, pp. 706–33. doi:10.1177/00953999922019058.

Index

195

CPSIA information can be obtained at www.ICGtesting.com
Printed in the USA
BVOW08s1707191215

430641BV00005B/9/P